SCOUTING FC...

Introduction

"The F O D"

Fred O'Donoghue

His Early Days

"Football's Scouting Nut"

A Scout at Various Clubs:

Darwen F.C. Liverpool F.C. Arsenal F.C. Rochdale F.C.

Blackburn F.C. Preston F.C. Blackpool F.C.

Life in the Thirties followed by a Partial Soccer
Autobiography and a Scout's Notebook

First Edition Published in 1996
(published privately)

Second edition published in 1999
In association with Firebird Books Ltd.
PO Box 327, Poole, Dorset, BH15 2RG
Tel: 01202 715349   Fax: 01202 736191

Fredrick O'Donoghue
Penwortham
Lancashire
PR1 9TR

Front Cover by Caroline Mynott
Student at Newman College, Preston.
Work done with kind permission of Kevin Quigley, Headmaster.

Number of Titles in one year (One)
ISBN No.1 85314 206 9

Note
The Author wishes to record the kind assistance of Blackpool Football Club in the
production and publication of this book.

Subscribers

A
G Ainsworth
D J Allan
S Allardyce
L Allardyce
T Almond
Mr Archie
J Armfield
Mr Armitage
D Armstrong
Mr L Ashcroft
Mr P Ashcroft
Mr Ashworth
J Astley
Mr Billy Ayre
B
L Bailey
N Bailey
N Baker
D Bamber
G T Bamber
C Banks
M Banks
U Banks
D Barnes
Mrs R Benson
S Birchall
P Black
M Bloomfield
C Boardman
M Bolton
J Borland
S Bowick
H Boyle
P Brannan
Gill Bridge
R Bridges
P Brown
J Buckley
Mr M Burns
K Burns
D Burrows
D Bushell
C
J Calligan
A Calman
A Cameron
N Canning
Carlisle United Staff
Mr C Carlisle
F Carr
L Cartwright
Mr F Casper
G Cassidy
Dr Cellicol
K Chadwick
J Chapman
L Chapman
Sharon Chapman
J Charnley
S Charnley
L Chenery
D Christie
R Clare
R Scott Clarke
D Clough
Mr & Mrs Comstive
M Connolly
Mrs Connor
R Cooke
Mr Corbett

A Cottam
E Cotton
Mr & Mrs Counsell
Alan Crawford
D Crombie
D Crompton
Mrs Cross
J Crumlehulme
R Cunningham
J Curran
E Cuthbertson
D
Mr Dagger
Rev G Dakin
G Darwen
Mr Davis
J Dean
I Dickinson
C Docherty
J Dodds
M Dolan
P Duffell
J Dunn
E
B Edwards
Tom Ellis
Tony Ellis
J England
F Eyre
Mrs Eyre
F
C Faber
M Fahey
D Fazackerley
P Fenwick
J Ferguson
C Finch
M Finn
T Finney OBE
M Fitzgerald
M Forrester
G Foster
M Foulds
J Furnell
G
S Galliers
S Gardner
R Garlick - USA RIP
Family
S Garner
T Gennoe
A Gibson
P Gibson
R & K Gill
R Glynn
Mr Goddard
V Godwin
D Gornall
Mrs Gowans
C Grainger
Mr Grand
T Greenwood
P Gregson
Mrs Griffin
Miss Grime
H
Miss Haines
Mrs Hale
Mr Hall
Mr Hamer
Mrs Hanson

Miss Harrison
T Hastey
Mr Hawkins
Mrs Haworth
Mr Hayton
S Hazelgrave
J Heald
P Heavey
Mr Heighton
Mr Hesketh
F Hewitt
D Higham
Josie Higginson
P Hildreth
D Hind
J Hind
H Holburt
D Hogarth
M Holgate
J Holland
Mr Holland
M Hothersall
Mr & Mrs Howarth
Mr Hughes
P Hunt
I
Mrs M Ianson
B Ibison
J Irvine
J
G Jack
R Jackson
M James
S Johnson
Miss Johnstone
Mr Jones
Mrs Joyce
John V Judge
K
M Keir
L Kershaw
K Kilbane
D Kolb-USA Family
L
Rev T Lakeland
Lancaster Uni. Local
Studies Department
M Latham
Mr Leaver
D Lee
Leeds United
Supporters
Mrs Linklater
I Liveredge
S Longworth
D Lucas
P Lynch
M
C Madden
A Maddox
P Mairs
M Maloney
R Mansfield
Mr Mariner
Mrs Marsden
J Marshall
Mr Jim Mason
Mr Mawdesley
A May
P McCann
J McCarthy

J McCullough
Mr McDonald
S McDonald
Mr McDougle
P McKenna
Lawrie McMenemy
Ian McMinn
J McPhee
Mr R Mears
F A Melling
Lee Merricks
Clive Middlemass
Mr F Miller
Matthew Miller
Mr & Mrs A M
Monaghan
John Mortimore
Lee Morton
Craig Moylon
C B Muir
Oliver Muldoon
J Murphy
M A Murphy
Mrs Maureen Murray
Mrs Sheila Myhan
Mr Henry Moon
Mr R Moon
Michael Morgan
Dave Munday
N
Frank Naylor
G Nelson
Gail Newsham
Tom Nichol
Tom Nicholls
Craig Nixon
Jack Noble
Mr P Nowland
D C Nuttall
O
A O'Donoghue
H o'donoghue
S o'donoghue
Vince O'Keefe
Teresa O'Neill
P
Joyce Pallardy
J Parker
R Parker
Tony Parkes
Bob Parkinson
Mick Parkinson
Stan Parkinson
Stuart Parkinson
Tony Parr
Colin Parsons
Mark Patterson
B Pearson
Tony Pepper
John Pickering
A Platt
Brian Pilkington
PNEOSC
Andrew Pope
Ben Porter
Mr David Porter
Steve Potter
Mr Keith Pyegrum
Q
Derek Quigley
Mr K Quigley

R
Mr Arnold Radcliffe
T Rambridge RIP
Mr W E C Real
Anne Richardson
I Rigby
Les Rigby RIP
Neil Riley
Philip Daniel
Robinson
Geoffrey Allan
Roscoe
Hazel Rowley
Philip Russell
O Rudenwall
Tim Rutter
S
Mr & Mrs B Salmon
R Saxton
C L Seed
Frank Sharp
Mrs A Shaw
Peter Shilton
Mr S Shockledge
Paul Sidebottom
Rick Singleton
J M Smith
Katherine Smith
B Snape
T
Mark Thistlewaite
Kevin Thistlewaite
Fred Tompkins
John Tougher
George Turner
Phillip Thomson
Gordon Taylor PFA
Rev. Canon Michael
Taylor
John Twentyman
Geoff Twentyman
Ted Taylor
V
Mrs A Vincent
W
L Watson
P Watson
Mr T M Watson
Michael Webb
N Webb
S Webb
N Webster
Martin Webster
Westleigh High
School
Val Whittle
Ernie Wignall
Mrs S Wilcox
J Wilde
A Wilkinson
J Willis
Leonard Wiseman
Brian Wood
Daniel Woods
Mr Darryl Woods
Martin Woods

Cartoon of the FOD by Mick Watson, English Electric, 1962/63

IV

Contents

When young Keegan was not up to much

FRED O'DONOGHUE, 69, chief scout at Blackpool Football Club, spent Saturday as usual, wrapped up in sweater and scarf watching a game with notepaper, pencil and voice-recording machine. Peering over his shoulder, you would see a mesh of diagrams and squiggles as he analysed the game with trainspotterish accuracy. This weekend it was Preston North End v York, to prepare Blackpool manager Gary Megson for a forthcoming fixture. Often he will have been out watching schoolboys in the morning. He could drive blindfolded to any pitch in Lancashire.

"In a first-team game the main things you watch are the set-pieces," says O'Donoghue with enthusiasm that belies almost half a century of being paid not very much by the mile to watch from muddy touchline and rickety seat. "Throw-ins, for instance. Do they go down the line or to the midfield? Free-kicks. Who takes them? What position does everyone else take up on the field? Who's in the six-yard box? Who's in the 18-yard box? Who picks up the 'keeper? Corners. . ?. All this is put into a report for Monday morning."

O'Donoghue's zeal for describing the minutiae of his trade stems from his time as youth coach for Darwen FC. Talent-spotting was an integral part of the job but visits to local libraries confirmed that there was no such thing as a Scouting Bible. He made a mental note to correct that.

Scouting for Glory has taken 15 years to write and a difficult period to publish. On the opening page he lists more than 350 people who stumped up advance money only for the original publishers to go

Eye for detail . . . Fred O'Donoghue takes notes during a match at Deepdale   Picture: STEVE YARNELL

bankrupt, taking their cash — and £700 of the author's — with them. O'Donoghue paid to publish it himself second time around with a loan because he wanted to honour those subscribers. The book is delightfully idiosyncratic ("My wife, Cathy, and I have been married for 47 years. As Catholics we don't talk about divorce. Murder, yes!").

Through his anecdotal story of working for Darwen, Liverpool, Arsenal, Rochdale, Blackburn, Preston and Blackpool, he reveals how top footballers are spotted — and missed — at the embryonic stage of their development.

He lists the qualities required of a professional footballer, six physical and 12 psychological, and provides guidelines for parents who can be as starry-eyed as their sons. "Think carefully before signing for a club outside your area. Avoid placing expectations on a child unrelated to tne child's ability," and so on.

In every sense it contradicts the image of the weasely scout beating a path to the door and obtaining a signature on the dotted line. "In my day you used to approach the parents, knock at the door and say: 'Hello. I'm Fred O'Donoghue from Blackburn Rovers.' 'Ave, come on in lad,' they'd say. 'I've been watching your lad today, he's not bad. Let's have 'im down for training.'

"Nowadays you've got to speak to the secretary of whichever club or the school authorities first. I have never approached a boy on a football field. They all know who you are and immediate attention is thrown on them. It's not fair to the boy."

O'Donoghue's claims to fame include discovering Franz Carr and Jason Wilcox and admitting to being unimpressed by Kevin Keegan. "Keegan was a clanger — well, I wouldn't say a clanger because I'm still puzzled about it," he recalls.

"Liverpool asked me to take a look at a young player. I sat down at Stockport, who were playing Scunthorpe, and I can't think what Keegan did all match. On the Monday morning, when I got back in my office — the traffic sector in Blackburn town hall — I reported back.

"The chief scout said: 'I don't know. Bill Shankly fancies him, Ronnie Moran fancies him, Bob Paisley fancies him, I bloody fancy him and even Roy Evans fancies him.'

"I said: 'Well, I can't think what he did,' and he said: 'I tell you what pal, you'll do for me. You're honest. You can only report what you see.'"

Steve Galliers' career has brought him most pleasure. "I took him to Blackburn and signed him on schoolboy forms. He was five foot nothing but his heart was as big as himself. I was mad at Rovers because they didn't take him on, so I took him to Chorley.

"He played against Wimbledon in the FA Cup and their manager rang me up and said: 'This Galliers. . .?' I said: 'Get him.' Wimbledon went from the Fourth Division to the First and Stevie Galliers was in the middle of the park all the way."

O'Donoghue did not intend to write social history, but that is his achievement. At a time when centres of excellence are relieving scouts' workloads at youth level, his story might one day read as the chapters on his childhood do now: as a bygone era with bygone values. Subtitled "Life in the Thirties followed by a partial soccer autobiography and a scout's notebook", his story of low-paid labour for the love of football is a salutary reminder of the community pride and loyalty that established our clubs long before they evolved into commercial institutions.

December 1996. A visit from the Daily Telegraph was "wow" good news indeed. Well done Sarah Edworthy, sports writer.

Scouting for Glory
by Fred O'Donoghue

The dream of becoming a professional footballer and playing before huge crowds at venues such as Anfield, Old Trafford or White Hart Lane, is one which motivates millions of youngsters.

Every week, on parks, playing fields and school pitches across Britain, the dream inspires tyros to a frenzy of effort as they attempt to emulate the superstars of soccer.

Their chances of progressing and becoming the next Cantona, Giggs or Ferdinand will depend heavily on their latent talent being spotted by individuals who never hit the headlines and who, even today, remain in the shadows of Britain's national game.....the football scouts.

Scouting for Glory is a book which, for the first time, reveals how soccer's stars and their first team colleagues are spotted - and sometimes missed - at the embryonic stage of their football careers by the men who regularly patrol park pitches and schoolboy games with a trained eye for homing in on the lifeblood of the game - fresh, new talent.

But Scouting for Glory is far more than a gloriously descriptive account of the role these key individuals play in football. The author also tells an evocative personal story of his childhood and adolescence in a typical Lancashire cotton town, Preston, which is as much social history as personal reminiscence.

The book is thus a warm autobiography, rich in local flavour, as much as it chronicles the author's association with big clubs such as Liverpool, Arsenal and Blackburn as well as a host of other football clubs.

Scouting for Glory also offers vital, solid common-sense information to parents with football mad children who dream of embarking on a career in the game.

The author has attempted to distil a lifetime's involvement in the game, including the amateur, part-time and professional levels, into a book which, he hopes, is as revealing as it is engrossing and instructive.

His manuscript has already received high praise from Tom Finney and his efforts to write a 'scout's bible' and the support of many top professionals in football such as Lawrie McMenemy and Gordon Taylor.

Above all else, Fred O'Donoghue was delighted that Manchester United boss, Alex Ferguson, agreed to write the foreword and chose the following words to sum up Scouting for Glory: "This book tells an amazing story."

Editor's Note 1st Edition

During the time I have known Fred, I have always found him to be a most genuine, honest and affable person, and it is obvious his hard work, enthusiasm and passion for football has touched many people involved in the game over the years.

I am sure Fred will not mind me mentioning that he left school at the age of 14 with very limited skills and embarked on a self-taught education in the Merchant Navy. Therefore, the culmination of the years and effort spent by him in producing this book, is a real achievement indeed.

As for myself, ironically, I cannot claim to hold a real interest in football. However, I would say that I found this book very enjoyable, amusing, but above all, human, and I'm sure (whether you enjoy the game, or not!) you will too.

Best Wishes Fred.

Lorraine Cherrington, Typing and editing   April 1996

Editor's Note 2nd Edition

This is the second time I have worked with Fred on his book. The first time was fairly traumatic with various things going wrong, mainly with the computer. However in the end Fred's pride and joy was published and to boot was very successful.

Myself and Fred have something in common we are both mad about football so when he asked me to work on this second edition I thought "oh no not again!". But then I had second thoughts, "name in print, fame at last, I'll do it". Only joking Fred.

So here we have it the second edition we hope you enjoy it, lots more to read and plenty of new photographs.

Good Luck Fred.

David Manock, Typing, layout and editing.   May 1999

Acknowledgments

I would like to thank the following persons for all the kind consideration and tremendous help they have generously given me in the publication of my book. Without their assistance and support, the task of writing what has been the chronicling of a lifetime's involvement in football would have been far more difficult and far less rewarding. I owe a very deep gratitude and sincere thanks to all of you.

Proof **Readers**:   Mrs J Harrison, Mr D Terry and Mr B Edwards
Special Work: Mr D Manock - A huge thank you
Chapter 12 thanks to Dave Crompton of Wigan FC.
Preview reading: Michael Dolan, Mr & Mrs S Allardyce, K Quigley and
L Kershaw, Manchester United FC.

Tape recordings, typing and corrections
Lorraine Cherrington, Peter White, Mr & Mrs J Howarth, John Morrell, Mrs Ruth Benson, Mrs Janet Kershaw, Mrs Hazel Rowley, Ken Durkin, Mrs Ann Platt, Miss Hazel Cartwright, Mrs Joyce Carden, Mrs Margaret Burscough, Steve Grand, Mrs Ann Grand, Jim Dean, Miss Ann Louise Jackson. And finally, but by no means least, Mrs Josie Higginson for the musical contribution. Also Vicky Oyston for an Operatic correction.

Extracts and photographs
By kind permission of the following:
Sir Tom Finney OBE, MBE; special personal photographs on loan, allowing for reproduction
Bamber Bridge Football Club; programme notes
Lancashire Evening Post
Lancashire Evening Telegraph
Chorley Guardian
Staff at Lancashire County Reference Library
West Lancashire Gazette
Leyland Visitor
Blackpool Football Club and all its staff
Manchester United Football Club staff members
And to all ex-members of the former English Electric Co Ltd (1950-1964) drawing office in Strand Road, Preston
Mrs S Wilcox, Mr & Mrs B Salmon, Mrs D Unsworth.
I owe so much to all of you.
Yours most sincerely
"The FOD"
Fred O'Donoghue

Extra Special Words..........

By

Sir Alex Ferguson   Foreword

Sam Allardyce of PNE, Notts County and ex Bolton Wanderers fame
Gordon Lee, Manager at Blackburn Rovers, Everton F.C., Newcastle F.C., Port Vale, PNE F.C. etc.
Brian Hall, Liverpool F.C.
Nobby Stiles, ex England, Man U.F.C.
Micky Burns P.F.A. Education
John Howarth, Burnley F.C.

Contributions by the following personalities:-

1.   Walter Horam, Comedian (top shelf)
2.   Jim Willis Ex-Leicester City etc.
3.   Bill Fox...sadly deceased, ex Blackburn Rovers Chairman
4.   John Howarth, Blackburn Rovers Secretary
5.   Bob Saxton, Manager of Various League Clubs
6.   Chris Holland, YTS Young Player from Blackburn, Ex-PNE, Newcastle etc.
7.   David Lee, Player Bury F.C., Southampton F.C., Bolton F.C., Wigan F.C.
8.   Gordon Taylor, PFA Secretary
9.   Harold Holburt, Top Scout at Various Clubs
10.   Jimmy Smith, Manager at Various Clubs
11.   Steve Grand, a very Personal Friend, Player and Coach

The production of this book would not have been possible without the help of many friends. I thank you all.

Foreword

By Sir Alex Ferguson

The Manchester United Football Club plc

Football is our National sport and many have written about the great clubs and players. This is probably the only book which has attempted to give an account of the life of a football scout. Fred gives an insight into the time spent on the muddy touchline and the comfort and hospitality offered in the Director's boxes of some of our famous stadia.

His pen portraits of some of the characters involved in football are written with humour and honesty. People not directly involved with football will enjoy the story of Fred's childhood upbringing in the streets of Preston.

This book tells an amazing story. Many people have been involved in football scouting and Fred has had the courage and devotion to put his experiences into words. This book is a 'labour of love' and soccer enthusiasts of all levels will welcome this well-told tale.

Sir Alex Ferguson CBE
Manager

A Few Notes

Once upon a time, an old cliche, as all good stories reputedly!! start, I decided, as there were no published books about scouts and scouting, to write a book myself. Helped along by Peter White of the Lancashire Evening Telegraph in Blackburn, I produced an instruction type of scouting booklet with one or two soccer anecdotes in its covers.

Several friends read the puny effort, including the famous Fred Eyre, author of "Kicked into Touch". Fred, in his kindly manner, told me that a lot more work was required on the project. Paul Agnew of the Lancashire Evening Post also had a look at the manuscript and thought he could make something of it. He said he liked it very much but dropped it for a more lucrative story - the Tom Finney book, which was very well done. (He didn't, however, return it to me).

I found writing about my childhood experiences exhilarating and very enjoyable. Different friends encouraged me to continue with my work and complete the job I had started. I hope you like my efforts.

F.O.D.

"Wandering Walter"

Preston's Top Comedian

Walt Horam - For the FOD

Congratulations to Fred O'Donoghue on the publication of his second book, (his first book was a purple 'un!). In his teens, Fred was a keen amateur sportsman. He excelled at cricket, soccer, ping pong and keeping a straight face when being interviewed.

Fred also sang in St Augustine's choir and it was rumoured that scouts from the Luton Girls outfit were after him but unfortunately for Fred he failed the medical.

Congratulations also to Fred for being appointed Blackpool F.C. main talent spotter. This reminds me that about six years ago I went to Bloomfield Road to help cover the game, Blackpool v Notts County, along with a commentator from Red Rose Radio. It wasn't a very good game and at the end of ninety minutes I was asked, "Who was the man of the match?", to which I replied, "It was one of the Morris Dancers." Over a drink in the bar afterwards I asked, "Will you need me again?", to which I got the classic reply, "Maybe, but don't hold your breath."

I'm closing Fred, don't forget the old maxim, "It's tough at the bottom, it's tough at the top as well, but you eat better!"

Cheers, Walt

Vauxhall Road Boy's School and St.Augustine's Church, Preston many year's ago pre war happy memories of my boyhood 1934—41. Also The Morning Star Pub, left-hand side

Chapter One

My Boyhood Days

I was born in a humble mill dwelling house, three up and three down, commonly referred to as a Cotton Mill Victoria breeding box, with the whitewashed back yard and the toilet in its place of honour. We were posh - ours was a flush toilet at the end of the yard. The place was Preston in Lancashire. Our home was No. 13 Livesey Street, off London Road. The time of my birth, later as I was duly told, was 5.30 p.m., on a Friday night the 17th of June 1927, pay night for my hardworking Dad, a four-loom weaver in the local Bank Top Mill not four hundred yards away.

The room in which I was born was specifically prepared by my mother's sisters who also lived in the same street at No. 2 and No. 3, my Aunt Agnes at No. 3 and Aunt Emily at No. 2, with their husbands, respectively Joe and Jimmy, as did my much-revered Grandmother, Grace. She lived with my Aunt Emily at No. 2. As you can see, families lived very close together and bonds were very strong in many local communities.

As in all cotton communities, Preston, Blackburn, Oldham etc., the areas were very poor, especially for the working mill classes at that time, yet no child or neighbour would starve; (go hungry, yes - starve, no). No-one I knew died through starvation in the Preston area where I lived. Some neighbour always helped out.

Clothes were patched and re-patched; bed coverings made from fabrics and old coats, and they were quite warm on cold winter mornings on the top of our bed which I shared with my brother, Albert, in our sparse bedroom with nails for our clothes behind the door.

Life in the early thirties was very hard and tragedies struck often and constantly. Death was a permanent companion and a regular visitor was the lady, (one in every street), who obligingly washed and laid out the unfortunate, children and adults, who had died of various maladies, i.e., mumps, scarlet fever, diphtheria and measles.

Many deaths occurred in childbirth, families were wiped out with tuberculosis. I could go on with many sicknesses which afflicted the people of our town. However, many more were born as birth control was still a thing of the future, and the population grew in spite of all disasters.

Almost all working people in my town in those days helped each other and loved to be called a good neighbour. "Have you got any sugar, Annie?" a neighbour would ask my mother. "Can you lend me 3d for his tea?"(meaning her husband),

"I'll give it you back on Friday," (pay night). Wages varied from £2 to £3.10s.0d, no National Health and Social Security, (DSS) in those days.

A mill worker's wage was subject, in a weaver's case, to slubs in the cloth, weft breaks, cop run-outs, beam tensions, oil, shuttle problems and, of course, waiting for the tackler. It was non-stop work, with the noise of three concords in full throttle blasting at the eardrums. Many became deaf but could expertly understand the hand talk across the mill alleys. Even today old mill hands use their toil worn hands expressively and exaggerate mouth movements, although their numbers are dwindling fast.

I was lucky. My home was a happy one, with love, warmth and kindness. I loved my sister Ella and the family around me. It was a strong unit and I felt secure in its sensitivity for other's feelings, within its compass. I loved the slow, glowing noise of the gas mantle over the mantelpiece, the friendly visits of nearby neighbours with stories of local happenings, and the neighbours who dropped off onions, cabbages etc., proudly from the allotments for Mum. People were very appreciative of such needed gifts.

The weekly visit of the doctor's debt collector was around 5 p.m. on a Monday night. It was a catalogue of perpetual bills. He didn't always get paid but was always welcome in my father's house. Then there was a twenty-year visitor, Tom Brindle, the Humane Assurance collector on Friday; collecting Life Policy monies for all the family, my father, my mother, sister Ella and brother Albert - 2s.6d in all, to be respectfully buried if the need arose. He was friendly, knowledgeable, always had a small cup of tea and told my mother, who had left this world for the next, that he was the agony aunt column upset. All the family listened to his prognostications and stories with relish and astonishment.

I loved the smell of newly-baked bread and barmcakes from the bungalow-range oven, sometimes with lots of butter, when we could afford. Indeed, the five senses were fully occupied in those pre-war days. As I have said, my grandmother lived with my favourite Aunt Emily. They sat near the fire telling me many Lancashire stories of days gone by. We all loved Christmas and the family party. Humble people, who gave what they could afford, but more especially, love with a big hug and a Merry Christmas and God Bless You Love; a word Lancashire people use so frequently. Happy childhood days.

Leisure time was taken very seriously. The football teams, cricket teams, street games, skipping, guinea pig, rounders, hopscotch, the local boxing gym at the London Road Gerry Lobby Pub, pigeon fanciers' lofts on London Road, fishing in the Ribble and Longton Marshes, local operatic societies, especially at St Augustines G & S Society, the local brass bands, church choirs, men's clubs snooker and billiards, society dog breeding and allotment holders. All these hobbies were taken so seriously that to be a somebody you had to be the best at whatever your leisure pleasure might be.

When I think of the three-score years that I lived and visited many lovely places at home and abroad I would not like to have been born anywhere else in the world. Amidst the toil, poverty and sickness of my boyhood days there was also love, caring warmth and real meaning to friendships and true loyalties to people.

The people of Preston, like many other North West Lancashire towns experienced similar mixed circumstances, knowing the true meaning of words like friend, neighbour, loyalty, love, sensitivity, truth and "ambition with honour". For a better life here and hereafter I would like to think that people of Lancashire still strive.

I have often thought of my forefathers. On my father's side they came from County Cork in Southern Ireland and on my mother's side from County Wexford. During the potato disaster of the 1880's many were forced to leave Ireland and seek work in England so as to be able to feed themselves and their families. It must have been a hard struggle for them in those harsh Victorian days. They were among thousands who came to Lancashire and records show that large numbers of Irish immigrants settled in the port of Liverpool and surrounding towns. Much has been written about their sad lot. How they would have to lodge with relatives in already overcrowded houses and work long hours in poor menial and labouring jobs.

My grandparents came to England and settled in Preston which had a growing Irish Community. My father was a Roman Catholic, yet my mother was Church of England and attended St. Saviour's School in Malt Street, Preston. When she was twelve she started work in the local cotton mill as a half-timer at first. From the age of fourteen she was in full employment for years until she became a married woman with children.

My parents were married in 1914 at St. Joseph's Roman Catholic Church, Skeffington Road in Preston. My father asked my mother to change her religion to the Catholic faith which she duly did and in fact became a better practising Catholic than my father. In the early days of their marriage they rented a house in Livesey Street, off London Road, about half a mile from Walton-le-Dale bridge. My father worked as a weaver at the local Bank Top Mill. I believe he was quite a good weaver and worked very hard but to supplement his meagre income of about £2.10s.0d to £3 a week he bought my grandfather's 'knocking-up' round. For the less knowledgeable reader I will explain. Every working day he would rise at about 4 a.m., to awaken his customers who lived in the nearby streets. The workers were so tired by the long hours they had to work that they couldn't rely on an alarm clock, but employed my father as a 'knocker-up'. He used a 16ft long bamboo rod on the end of which were tied four very thin steel wires - splayed fan like, about one sixteenth of an inch in diameter. Each morning he would go round to his customers' houses and gently rattle the splayed wires against their bedroom windows. He would listen carefully until he saw the curtain twitch or heard a voice calling, "Reet Phil I'm up now, tha's awreet lad tha' can gooa." That knocking-up stick was precious to him as his means of earning 4d a week from each of his customers. It was locked up in the lobby every night as he was frightened that someone might come and take it away. That was strange really because we had no lock on the front door of the house, just a bar. Looking back, would anyone steal a knocking-up stick? No, I don't think so, Dad was playing safe.

His customers would be going out to work at differing times. The earliest up were the postal workers who had to be in the town centre for quarter past four each morning. Next at four thirty a.m. were the fishmarket men who in those days walked down to Preston railway station to be buying and selling fish between five and half past six.

Next came the cotton-mill hands - the weavers, spinners and doffers; then the local engineering workers, the fitters and turners. Many of the Leyland Motors lads cycled from Preston to Leyland and back every working day of their lives. I well remember one chap, Tom Judge, whose son John was my pal at St. Augustine's Boys School. Tom would cycle eight miles to work, I can see him now riding down London Road when I was taking my morning newspapers round. He would leave home at about seven a.m. to clock on in Leyland motors factory at half past seven. Then he would cycle home again at about six in the evening. When I saw him I could see as a young boy that he was absolutely shattered. Life was hard in those days for the working men of our towns and especially during the war.

As I have said before there was no Social Security or National Health Service and factory workers and mill hands were fined for being late for work. So it was my father's job to get those men out of their beds and off to work by rattling at their bedroom windows. In 1939 he had about sixty customers paying 6d per week and he also earned £3 for a forty-eight hour week weaving at the cotton mill, Saturday mornings included. The value of the pound was four times more than today's value at least. However we were poor people and my parents knew it.

He would collect his "knocking-up" money after tea on Friday nights. My mother had sewn a double pocket into his big topcoat to take the weight of the coins. He would set off after tea at seven o'clock and it took him about two and a half hours to do his round At every house they would want to have a word with the 'knocker-up'. My Dad was a good listener but he didn't speak much himself. (He used to say that God had given us one mouth and two ears. If he had intended us to talk more than we listened, he would have given us two mouths and one ear).

When he came back he would spread the money out on the big dining room table in our home in Livesey Street and my mother and I would sit down together to count the coins. I can see her now separating them into one shilling piles of copper and silver and adding them up. Usually there would be about twenty-seven or twenty-eight shillings.

There were some customers who weren't in when Dad called, or who were bad payers so my brother and I were given the task of going a second time to those houses at Saturday dinner-time. We were given a penny in the shilling back, so if I collected four or five shillings a very welcome four or five pennies were added to my meagre spending money. Twopence would take us into the Empire Cinema in Church Street on Saturday afternoons to see Flash Gordon, Buck Jones, Tom Mix etc., and with a Fry's Cream bar and a hap'orth of wine gums I was rich! The Plaza and Guild in New Hall Lane were also popular venues with me.

The money my Dad earned from his early morning job was put to good use. Ours was the first house in the street to have electric lighting. The old gas mantles and fittings were taken out and electric wiring installed. My mother was really thrilled especially when the neighbours would ask, "Can I have a look at your lights Annie?" She would bring them in and switch the lights on and off and they thought it was wonderful - no more lighted tapers or matches for the gas mantles!

We also bought our first radio-set. That was an Echo which was fluid battery-powered. It was marvellous to be able to enjoy hearing all those pre-war singers and bands - Ambrose and Henry Hall and so on. Again our neighbours and others would come in to listen - 'always when Dad was out'. My "Mam" loved company.

Eventually about 1940 my father had to give up the 'knocking-up' round. The war had started and every village, town and city in England had to be 'blacked out'. Street lights were either switched off or reduced to a dim glow and every chink of light in houses or buildings had to be hidden by thick black curtains at the windows. The winter of 1940 was a particularly hard, cold one. The River Ribble froze to a depth of about twelve inches and the pavements were covered in ice and snow. As a youngster then, I was delighted with the snow and ice but my father found it very difficult underfoot. He fell several times and was very badly bruised. He had started working for the English Electric Company at Salmesbury where Halifax bombers were built throughout the war years. So, he realised the time had come to give up his early morning job. He missed the extra shillings but at least did not have to contend with the icy-cold mornings any longer. My mother was relieved too. She had seen how very hard he had always worked - she loved him very much and found great joy in caring for him as she did her children, Ella, Albert and I ("Our Freddie"). Dad's name was Philip but she always called him Dad.

Early Football- Preston North End Cup Final

During these years my father was quite a well-known referee in the local amateur football leagues - The Preston and District; the Catholic and the OLD YMCA. He would come home from refereeing matches on Saturday afternoons and talk at great length about the game of football and the day's play. I suppose this was where my interest in the game started and I began to dream of one day becoming a soccer star.

We lived about a mile and a half from the famous Preston North End's football ground at Deepdale which was then attracting gates of 20,000 plus. There were a lot of big families in our street, the McEvoys, the Topping brothers, the Rambridges, Billingtons and Jollys. We were all football mad and each Saturday four or five of us, aged between about 8-12 years, would walk up London Road to the North End ground. In the last ten minutes the gates would be opened ready for the usual rush to the exits at the end of the game. We were all little lads but somehow we managed to squeeze our way through the crowds. Some of the chaps would say, "come on lads" and help us through to the front. There we would sit on the cinder track right next to the pitch and watch the last ten minutes or so of the game. It was a great atmosphere and how we enjoyed being there with all that crowd of people! The Preston North End players became our idols.

Then we would return home and play for hours and hours with a sixpenny tennis ball, or any available old ball. The nearby park, 'Smith's Recreation Ground' was our favourite pitch and there we would play until the park-keeper, (Billy Durham), chased us off. As you can imagine we became very proficient with a small ball. Having played through the years from 1934 to 1939 I didn't realise then that football was destined to play a major part in my future life.

But I must go back a bit now, if I may, to my younger days. One of my earliest memories was of being taken by my mother one September morning in 1930, when I was three years old, to school. Children could start at this young age because we lived quite near to the Infant's School which was in Carr Street. It belonged to St. Augustine's parish and was next door to the Girls' School. Boys attended the Infants' School until they were seven, then they moved on to the Boys' School.

On the first morning I arrived, feeling bewildered and frightened. Mum and I were met by a kindly nun, Mother Martha. I clearly remember her, dressed completely in black with a chalk-like gaunt appearance and without any facial expression as she said, "Oh hello Mrs O'Donoghue, is this little Freddie?" Then she looked down at me and smiled, I can see that nun's smile now. Full of kindness and warmth, I could almost feel the warmth, and off I went with her, hand in hand, into the school. I vaguely remember those young lads who were in my first class and I particularly remember one of the girls, red-haired, my Cathy. Eighteen years later I married her and now we have been together for over 50 years. (As Catholics we don't talk about divorce. Murder, yes!!).

Even at that young age, four or five years, we would always play with a ball at playtime in the schoolyard. Often we would be told to put it away, before we broke a window but the ball was always in the court at St Augustines - even in the Infants' school.

When I was eight years old I was asked to join the Church Choir and I sang with them as a boy Soprano until my voice broke when I was fifteen. My friend, John Judge, was also in the choir and I well remember the other boy singers - Jack Garner, Ronnie Norcross, Bernard Judge, Leo Bateson, Jack Bentley and Harry Worswick, etc., etc. I was delighted to be selected for the choir because we were often excused lessons to attend and sing at funerals and other important services in the Church. We had special music lessons and had to learn the Latin in which most of our church services were sung. If an important person or a priest died we were asked to be in the choir at the funeral. We would go up into the choir loft and sing a solemn Requiem Mass, 'The Dies Irae', and other hymns with sad Liturgical Motets. Our training was thorough and we were often complimented on our singing by the learned clergy, and Doctors of Divinity of the Church, the Canons and Bishops, etc.

I found that I could learn and remember tunes easily and had no problem singing solo parts. I had developed a bad stammer which deeply affected me but it didn't show in my singing. On Christmas Eve of 1938 I was chosen to open the beginning of the Midnight Mass by singing solo the first line of 'Adeste Fidelis', (O come all ye faithful). "Adeste Fidelis Laetie triumphantes, Venite, Venite in Bethlehem", I sang out confidently - all traces of my usual speaking stammer disappeared. There was then a short pause before the full choir joined in 'Natum Videte' and I became aware of a slight sobbing noise coming from the church below me. It was my mother, she was in tears, not able to believe that the boy soprano singing before all the clergy and congregation was her little lad Freddie, overcoming that very bad speaking stammer he had unfortunately acquired. Many times in later life she recalled to me her feeling on that Christmas Eve, and often asked me to sing Danny Boy, Rose of Killarney and Mother MaCree etc. She loved to hear me singing, which I did for her.

Here I must say how much I appreciate the good musical education we received from St Augustine's Boys school staff. It started in me a lifelong interest and pleasure in good music. John Judge and I spending many hours in the choir loft at St. Augustine's Church.

John's father, Tom Judge, was a member of the parish Amateur Operatic Society which produced a Gilbert and Sullivan Opera each year from 1914 until the 1939 war started. John and I would go and stand behind the stage watching the rehearsals - it was a revelation to me - I saw all the G & S operas, - Trial by Jury, Ruddigore, Princess Ida, The Mikado and the Gondoliers - and learned a lot about singing and stage matters. Not forgetting the Gilbertian wit "As well as". The words spoken and the comic innuendoes became meaningful to this little lad.

St Augustine's parishioners did not just attend a church that stood on the corner, the church was the centre of their lives, a vibrant complete community, and as I grew older I became involved in that way of life. At Whitsuntide we took part in the annual walks around the town centre. Our mothers saved a few pence each week for new outfits which came from Frank Wilson's shop in Avenham Lane. All the parishioners' children turned out, smartly dressed in their new clothes for the Catholic Procession. We were very proud to walk behind St Augustine's banners. Proud of our religion and our Catholic Faith but most of all proud of the church which we loved and its people therein. Yes I certainly lived in a tightly knit community that sought an attainment of culture and education of its parish people.

Besides the choirs and football my interest spread to other sports. I was a member of the school cricket team and then became involved in boxing. There was a club for young lads in Starch House Square, near to the old Majestic Ring Stadium. I joined this club with school pals, Stan McCarthy and Ronnie Sinclair and my parents encouraged me to continue boxing, even after I had my big nose smacked once or twice. I was quite taken up with the noble art of self defence and once again I was in dreamland! If I didn't become a soccer idol like my heroes, Jimmy Dougal, Frank and Hugh O'Donnell or George Mutch, then maybe I would become a champion boxer, another Len Harvey, Larry Gains or Tommy Farr. Maybe a Joe Louis, my favourite fighter of those days. I was very fortunate to watch him at Santos Football Ground as 4th Engineer SS Lalande 1950. He beat the Brazilian champion.

Another hobby was fishing. As a young boy of six or seven I had been taught to swim by my Dad in the sluices and pits on Longton Marsh. As I grew older I would go fishing there with him after attending church, 7 a.m. Mass on Sundays. Sometimes the Toppings, McEvoys and Rambridge brothers came with us. We would cycle on our pushbikes up to the Golden Ball and then down Marsh Lane onto the marsh to fish for Snigs, (eels). Note that we went to Mass first. If we didn't we had to account for it at school on Monday morning. Our names were called out from a register by the teacher, "O'Donoghue, Mass and Communion?" "Sir," was the reply which was recorded. Woe betide anyone who answered "No sir". An Inquiry usually followed, if sick you were excused. Mass was a must in St Augustine's Boys' School. It was a mortal sin to miss Mass on Sundays, condemned to hell for all eternity if you had died.

Football however was the abiding love of my life. I had progressed from the tanner ball in the streets and school playground. Sometimes we had to give the school goalkeeper some practice. He stood against a blank wall on which chalk posts had been drawn and we young hopefuls queued up all the playtime to have a kick. Football in the schools was very competitive then. All the boys wanted to play in the town Ord Cup Competition. All lined up to have a shot at the goal. If you scored that made your day.

In 1938 when I was eleven, my heroes, Preston North End, got through to the F.A. Cup Final at Wembley. Our local greengrocer had earlier promised that he would get two tickets and take me down to Wembley for the Final. However, he couldn't get any tickets, so instead he took me to the opening on April 14 1938 of the new Ritz Cinema in Church Street, I can't remember the film!

The Final was played on the 30th April. I can still remember the squad that lined up for PNE - Holdcroft, Gallimore, Andy Beattie, Shankly, Smith, Batey, Watmough, Maxwell, Bob Beattie, Mutch, O'Donnell - they were my gods, the idols of my school days. On the great day I listened to the match on the radio with my father. The neighbours who had no radios were all crowding round. It was all too much for me and I started pacing up and down. My father said, "Go on get out, go and play on the park". You did what your father told you in those days, so I went off into the nearby park and sat on a swing. It was, I assume, about ten minutes past five and suddenly all went deathly quiet. Then there was an explosion, a cacophony of sound that was deafening - "unbelievable". I rushed out of the park gates and saw the street filling with people. They were dancing, singing, hugging each other, - "Preston has won the cup, Preston has won the Cup" they called. I was overjoyed, everyone was overjoyed. It was amazing to hear the sound and see the joy of my own Prestonians. Mutch had scored from a penalty after being brought down. The referee's name was 'Jewel' and I remember thinking, "My God what a jewel, what a day, what a game'. That match had a great effect on me and football came into my life in a big way. I began playing every hour that I could.

There was no television to watch in those days remember. You used your imagination and dreamt of football idols. At about this time someone managed to get hold of a real caseball and we lads played regularly on Frenchwood recreation ground, ("The Rec"). We lost this pitch when it was ploughed up and used for growing potatoes in the wartime 'Dig for Victory' campaign. So we moved over the Tram Bridge and sneaked on the school playing fields belonging to the Catholic College and the Technical School and played there, many, many hours.

We were practising then at school for the Ord Cup and the Scanlan Shield. One of the boys in our school was emerging as a very fine player. He was Tommy Hough. I knew the family, who had been customers of my father's knocking-up round. Tommy was a big, strong lad. He was picked for the Preston Schoolboy's Team in preference to Tom Finney because of his height and strength. All the school was agog when he was selected for the team which went to play down in London. He was the school hero and certainly won the accolade for football with Tom Finney sitting in his shadow.

There were other good footballers in St Augustine's Boys School team - Tommy

Loughlin and centre forward Alfie Ingram, both useful players. With all my enthusiasm I felt that I could never match up to these lads. I always seemed to be near the frame but not quite in it.

In 1936 Preston Schoolboys forced a draw with West Ham at Upton Park. All the local schools lined Fishergate in Preston to welcome home the Joint Champions of the All England School Shield Knockout. How we cheered our Tommy Hough. Tom Finney was the team's reserve, Hough keeping Finney out of the squad at that very happy time, then the war coming along to destroy Hough's promising football career.

Grandma Garlick and Aunt Emily

Dad and Fred, Longton Marsh 1938

Fleetwood Lifeboat Crew, 1936. Uncle Larry Bond standing far right

Chapter Two

Double Bronze- Grand National

My moment of glory was soon to come. When we were old enough the whole of my school class was taken to Saul Street Baths to learn to swim. I was already a competent swimmer, since my father had taught me at a very early age on Longton marsh. For years my pals and I had enjoyed swimming down at the Church Deeps in Walton-le-Dale, also at Saul Street Baths in Preston. My first visit to the baths with the school class however ended in disaster.

The master from Class 4, Mr Bill Doherty, was in charge of our group. We were marched down into the bath basement to change amongst the heating boilers and pipes. The cubicles were reserved for paying customers not poor little schoolboys from St. Augustine's. The basement was our lot in which to change.

As we went into the huge pool room, my friend Gerald Adams and I left the main group who were lining up at the shallow end. Showing off a bit, we were a couple of daredevils, we both dived in at the deep end and swam the length of the pool, thirty-three and a third yards to the shallow end. There we were hauled out by the swimming coach, Mr Worthington, who told us off in an aggressive way for being so stupid and brash at our first visit. We spent the rest of the lesson sitting up in the balcony in disgrace and got caned when we got back to school by a very annoyed school teacher, three strokes on each hand. It hurt and we didn't do it again.

The coach had obviously been impressed for shortly afterwards he began to train Gerald and me with a view to entering us for the Bronze Medallion in Lifesaving. None from St. Augustine's Boy's School had ever achieved this standard, Intermediate Certificates, "Yes", but not Bronze Medallions. We were so keen to succeed. We spent weeks training for lifesaving. It was a difficult course, but we stuck at it. On the day of the test we each had to swim a long distance and then retrieve a very heavy brick from the bottom of the nine foot deep end of the water. Next we had to rescue a fully dressed lifeless person, a bath side attendant, dragging him along and getting him safely out of the water with a resuscitation demo as well. Thanks to our coaching from Mr Worthington we both succeeded. We were the first two boys at St Augustine's to receive the Bronze Medallion and we both felt ten foot tall.

The headmaster Mr. W. Moulding lined up the whole school in rows - classes 1 to 7 - he was so proud and so were we, when he announced, "These two boys, Gerald Adams and Frederick O'Donoghue , have attained a 'first' for this school. They have both been awarded the Bronze medal in Lifesaving. It's splendid news and I am delighted to present them with their awards. Come to the front of the lines please".

That was in July 1941 and now over 50 years later that medal is still as impressive, made of heavy bronze and in its special box. A happy memory of bygone youth.

I remember too, how pleased my parents were when I took the medal home. They had not known we were entering for it.

Looking back I wonder would I have been better advised to concentrate on just one sport or hobby and perhaps achieve a high standard in that? Instead I had so many interests, swimming, boxing, soccer, cricket and particularly singing, that there was not time to become more than just accomplished in any one. But, I have had years of pleasure from them all and in my lifetime I have met so many people through my varied interests.

I was fortunate to have relations in Fleetwood and spent several happy family holidays with them. My father's aunt had married a trawler skipper named Larry Bond. His sons were all fishermen and one or other of them would accommodate my brother, sister and me during the school holidays. They were great times, fishing in the River Wyre, swimming in the public pool, sailing across on the ferry to Knott End.

I remember it all so well especially the occasion when my Uncle Larry took me out to sea for three days fishing for prawns and flatties. His boat was a thirty footer, The Arctic Queen sailing from Jubilee Dock. I am pleased to say that I didn't' even get sea sick although it was my first long sail.

My parents were keen members of the Labour Party in Preston and not just in name only. At election times they would go out knocking on doors canvassing for such salt of the earth candidates as Billy Beckett, Mary Wignall, Jimmy Henry and Joe Lund. They also supported Edward Shackleton at the General Election, representing Preston South as M.P.

My parents were well-informed and could be heard discussing working class heroes of the past, such as the Tollpuddle Martyrs and Keir Hardie. They enjoyed their Saturday weekly night out at London Road Labour Club. There was a pianist on Saturday nights, and sometimes Dad would have a game of snooker or play at cards on Sunday dinner times. Mother always took politics seriously - more so than my father. She spoke well and was often called to give public speeches at local election times in various schools. On one occasion she addressed a large audience in the Free Trade Hall in Manchester. She was a long time member of the early Labour Party in Preston. A catholic convert who made sure we attended church services. She was a tremendously jolly character.

Mother also had her more serious side. Our house in Livesey Street was always open for visits from the neighbours. They were all her friends and everyone loved her. As my father worked long hours and she was kept at home by ill health they would come visiting. Mrs. McEvoy, Mrs. Topping and Mrs. Turner and many others. She had a gift of 'reading cards' and enthralled the ladies by telling their fortunes. She knew all the techniques, expressions about dark strangers, letters, predictions and so on. They would pay her a penny for her 'readings' but I could never get her to tell my fortune, nor could anybody else of the family.

On one particular occasion I was at home sick from school and it was the day of the Grand National Race at Aintree. My father was out working. Five or six of these ladies came in our house and decided to have a bet on the 'Big' race. They all chipped in a couple of pence but couldn't decide which horse to back. So I was called to make a selection from the list of runners. I looked over all the names and one that appealed to me as a boy most was obviously "Battleship". Someone ran up the street and put the each way bet on with the bookie's runner, a chap called Chris Halliwell. He had a clock-bag which was closed just before the races so they managed to place their bet just in time. Everybody crowded around the radio in our kitchen. Mrs. McEvoy with her 'Hedges' snuff, and the others all sniffing snuff and listening eagerly to the broadcast. Well, you can imagine the scene when Battleship came in first at odds like 33 to 1 or so!!

They were so excited they grabbed hold of me, kissing and hugging me - I had never been so popular in my life! Of course, that was beginner's luck and when they asked me later to try again I was not so lucky the next time which was the following day. The wonder-boy horse-selector faded from fame!

Yes, my mother was very popular and made friends everywhere. They would call in to seek her advice and tell her their problems. Before she became ill she would be the life and soul of the party - telling jokes, singing and dancing. You would hear them saying, "Annie's here", and she was not above taking a pinch of her friend's Hedges' snuff when Dad's back was turned. She was a great character, I loved her very much.

War

Hitler (Adolf) - Merchant Navy

During the years 1938 and 39, I could feel a change coming over our house and community. My father kept talking about this mad man - Adolf Hitler - who was marching across Europe and would have to be stopped. There was talk of war. My

Dad changed his job and started at the English Electric factory in Samlesbury which had been turned over to producing military aircraft. When the war against Germany was finally declared, things began to change rapidly all around us.

One of the first men to join the army was my Uncle Joe who lived in our street with Aunt Agnes. He had been in the Territorial Army so was recalled immediately the war began and served with distinction in France, defending the Maginot Line. Later, in the war in 1943 he had to be discharged from the army after suffering serious wounds to his spine at the evacuation of Dunkirk.

My brother Albert, who had Matriculated at Preston Catholic College, had been employed in the drawing office at English Electric and was drafted away from home to Belper in Derbyshire. For the rest of the war he worked there on secret war work. He wasn't allowed to tell us any more than that, but I understand that Rolls Royce and tank engines were involved. Also he was exempt from serving in the services as his job was in the 'Highly Reserved' category. He tried to join the RAF but was turned down. He also tried the Merchant Navy but his job was considered more important.

All the other eligible lads from the Livesey Street area were 'called up' into the Armed Forces and some never returned, including two of the De Santis brothers and my friend Tommy Rambridge. Tommy was in the Royal Navy and was killed off the Hook of Holland in 1942 at 18 years of age, 3 years older than me. All the other men and women who were not in the services, being either too young or too old, or unfit, were obliged to work on war work in the local engineering factories. There were some very big works in the Preston area, Leyland Motors, English Electric Company, The Royal Ordnance Factory at Euxton and the Royal Navy/Preston Dock, all a hive of industry working twenty-four hours a day turning out munitions, aircraft and vehicles for the services.

My mother, ill as she was, made her contributions to the war effort. The government had opened places where workers and others with passes could obtain a cheap, basic, hot meal. Most of the local cafes had been obliged to close down or reduce their menus drastically due to the rationing of foodstuffs. So these "British Restaurants" were desperately needed, opening daily from 12 noon to 2 p.m. My mother used to go down to Church Street and give a hand there serving meals, simple meals, lots of spuds, cabbage, spam and corned beef.

At the beginning of the war in 1939 I had a paper round delivering newspapers for Mr. Edmundson, the newsagent, in London Road. I would be up at 6.30 a.m. each morning to start my job and as I walked the round I would often read the headlines of the newspapers - the Daily Dispatch or the Daily Express. In this way I learned a lot about the progress of the war and followed events and the different battles very closely. I had particular interest in the happenings at Dunkirk as my Uncle Joe was there.

The newsagent paid me half a crown per week, (i.e. about 12p in today's currency), which I was allowed to keep for spending money. I would use it for boxing kit, football kit and also for sheet music, some of which I still have today. I loved the Big Band Sound and occasionally would buy a gramophone record of Glen Miller or Harry James and other top big bands. My school boyhood days came to a close in August 1941 and at 14 years of age I started my apprenticeship with Whitehead's Foundry on Syke Street, working 50 to 60 hours a week on war work. Engineering the hard way - heavy work and long hours. I learned about the working side of life.

John Whitehead's was a well-known Iron Foundry and had been making brick and tile machines for the past 100 years at the Albert Works in Syke Street, Preston.

I started at 7.30 a.m. and finished at 5.00 p.m., with one hour for dinner and you clocked in and clocked out. Quarter of an hour was stopped out of your pay if you were two minutes late in the morning or afternoon. My first week's wage was twelve shillings and sixpence. My mother gave me back the two shillings and sixpence and gave the rest of my wage to the church. I heard the Reverend Canon Prescott say. "A mother and her son have given the Church his first week's wage. May God Bless him and his good parents". That was a common practice for Catholics in those days at the nearby local churches.

The first six months I was the 'canlad', going for pies in Cross Street, chips and fish and also fags, if I could find a shop that had them. It was a very difficult time for things like fags and pipe tobacco. I also had to brew up around 12 noon for the turners and fitters in the works.

My position at the foundry was an apprentice fitter. One of the turners was a chap called Walter Ellis. Funnily he would say, "Fred", in very cultured tones, "Would you proceed to the nearest tobacco establishment and procure for me some selected pieces of the vagrant weed. Woodbines, Players, Kensitas, Park Drive, Capstan, Craven A, State Express they would be more than welcome to your friendly compatriot and mentor. However, if unable to procure the aforesaid, purchase the dastardly abomination of all abominations, Spanish Shawl or Turf, which I must say Frederick is horse shit in disguise". Of course all the chaps nearby would burst out laughing. He always described fags as the vagrant weed. Characters abounded at the foundry. I could go on and on.

After six months as canlad and general dogsbody I was seconded to Jack Airy, the top fitter at Whitehead's. The apprenticeship began fitting on various machines, boiler surveyors, boiler scaling, safety valve settings and renewals. Lathe work on shafts, castings, brass, pump and hydraulic work. Oddly the war helped young lads in engineering with many skills, the fact being that a lot of our young fitters and skilled machinists were in the services. Lots of the senior tradesman's work was loaded onto the young 14/15/16year old kids. I was going to night school three nights a week studying Maths, English, engineering drawing - and science subjects and working all hours. On Saturday and Sunday I was working for Balmer's Ship Repairers on Preston Dock on Navy vessel ship repairs. My apprenticeship was whizzing by. I was 19.

My pals Bob Parkinson, John Judge, Alfie Ingram, Arnold Radcliffe and Ged Connor had been called up in the armed forces. This upset me, I wanted to join the Royal Navy. National Conscription was in full force but I was in an exempt occupation. The Navy Recruiting Officer at Pole Street turned me away. He did say however I could be given priority from more exempt occupations by volunteering for the Merchant Navy, who were crying-out for ship's engineers, or become a Bevin Boy down the mines. I didn't fancy that. So I applied and managed to join the Merchant Navy as a Junior Engineer, a kid of nineteen years of age. Dad objected, Mother cried, but I was determined - away, away.

Stan Grandidge was Whitehead's foreman fitter. He was mad at me for leaving the firm at this particular time, with its full order book, and I was surprised at his vocal objections to my leaving. I did manage, however, to get away in November 1946, after much argy-bargy with him.

A brief sketch of my Merchant Navy days from 7th November 1946

First Boat - S S Defender

5th Assistant Engineer - Harrison Line. Built 1914, an old lady, 5280 tonnes, steam ship, 6 boilers, quadruple steam expansion engine. Scotch marine boilers, hand fed. Coloured Indian seaman stokers. A trip to India calling at all relative ports to Calcutta and return. Terrible riots in Calcutta. Saw Mahatma Ghandi in Chowringee, thousands swarming round him. Gurka troops on board guarded our ship. Signed on 6th January 1947 in Manchester, Salford Docks.

Second Boat - S S Strategist

5th Assistant Engineer - Harrison Line. Was 3788 tonnes with triple steam expansion engine, coal fired boilers and a Liverpool crew. I joined the ship's football team and cricket team. Trips to West Indian islands with exports from the U.K. Barbados, St. Kitts, Antigua, Trinidad and other small islands. Great trip, very happy. Signed on 9th July 1947.

Third Boat - S S Senator

4th Engineer. American all welded designed Sam boat. Oil fired boilers, triple steam expansion engine. Trip was to South Africa with U.K. exports, Suez and round the Cape. No sport on board, a tough trip with the sad news of my Mother having a stroke. I was in Capetown, the company would not fly me home to see her. I was devastated. She passed away later when I arrived home and I was with her when she died.

Fourth Boat - S S Lalande

4th Engineer, - Lamport and Holt. Triple expansion engine oil fired boilers. South American run. Santos, Rio de Janeiro, Bahia Don Salvador etc. A great trip. Made a lot of good English friends in the Capital of Sao Paulo. I saw Joe Louis fight the Brazilian Heavy Weight Champion at Santos Football ground. The fight lasted two rounds. Spoke to my boyhood idol the Brown Bomber. A good trip but I felt lonely, missing Cathy and family. Six months away was a long time.

Fifth and Last Boat, a tanker - The Pass of Ballater

3rd Engineer - small petrol tanker. I joined her in the Mersey. A complete nightmare. Came finally home for good on 5th July 1950. Sailor home from the sea - being married - it's time to settle down and get back to family, FOOTBALL and other matters.

English Electric

Ronald Hesketh - Drawing Office Days
Now sadly deceased

Most of my playing days were of course with St. Augustine in the Preston Catholic District League. I had played odd games for the following clubs in the district, English Electric (now BAE), Higher Walter Mills, Fulwood Amateurs, semi-pro matches for Fleetwood, Darwen and Lancaster city and I had also captained the Catholic League Team for the area.

As I worked in a large jig-and-tool aircraft drawing office, my comings and goings were all well known, even in the local rag, the Lancashire Evening Post. A well-known cricketer and ex-PNE footballer was Ronnie Hesketh who was larger than life and worked on the next drawing board to me. Both of us luckily were sent down to Lillieshall on a coaching course with the Walter Winterbottom F.A. Coaching School.

Ronnie was a great lad, a giant of a man 6' and 14 stone, who pulled my leg something awful along with others, Frank Miller, Peter Hamer, Harry Yates,

Freddie Mawdsley, Ces Burton, Terry Carter, Ken Simpson, Harry Eaves, Terry Rodgers etc. etc. All these chaps worked within shouting distance of each other in the huge drawing office at Strand Road in Preston.

They made my life an open book. Hesketh on a Monday morning after St. Austin's had won a match would bawl out, "You've never seen anything until you've seen the FOD in full flight on the wing." My position of course was outside right.

When I walked into the office I was sometimes greeted with voices singing, "Fo De, O, Do, Do". The last of my playing days lasted three years. I was going to retire on my wife Cathy's instructions. A cartilage removed, ten stitches in my right eyebrow, broken wrist, other odds and sods. She was worried about my being off work and my three children to boot. "Fo, De, O, Do, Do" later became my Preston North End coaching theme song in Northern Ireland with the Under 14's squad (PNE).

At the end of the footballing season, (foolishly), I would announce my retirement then three months later, (August), make a spirited comeback and this went on for about three seasons. As you can imagine, Hesketh and the jig-and-tool drawing office was in full chorus, especially when these events of mine appeared in the press. (Oh my, I was in trouble).

Even my local operatic society, St Austin's took part in mercilessly ragging me about it. It was all good fun. The leading ladies threatened to go on strike if I didn't retire! The Big Spoon Man, Hesketh of the drawing office, then decided to ask all my work pals to write, as he put it, an ode to the FOD. Here are some of my pals' thoughts and a sketch of me in full FOD match kit.

SOME SAY HE WAS A HUMAN,

SOME SAY HE WAS A GOD,

THERE'S BEEN MANY INVITATIONS,

BUT NONE QUITE LIKE THE FOD.

(THANK GOD)

"Farewell Freddy"

(A Tribute to the GOM)

THE YEARS ROLL BY AND IN THEIR WAKE,

LEAVE NAMES OF MEN WE N'ER FORSAKE

GREAT AND DARING, STAUNCH AND TRUE,
BUT NONE LIKE "FOD", I'M TELLING YOU!!
(Published by the FOD mutual admiration society in conjunction with St
Augustine's FC and ladies of his operatic society)

Memo No. ST.AU.FL.CR.00.00.BL

Tribute to the GOM

A very sad occasion for the office, yes the FOD has at last burned his boots, the game will miss him, we will all miss him. Will anyone interested please pay tribute below as to what we all think of the GOM.

To one who has played with and against FOD for a number of years this is indeed very sad news. On each of the previous occasions when he has "hung up his boots for good", his love of the game has always dragged him back into the fray. It seems sad to think how we shall no longer see the "skills" of the game which FO'D always tells us are his greatest assets viz:- the electrifying burst of speed, the beating of the full back with Owd,lad, the drawing of the defence and the final "clipping" back of the ball from the goal line. These talents are very rarely seen these days (especially from FOD) and I mourn their passing. Who can forget also his sterling displays at full back when his team were up against it (they are still up against it), or the time when he starred in a championship team for English Elec First XI, (could we ever forget the four games he played when they were short), and was rewarded with a trophy. I feel sure that the Catholic Football League will honour him in some way for his efforts. A medal from Pope John would be appropriate I think. For my part I would like to wish him a very happy retirement, (till next season comes around), I express the hope that perhaps the first to benefit from his unhappy retirement will be the landlord of the "Morning Star" on match days.

All the best FO'D, perhaps St. Augustine's FC will show immediate improvement.

Frank Miller

**'DOF' NI RETTEB YALP LL'UOY
STOOB RECCOS THGIEWYVAEH**

No words can describe the GOM in full flight down the right wing and his accurate chips (not fish and) back from the by-line.

This news is a sad blow to amateur soccer, the FOD was always a credit to the game, always immaculately turned out in Alec James type shorts, I suggest an illuminated address or some such honour for this all rounder.

This player has retired three or four times already.

I am sure Mrs. FOD did the right thing in burning his boots, why the hell didn't she burn them eight years ago then he couldn't have made a comeback. 'FOD' Lightweight shorts are the longest.

In closing, my heart is heavy to think that the maestro will not grace the parks of Preston again, but this may be a blessing for all the younger players who will no doubt benefit from this very, very sad occasion by gaining soccer knowledge from this widely travelled sportsman.

"BROKEN HEARTED"

R Hesketh.

Not knowing beforehand that a certain FO'D played footbrawl, it comes with some surprise therefore that he is retiring "again". The fact that he has reached this late date before announcing his retirement, seems to me all the more sportsmanlike; as the relief of his compatriots will only be overwhelmed by the sheer joy and happiness of Preston footbrawl fans in general - (Note "the" General), because if he had retired ten years ago, what would these Preston Footbrawl fans have to look forward to in 1962 besides Div III "Footbrawl". I suggest a compulsory retirement after the last three retirements.

MAN'S GAME LOVER

Terry Rodgers

They say "Old Soldiers never die" perhaps this FOD has the same qualities. Anyway he's forever telling us about his qualities. So I suppose we must be unlucky once again.

The saddest thing of all is all these young footballers who have played alongside him and how he has helped them. Who can they look to now? I mean who else could be so bad as to make others so good. No-one has ever given crows more enjoyment, nor made Referees and Linesmen's jobs so enjoyable - laugh!!

No-one has said so much and done so little. One could write a book on how he says he'd played and all the teams he says he's played for and probably be done for libel to boot. Yes, no-one has even been so low before and I think you will all agree no-one could be so again.

I well remember making an utter fool of myself as full back when FOD was on the wing - both on the same side. After the game he was heard to say, "what a ———— - I'd made of myself", but I remained happy having seen more of the game from my full back position and especially noted the right wing.

This must be it!! SEVEN times he has come back but even he can't have the neck to do so again. Or perhaps he has. Well ——

Harry Eaves

WELL PLAYED FREDDIE, WE ARE SO "GLAD"
(SORRY "SAD") TO SEE YOU GO.
THIS MIGHT BE THE END OF A GREAT (?) ERA FOR THE CLUB
"ST AUGUSTINE'S CLUB FC SUPPORTERS CLUB"

NB. PER ARDU A ET FOD, PRO DEO PRO FOD

Anonymous - possibly Terry Carter?

This is a great loss to the game, indeed but it is opera's gain!!

Lilleshall will never see the likes of him again, as you know the FOD set the place alight with his brilliance. Well really it was Walter Winterbottom who set the place alight after watching the FOD, he said if that's what they produce it should be burnt down. After FOD and Hesketh watched the recent England -v- Hungary game, what terrible fiendish manifestation can I think of next, for the cathedral of football, Walter Winterbottom, and the FOD.

Keith Lever
The twisted knave of Jig and Tool.

As a GOM fan for years the news of his impending retirement has left me speechless. Dare I suggest that he teach a certain member of R. Hesketh's football team a little gamesmanship or shall we buy them both retirement gifts.

One think is certain now, the GOM - FOD will be spending all his spare time with his operatives - so I remain, still one of the FOD's most ardent fans.

"OPERATIC CRITIC" or "FOOTBALL FAN"

I would like to see some of our rougher players burnt along with FOD's boots.

Ronnie Whiby

Play the Game

Poor! Poor! sad and broken hearted FOD but I ask myself is this another stage play with FOD once again taking the lead part, or is the burning of boots in some twisted way (KNOWING FOD) a "Joan of Arc" sequel. Anyway I'm hoping that this magnanimous gesture will not be marred by another return to the game.

Instead of burning the boots I wish he had left them laced on his feet and then hung them up!!

Harry Yates

Ode to ye Ancient Footballer

Unlike so many and like such a few,

Retirement to FODDY is nothing new,

Footballing o'er from this day on,

Who will the burden fall upon.

Of oft repelling the ferocious foe,

For he had told us so often, well do know,

Of the times FOD has netted that leather ball,

The truth of the story we cannot recall,

But I think St Augustine's will soon find out,

How to start winning, without a doubt.

Anon (Admirer)

You'll be a little lovlier after the match

with 'FOD' soap for footballers

(without the 9gm ounce perfume)

FOD's final (we hope) retirement from the game will come as a great shock to all opera, (sorry football), fans.

Fortunately I never had the pleasure of seeing him play, but I heard all about his great feats on the field - from FOD!

May I suggest that Frenchwood Rec be closed forever, in memory of a true sportsman.

Jim Irvine now sadly deceased

FOD's skills explained

He gathers the ball, beats one man, two men, three men even four, then he's only the Goalie to beat, but what does he do, he beats the keeper with a swerve, twist and pivot, (consecutive moves these), then with a nonchalant grin and wave, (as much as to say, "you know how it is"), he side steps over the ball and cracks it into the net. Result - Lostock St. GERRARD'S 1 St AUGUSTINE'S 1.

This is a piece of the Sports news printed in the Catholic Racing Results on 16th August 1956. The scorer at this game as if you hadn't guessed was - wait for it - YES FOD!!! I should know, I wrote it.

After this game, FOD was ceremoniously thrown into the River Ribble by his team mates along with one cut block of cement. Still FOD you remain -

THE GREATEST LITTLEST MAN OF FOOTBALL I HAVE
HAD THE GOOD FORTUNE TO MEET

Mick Watson

Glide past the fullback with 'FOD' non-skid football studs

It is a pity with a heavy heart that this news was received. However it seems a pity that his bloody voice hasn't broken so ending his singing career. I'm afraid we'll still have to suffer his feeble efforts at some of our informal functions. Like Santa Lucia and Vesta La Giubba, if you know what I mean.

Ken Barnes

This memo recalls for me a happy memory of the phantom FOD taking a penalty. The team 3 - 2 down, two minutes to go, the police holding the crowd back to the touchline.....

The FOD strolls up, quietly, confident, an air of anticipation on his countenance, the crowd hushed. He shoots.............a goal?............NO, about 8 rotten feet wide.

Hard luck Foddy.

No Foddy, don't hang them up, burn them, you might decide to play again.

Fred Mawdsley now sadly deceased

The Old Invincibles

Well Foddy the memo paying tribute to you is almost closed, thinking back over the seasons I can only wonder how fabulous you really were, and where on earth you learned to play the way you did, I think it was the continental style before they started playing it. Not the Hungarian Style as you and I know.

All the best in your retirement FOD. GOM NBG FL FH.

Ronnie Hesketh RIP

No wonder Mr. Wilson cancelled the TSR2 Project. I found myself redundant. With a bit of luck I found work at the Town Hall in Blackburn and lived over there for quite some years.

Fred, Gibralter, 1947.
SS Defender

Fred & Cathy, 1946.
While serving on the SS Defender

Fred on Flying Fish Day.
SS Lalande, South Atlantic 1950

Chapter Three

Short Stays

Darwen F.C. : Liverpool F.C. : Arsenal F.C.

I'll begin by talking about my early introduction into semi and professional football, working with managers with little anecdotes along the way starting with Paddy Sowden at Darwen Football Club.

I was working at Blackburn Town Hall at the time when I met Paddy Sowden. Paddy had a grocer's shop on Duke's Brow in Blackburn. Paddy was a very affable sort of a chap, a good footballer. He was understudy at Blackpool for a long time to Stanley Matthews and had a lot of experience. He was also a full badge professional coach and worked for the Lancashire Football Association and this is where really I met him on a coaching course. I also saw him down at Lilleshall and joined his primary preliminary course class at Preston, many years ago. Paddy was a smashing player, a good coach but he worked for a very, very poor club, Darwen. He picked me up on Tuesday and Thursday nights and we would go out to the Darwen ground called the Anchor and do the training and coaching. I was reasonably fit and turned out in the odd game for the reserves. However, the old legs weren't what they used to be so Paddy used to ask me to do a little bit of scouting.

Paddy left Darwen and joined Les Shannon at Blackpool. He was later to go on to Luton FC with Harry Haslam about 1970-72. When he was with Harry Haslam at Luton, three of my pals and myself, decided to go and visit Moscow. I rang Paddy up and said were going to Moscow and would be flying from Luton. We wanted to stay overnight and said that there were four of us going. Would he find accommodation for us in Luton? He sure did, he also arranged for us to see a match the day before we flew out to Moscow. He had arranged for us to stay at The Red Lion Hotel in the centre of Luton and was there to pick us up and escort us. Paddy really looked after us.

The same day we still had a lot of time on our hands so he took us along to see Harry Haslam, which was a joy itself, a Lancashire lad. He was picking up phones and saying "Hello Matt, is that you?", obviously talking to Sir Matt Busby. Luton were playing an Italian team that night. I think it was Bari and Harry arranged directors seats for us, of course, the best seats in that elite circle. As I recall Paddy was always very affable, very friendly and certainly went out of his way to make us feel welcome at that particular time and has kept in touch with me these last 30 years.

As I said before, Paddy left Darwen Football Club and I assisted for a few weeks.

Darwen owed me quite a bit of money in travelling expenses. I was supposed to be on petrol expenses, but I could not expect Darwen Football Club really to pay any kind of expenses, due to the very low income that they had from a sparse support. Reluctantly I handed in my resignation to Jack Howarth, Mr. Darwen F.C. himself, who was a workaholic for the Club. You name it he did it.

In trying to raise funds I became interested in organising a concert. I approached Leyland Motors Brass Band and asked Ernie Appleyard, the Conductor, whom I knew, if the lads would come over and play at the Free Gardener's club in Darwen. Sure enough they agreed. We had tickets printed and I distributed them to all the connections at Darwen Football Club, the different directors, Bob Eccles; Jack Howarth who was the Club Secretary at that time, and we managed to fill the Free Gardener's club to listen to Leyland Motors Brass Band. I also asked a top comedian in Blackburn called Jimmy Quinn to come along and do a turn for the football club for free. Jimmy did of course, a good lad Jim. Leyland Motors Band charged a nominal fee of £15 for twenty players or something like that. We made over £300 on that particular night which taught me a lot about raising funds.

Trying to get money together for a poor club is a tough job. The gates had fallen very dramatically and it was a shame to see the decay at Darwen football ground. I remember playing there for Lancaster City many years prior to 1947 before I joined up, and there were 2 or 3000 on the ground. It was a shame to see the club slowly dying. Darwen F.C. even made a draw (F.A. Cup) with Arsenal F.C. in the halcyon days of the club (Pre-War).

Later, funnily by strange coincidence, I was invited by Ernie Appleyard to sing with the Leyland Motors Show Band along with Blackburn's Kennedy sisters, a great trio, in various concerts usually for charities. One concert which stands out was the Blackburn Mayor's Gala Show on Bonfire Night in November 1972. Happy, busy days. It was time to change my footballing interest at Darwen F.C. for different fields.

At that time there was a boy called John Waddington who was playing in the Darwen set up. I knew Tony Waiters, who was a coach and goalkeeper at Liverpool. He had seen me scouting up and down the circuit. I gave him a ring, "Tony, I'm leaving Darwen Football Club".

He asked me, "Are there any players there Fred that you fancy?".

"Well", I said, "there is really. A lad called John Waddington. He's a centre back and also plays up front for St. Mary's College and Darwen Reserves. He's only a young lad, 16 or 17". I think he was sixteen at the time.

Tony said, "Fine", and the next move made was a trial, to cut a long story short John Waddington moved from Darwen Football Club to Liverpool Football Club. He did very very well.

He was in the B Team and then the A Team and then the reserves and resulting from that Tony said, "Fred, why don't you send a letter to Bill Shankly,? I can get you a job doing a bit of scouting in your area". That was the Preston, Blackpool and Blackburn area, and I said, "Fair enough".

I duly sent a letter off to Bill Shankly at the end of that particular season and the reply came back from Shanks that he would review the situation. Then, lo and behold, I became a Liverpool scout and everybody was surprised. It also appeared in the local papers. 'Fred O'Donoghue appointed as Liverpool Scout in the North West area'. I was elated. One of the lads I took was my old drawing office tormentor, Ronnie Hesketh's lad, Tony, not a bad all rounder. (Cricket especially).

I began taking boys down to Melwood. Tony Waiters and I became great friends along with Ronnie Moran, and Joe Fagan. Three or four of the lads did very well, David Moran and Peter Lamb, appearing in the A and B Teams. I didn't do too badly really, but that particular year Liverpool became involved in the FA Cup Final.

I'd seen Bill Shankly on two or three occasions before and had spoken to him about various players within the area. You've read and heard lots of stories about Bill Shankly from all the different players; I found him very direct. His language wasn't the King's or the Queen's but more strong, Scotch/English of a vulgar kind. Bill Shankly was a law unto himself.

I saw and read in the Daily Mirror, about Shankly handing out Cup Final tickets to schoolboys in Liverpool because they were wearing Liverpool shirts and shorts. This was when Liverpool was in the FA Cup Final with Leeds at Wembley.

My son, Stewart, was absolutely crazy about this Liverpool team so I wrote a letter asking for two tickets for this particular match at Wembley. Peter Robinson who is now the Chief Executive Officer, and was the Secretary in those days, sent one ticket. I rang up Bill, "Bill, it's Fred O'Donoghue here. I've only got one ticket. Stewart my son is only 10 years old and I would like two tickets to take him down to see the final".

Bill said something in Scottish and then I got a mouthful of language off him and I couldn't understand this. I was hurt, so I sent another letter to Peter Robinson indicating that I was going round the North West area looking for boys to play for Liverpool FC. One was already appearing in the reserves and looking a very good player, (that was John Waddington of course). I said I had seen in the newspaper that Shanks was giving out tickets willy nilly, or so it appeared to me. It may have been a publicity stunt, this I don't know. However, it looked very, very bad to someone who was working for the club, earning nothing really apart from petrol expenses and here he was giving tickets out. Sadly, I never got a reply.

I then asked Geoff Twentyman who was Chief Scout there. Geoff couldn't help me. He said he had no tickets left. Ronnie Moran of course, he couldn't help me. He was only a coach there at that particular time. Ronnie said, "Well, I wouldn't worry about it so much Fred. Leave it till you've been at the club a bit longer until you ask for an extra ticket. I'll try and get one", but Ronnie couldn't. I was still adamant about this. I managed to get one off John Carey at Blackburn Rovers for our Stewart.

In August that year I got a letter from Peter Robinson who thanked me for my services as a scout for Liverpool Football Club, but they no longer required me. I was most upset. I drifted angrily away from Liverpool Football Club. Obviously I'd been sacked. I decided then to try elsewhere, however more change quickly came my way.

The phone rang in my office, Ext. 322, Blackburn's Traffic Section Engineering Department. A phone call from Gordon Clarke who was then chief Scout at Arsenal FC. "Fred I believe you've had a bit of a barny with Bill Shankly and the Liverpool set up".

I said, "Well, yeah I have", and explained what it was really about.

He said, "Do you want to do a bit for us, for Arsenal?" This was an honour indeed and I joined the Arsenal Football Club and that basically was the sorry story of Liverpool and my one and only sacking in football. However to return to Liverpool FC, I had one or two happy moments with the staff.

Expenses from Liverpool FC   Letter from Bill Shankly, 1970

I remember going down to Melwood on my Sundays. I remember taking trialist boys down, taking my son Stewart to see games at Liverpool when Ronnie Moran would give me a ticket for Stewart. I made friends with Rueben Bennett, and Tom Saunders, now a Director. I played with the Staff v Apprentices odd afternoons when I was down there, and enjoyed it. By the way, Staff always won.

FOD'S big clanger - Kevin Keegan

(Turned Down)

One Friday night while I was working for Liverpool, I was instructed by the Anfield chief scout, Geoff Twentyman, to go to Stockport to take a look at a young Scunthorpe United player - that's right - the one and only Kevin Keegan, then virtually unknown.

The report I sent back was not very enthusiastic. Kevin must have had one of those nights, or at least that's what I tell myself every time his name is mentioned. Anyway, Geoff persisted and the rest of the Keegan story is common knowledge with his fairytale rise to stardom with Liverpool and England, eventually leading to a half a million pound transfer to West German Club, Hamburg. Incidentally, at the same Friday game was Frank O'Farrell, then, I think, with Leicester. Little wonder perhaps that I have a very high opinion of Geoff Twentyman as a scout! He's the top man for me.

You will always find a number of ex-professionals, like Geoff, in the ranks of soccer scouts, though I think it is fair to say that the bulk of the scout army is made up of people from many other walks of life. Especially at youth level and schoolboys.

Quite a lot of former players retain their enthusiasm for the game and while wanting to steer clear of the pressures of management, have a hankering to maintain their connection with it. Cynics would argue the opposite, of course, but there are many players who hang up their boots and wish to put something back into the game that has given them so much and usually do a bit of part time scouting. To conclude, Geoff said Shanks, Ronnie Moran, Bob Paisley, Tony Waiters, Joe Fagan, all of 'em fancy Keegan, even Roy Evans. That makes you the odd man out!" I stuttered "How wrong could I be'." He laughed. "I'm human too", he said. "Forget it, you'll do for me. You're honest".

Shankly - he must have been the greatest after Bob (trophy wise) Paisley - everybody said so. I didn't see it like that. I saw that Shankly was his own man and I admired him for that. He was a ferocious kind of a man who had great changes of mind and you could never really get close to the man. Being honest, I didn't really get to know him. He had so many connections and so many people that he was dealing with, day in and day out. He was a megastar manager, there was no question about that, a megastar manager. I regret having read the Daily Mirror that day.

Later however when I met Bill Shankly at a game with Blackburn Rovers reserves he came across to me in the old, big boardroom at Ewood, shook my hand and inquired about my health. A big, big man, I admired him really despite the fact that he had sacked me. Eddie Quigley who was stood next to me remarked, "I didn't know you knew him, Fred?"

My reply was, "Eddie, I don't, I really don't". (He puzzled me)?

Brian Hall was a player for the Anfield Club when I was scouting for them, a scintillating player, a flank man in a very good team. I had watched both Brian and Steve Heighway on several occasions. It was ironic that, twenty years later, I signed Brian's son, Andrew, on schoolboy forms for Preston North End. Brian became part of the coaching staff at Preston North End.

Brian Hall, how the lads loved him, as did I. His skills, his own personal panache of pass and move. Over the years at PNE I got to know him and the family very well. Happy days with Brian at PNE. Also I will not forget Ronnie Moran at Liverpool, my coach supreme and a very old friend.

"Arsenal here I come". In the North West area at that time there was a scout for Arsenal FC called Harry Woodhouse. Harry was a big name in the scouting fraternity. He was the one that had spotted England Schoolboy, Trevor Ross, who signed for Arsenal FC.

So I joined Arsenal Football Club. It was a different game. The standard of player that they have there is absolutely top class, international level. The boys that go to Arsenal have to be of a very high standard indeed and I realised this when I visited the training ground. The young players, 14, 15 years of age were all exceptionally good players.

Harry Woodhouse it seems had told Gordon Clarke about me and about the places that he'd seen me, mostly on town team games in Burnley, Preston, Blackburn, Bury and Bolton and I think that's how I got the job really. It was Harry Woodhouse who prompted Gordon Clarke to give me a position as his assistant in the North West. I began working for Arsenal. That particular year Arsenal appeared in the Arsenal v Leeds FA Cup final. I thought, "Aye, aye, here we go again, I'm going to get left out". I hadn't had much success with regard to trialist schoolboys because of the high standards involved. There were not many England class schoolboys knocking about up north at that time apart from maybe Tommy Caton and Trevor Ross, and lads like these, I had no chance of getting anyway. So, I expected another single ticket. But no, Arsenal style, I got two tickets for me and my wife Cathy; the train tickets from Preston down to London, to stay in one of the top hotels in London. To go down on the Friday night, have dinner on Friday night, full English breakfast, lunch at Highbury and on to the game at Wembley, not far from the Royal Box. I could actually see the Queen.

I watched Arsenal get beaten by Leeds in that particular match. Each of the wives was given a red carnation with a £5 note in an envelope. The pre-match banquet was sumptuous and then back to the hotel at night time to a first class meal and breakfast in the morning. All paid for by Arsenal Football Club, I had never seen so much wealth in all my life in football. Wealth abounded everywhere, the clothes, the food, caviar, the top business connections, it was absolutely unbelievable what we saw. Cathy who is not very much interested in football was certainly interested about the weekend stay at the Arsenal's expense. We often recall that weekend in London. Moet Champagne and Dover sole.

I wasn't at Arsenal very long because of the scarcity of English schoolboy stars. I was at the end of a telephone line most of the time with Gordon Clarke and Ernie Collett. At one particular meeting, while I was down in London, Bertie Mee came along to talk to the scouts. There were a lot of scouts, forty to fifty I would say would be a moderate estimate. I didn't exactly know how many there were but there certainly seemed a lot of scouts. But I was beginning to think I was just a number at the end of the telephone line. I sent my petrol expenses down to Nobby Clarke and they were paid promptly, without any fuss, but I was losing interest in a club that I couldn't get my teeth into. Remembering my Darwen FC days and the involvement, I needed a challenge. It came sooner rather than later.

Rochdale F.C.

I was down at Rochdale one particular time watching a player for Gordon Clarke. Fred Radcliffe was the Chairman at Rochdale FC, and I had met him previously while doing business for Blackburn Corporation. He was the spring manufacturer in Rochdale. Blackburn Corporation had bought various components from Fred Radcliffe.

"Fred, what tha' doing", (in broad 'Rochdale - Lancashire' if there is such a thing). "Fred, what tha' doing working down yonder for a club you can't get no satisfaction from?"

I shook my head, "Don't know", I said. I came home that night and said, "Cathy, I am at the end of a telephone with Nobby Clarke". Telling her about Rochdale.

"Fred Radcliffe," she said, "is right".

I rang Fred up on the Monday morning from the Town Hall. "It's Fred O'Donoghue, what were you thinking for me?"

He replied, "Chief Scout".

Cathy and I had three children.

I said, "If I take the job on as Chief Scout," (he said, "yes"), "how much will that work out at?"

His reply was, "£3 a week for telephone expense, your petrol expense plus car repairs and 6p per mile. It's nothing really, but you will love it with us, Fred, this I'm sure!"

I reckoned it up. It was miserly, but I love football, because it wasn't any kind of money really. The nut I am, I love doing it. I finished at Arsenal, spoke to Gordon Clarke and thanked him and Ernie Collett, who was his assistant scout, for kind attentions, and became a member of 4th Division Rochdale Football Club. Nobby Clarke and Ernie Collett understood my feelings and graciously accepted my written resignation with their best wishes.

Now joining a football club on those kind of terms could cause problems. It's not the Manager that asked me, it was the Director-Chairman. There is a difference and I said to Fred, "Listen, you'd better make it right with your Dick Connor. I don't know Dick Connor or Peter Madden who is his assistant. You'd better get that right before I join you because he's going to be watching me. Tell him I've no ambitions to be a Manager, or an Assistant Manager, but I'll certainly do the local scouting as we've discussed". A little bit later another phone call, - honestly the phone (Ext. 322) at Blackburn Town Hall was more like the soccer hotline than the traffic management side of the business. It was Dick Connor, "Fred, I'd like you to come down and see me and Peter". I said, "Yes alright".

Off I went to Rochdale and sat in the little manager's office. Beryl was the Assistant Secretary, a bonny girl Beryl. She caught my eye as soon as I went in. I said, "I don't mind working here with such pleasant faces around me". Dick Connor smiled, sat down with me and Peter Maddon. We thrashed out a kind of policy which could only be done in a small way because we were limited, no cash, just limited resources which I'd experienced of course at Darwen.

Rochdale I found very interesting. Possibly it set me off on my path, with whatever glory that scouts may get. The first megastar in my book was John Waddington of Liverpool FC, but there was this lad called Alan Taylor. Alan was a lad from Morecambe, a former apprentice at Preston, who didn't make the grade (so Alan Ball Senior said). I'd heard that he'd been released from Preston and that he had started to play for Morecambe reserves. I rang a friend of mine up there, former Darwen player Sean Gallagher, who had played with me and Paddy Sowden. I asked about this lad coming from Preston and Sean rated him. I went to watch him a few times in the Morecambe reserves and I recommended him very highly to Dick Connor. He was very fast, not a lot of trickery about him but very, very fast. He could ghost past players, and he looked above his class in Morecambe reserves. I came back repeatedly and told Dick Connor about this lad in Morecambe. Jimmy Birket, Manager of Darwen FC, who later worked for me at Blackburn Rovers, saw him at Bradford Park Avenue and gave him a good report. Also Stan Howard at Chorley Football Club came back with glowing reports. Again I recommended him. We decided then not to go for him but to leave it until the end of the financial year. Financially, Morecambe were struggling. I'm sure they'd have snapped our hand off if we'd offered £2,000. Anyway the deal was done at the Bull & Royal in Preston. It was £2,500. £500 a month for five months and basically that's how Alan Taylor joined Rochdale. By this time Dick Connor had unfortunately been sacked, along with Peter Madden. Walter Joyce became the new manager of Rochdale Football Club assisted by Dennis Butler and of course myself who did the scouting, the legendary Tom Nichol doing the Office Admin with Angus McLean and pretty office girl Beryl. I had a homely feeling about the club. The cleaner, a buxom lass, always greeted me with, "Hi Fred, are you alright?" It was nice.

Alan Taylor went on to do great things with Rochdale Football Club. Different managers came down; Ken Furphy who I spoke to at great length; there was Ron Greenwood from West Ham, also Harry Haslam and a posse of league managers who I was getting to know by this time. I spoke very highly of Alan Taylor. Alan of course went on to West Ham glory, when he was sold by Rochdale for £75-85,000 - you never really got to know how much, but it was a lot. I got a letter of thanks from Rochdale Football Club. Also a wine set with a decanter and glasses with the Board's appreciation for what I'd done. It was very satisfying to see Alan Taylor go on to Wembley and win the cup for West Ham. We've kept in touch over the years.

The top man at Rochdale when I worked there was Tom Nichol (who is still there). No praise is high enough for this man, always available, did every job at the Spotland Club and assisted me in every way, loyal to the cause on Mickey Mouse money. Tom is one of the unpaid giants of our National game.

Walter Joyce had been a player at Blackburn and Burnley, was well respected in the game and knew the game inside out. Rochdale was his first club as a Manager and on the day that he came down to Rochdale, Chairman Fred Radcliffe rang, "Fred, you'd better come and meet Walter because you don't know him". Dennis Butler, ex-Bolton player had been moved up to his assistant. I duly went down to Spotland. Chairman Fred introduced me to Walter who said, "Come on we'll go and sit down in my office and we can talk about different areas and the different lads that you've brought down".

We went into his little office there as Secretary Beryl gave a warm smile and said, "Hello Fred, do you know the new manager?"

I said, "No, but I will be doing in the next ten minutes," Beryl was a joy really, always very pleasant and said the right things. I went into the office with Walter and we talked about this and that, the players that we'd seen also the players that we'd like to sign on, if we'd only more money, and things like that. The phone rang and he put his hand over the mouthpiece, "It's Tommy Docherty". "Hello, it's Walter". The conversation went something like "Well, yeah it's very kind of you to give me a ring Tom but, well, I've just been appointed, this is my first day".

When he came off the phone I asked, "What was that about Walter?" and he said, "I've been offered the Manchester United Youth Team Coach job and I don't know what to do Fred".

I said, "But you've only just taken the Manager's job here at Rochdale".

"Yeah, I know that. Tommy Docherty wants me to think about it and to let him know within the next twenty-four hours what I'm going to do. Do I want the Manchester United football job or am I going to continue here at Rochdale."

I said, "Take your time about this one".

We went on talking about things as previously, then it came up again. He said, "It's on my mind Fred, I can't concentrate. I'll have to make a decision. I want to make a decision now".

"Well, wait a minute Walter", I said. "Tell me what do you want to be most of all". I repeated, "What do you want to be?"

"I want to be a manager," was his reply.

"Well you've answered your own question really. Tell him that you want to be a manager.".

Probably that's about the worst advice I could have ever given Walter Joyce because looking back in retrospect I think if Walter had gone to be the manager of the youth team at Manchester United he would have been a mega-youth team manager at this moment in time.

Walter picked the phone up, "Tommy? Walter, I've thought about it and I know it's only been half an hour since I spoke to you, but I want to be a manager Tom more than anything".

I could hear a Scotch voice saying, "Well best of luck to you, best of luck". He put the phone down and then we continued.

Walter Joyce worked very hard at Rochdale. He used to mow the pitch, roll the pitch, mark the pitch, do a secretary's job, pay wages; Walter Joyce was the workaholic of the lowly Rochdale Football Club assisted by Tom Nichol. Mr Loyalty himself..

Walter is a powerfully built chap, he also has a very charming and pleasing personality. His apprenticeship began at Burnley along with another compatriot of mine, Jim Furnell. His knowledge of the game and his vast experience makes him stand out as one of the North West's top men in soccer circles. A player at Burnley, Blackburn, Oldham; he had been to Huddersfield, Bolton, Crewe, Preston and now at Bury helping out. He has known all the ups and downs at all levels of the game. A canny lad, he made a bob or two and later at Preston I called him the St. Helens millionaire. He loved a bet on the horses.

My first experience with him as manager at Rochdale was when he sent Dennis Butler, his assistant and myself, to sign on Leo Skeete. He was a tall, skilful striker whom we had been watching at Ellesmere Port. On that particular day Leo was playing at Wigan. Walter rang me up. "Fred, meet Dennis at Wigan's Springfield Park and get Leo to sign. I've done the homework with the Ellesmere Port Chairman". Dennis and I watched the game, which Wigan won, but we both liked some of the skills that Leo had.

After the match we went down into the dressing room and completing introductory formalities took Leo into the secretary's office, kindly lent to us by the Wigan manager, who I think was Gordon Milne, ex-Liverpool, at that time. Dennis produced the League forms and an offer was made to Leo. Looking back it was Mickey Mouse money, but Leo accepted. Dennis put the forms on the desk to be signed.

Leo slowly paused. "Excuse me", he said and took out of his jacket pocket a box which contained contact lenses. "I'll have to put these in first, I can't see as good as I should," and returned to the visitor's dressing room to use the mirror.

Dennis looked at me worried. "Bloody-hell! Did you know about that?"

I said, "No. Stop worrying. Think of Nobby Stiles". In those days players with contact lenses were not top of the pops as far as football went. After a while Leo came back and signed. Dennis and I shook his hand and wished him all the best. He did well at Rochdale and Walter Joyce was suited. I may add that Dennis and myself had one or two queer feelings that day!!

I became more involved with Rochdale and Walter - going to his home, meeting his good wife, Doreen, a smashing girl, his son Warren and the rest of his family. We became firm friends. The one trip with Rochdale I'll not forget was a Friday night match with Bournemouth, (away). Tom Nichols, the wonderful evergreen top man at Rochdale was unable to go as sponge man. I volunteered to do the task. At 8 a.m. on a Friday morning, a cold wet November day, I climbed on the rickety old bus. Players were half asleep. Walter with an angry voice: "Skips on board?...Fred".

"Yes Walter" I said. Everyone was bad tempered. Breakfast!! God knew where it was. No motorway stops in those days. No motorways! The way we went the driver got lost!!

Menu for breakfast - toast and tea, no bacon or eggs, "Not much money to spare", Walter thoughtfully said. "I'll have to watch the cash"

Six hours later lunch. "Ha, Ha", this was better - beans, and toast with an egg, (in the singular), poached or boiled and only one per player. Those that didn't like eggs took them and gave them to the chaps who did. I was lucky I had two. We were all weary but wow - it's Bournemouth. 'Oh, I do like to be beside the seaside' - what a silly song I thought.

At 5 p.m. we went for a walk on the cliff type sea front, Walter telling all players to stretch their cramped-up legs and be back at the flipping bus for 5.45 p.m. At 6 p.m. we had arrived duly at the Bournemouth Dean Court Ground for the 7 p.m. kick-off. I ran on the pitch three or four times attending tired legs and weary mind. We got beat of course!!

The journey back I thought was the longest I'd ever ever made. Stiff sore bum, the meal on the way home was half cooked, some of it cold - chicken fricassee they said!! We arrived in Rochdale at 3.30 a.m. back home in Preston 4.45 a.m. I vowed, never again, to go all that way and get beat. It wasn't pleasant. However, the wind of change began to blow again.

I was about to leave Walter and Rochdale to join Blackburn. But the harsh life of some of our poor clubs is very real indeed and football needs to address the issue, with T.V., financial aid, and more football pool donations. Richer clubs have become more greedy, with money becoming the curse of the National game at all levels, and Court Writs on many 2nd and 3rd Division Clubs. Money is now the God the time has come for a National Football "Revolution" of change. Greed is the root of all evils in our expanding National game. Players, Directors and Clubs alike. A lot of them are guilty of greed. More wanting more; and Sky television dictating when our teams shall play Sundays, Monday, etc.

These predators of greed and power. What a shame, what is going on in our Country. The dog used to wag the tail, now the tail wags the dog - if you know what I mean. Gallant Mr. Bryan Gray, Chairman of PNE in the Lancashire Evening Post January 14th, 1999 is quoted as stating that the huge amount of money from Sky TV and BBC is having damaging effects on the game in lower divisions how right he is. His solitary support for the Office of Fair Trading (OFT) is courageous and ? PNE being the one and only club in England to back the OFT and have sent a 90 page report to the proceedings that the existence of lower league clubs are now seriously threatened. Well done Bryan. May I also add the agents in the game have multiplied tenfold these last few years. They remind me of vultures clawing, biting and picking the unfortunate victims. I hope the PFA will take note and action the goings on of this unfortunate equation.

Chapter Four

Ken Furphy - Blackburn Rovers FC

Ken Furphy had seen me at various schoolboy games in Blackburn on Witton Park, Pleasington and on different school grounds along with Jimmy Baldwin and Harold Readett. Harold Readett was the chief scout at Blackburn Rovers and knew I'd taken boys to Liverpool, also Arsenal and now was taking boys to Rochdale.

Ken Furphy came round to me on Witton Park and said, "Fred could I have a word with you?"

I didn't know Ken Furphy. I knew he was from Yorkshire somewhere, and he'd come up from Watford FC to be manager at Blackburn Rovers. Although I had spoken to him at Rochdale F.C (re: Alan Taylor queries)

I went to one side with him and he said, "How would you like to be the Chief Scout at Blackburn Rovers?"

I looked at him incredulously. I was working in Blackburn at the Town Hall as I've said before, in the traffic management section and here I was being offered the Chief Scout's job at Blackburn Rovers. He followed that quickly by saying, "It's not much money Fred but if you come I can give you £10 a week and petrol expenses". I said, "It's kind of you Ken. I'll have to think about this". I was thinking about Fred Radcliffe and Rochdale; Walter Joyce and Alan Taylor and the friends that I'd made like Angus McClean, Beryl and Tom Nichols. I thought of all these friends. Here I am talking about going to Blackburn Rovers, but it made sense.

My wife Cathy said, "Fred, it makes sense. What are you waiting for? You love football, you're in football, why the hell don't you get down to Blackburn Rovers and get working there? It's the town where we live." We lived on Revidge Road in Blackburn. She went on, "This is the place to be, not travelling all the way to Rochdale two nights a week, also Saturdays and Sundays. Get yourself down to Blackburn Rovers."

I rang Ken Furphy and we arranged a meeting. Ken was one of the most competent managers that I ever met or worked with. I'd met Bill Shankly, Bertie Mee, Dick Connor, Walter Joyce and now Ken Furphy, a grammar school educated lad who had a family; wife, son and daughter. He lived in Blackburn and here he was inviting me to come inside. I felt very, very elated. I had a head like Birkenhead, I certainly felt on top of the world with obvious recognition as a scout.

He took me into the offices and introduced me to Mr Fryars who was the Youth Director. Mr. Fryars, I felt, didn't particularly like this appointment. Ken told him in no uncertain terms, "This is my Scout from now on. Do you understand me Mr. Fryars?" There was an obvious clash between the pair of them.

Mr. Fryars, irritated, snapped, "What's to become of Harold and Jimmy?" (that was Harold Readett and Jimmy Baldwin).

"I'm not concerned. They can carry on scouting if they want. They've been here many years, but this is my man. Do you understand me?" stated Ken Furphy.

I could see Mr. Fryars was really upset. Ken took me from the top offices at Nuttall Street down to the small offices below, gave me a desk, telephone and a file of information. He then handed me a list of scouts and left.

Mr Fryars, who had followed, turned on me and said, "From now on all the expenses that you incur must come through me. I'm responsible. I'm the Youth Director at this club".

I felt a lot of hostility really from Al Fryars, but was later to find him a very warm, and very conscientious man in many ways. He was very tight with the money and he wanted to know where every penny had gone. Mr Big Al Fryars was in the cattle business. He used to buy and sell cattle and the staff christened him 'Big Al' because he wore a very large trilby. It was more like a John Wayne western hat. He was a lively member of the Board at Blackburn Rovers at that time with Bancroft, Keighley and Ibbotson etc. There was quite a bunch of rich men on the Board at that time. But, as I stated before, 'Big Al' made it clear, "I want to see every expense in detail".

Suddenly from a Chief Scout at Rochdale where there was only me doing the scouting really, I became in charge of eight scouts on the Blackburn Rovers scouting team. Some of the scouts were on a weekly wage. There was Jimmy Baldwin on £3 and Harold Readett, who was the Chief Scout at that time, and who resigned a little later, was on £5. With my wage the total wage bill for scouting activities within the North West for Blackburn Rovers was roughly about £30 per week. Big Al also made me responsible for the accounts of the scouts. They got mileage at that particular time of 6p a mile and I was responsible to Mr. Fryars for showing him the monthly accounts, making sure the mileage was right.

In all fairness Blackburn Rovers FC had very, little money at that time. They were scrimping and saving, trying to make ends meet and I was responsible for paying the scouts concerned. Payment of these cheques was made by John Howarth, who was a very young club secretary. They didn't earn much those scouts. I think the most would be about £10 to £12 a month and they'd spent hours and hours on pitches all over the place.

In Wales they had a great Welsh connection, Gwyllam Morris, a scout who brought along Roy Vernon, Mike England and others. He wasn't really a scout, he didn't know much about football but he kept his ear to the ground and got a list of these lads and good players in the area. I was later to visit him and stay with him for a week in Pwhelli.

Slowly, I became established at Blackburn Rovers. It was a daily routine of finishing my work at the town hall at 12.30 p.m., jumping in my car and going down to Ewood, picking up the mail, the trials, the scouts, the schools , the teachers, all the bric-a-brac that goes into scouting and then returning back to my desk at 1.30 p.m. at the Town Hall. I enjoyed the life, enjoyed going to different games, the Reserve Team games to A and B team games.

After I'd been there two or three months Ken Furphy said, "Fred, I'd like you to take care of the A team and Tommy Howarth take charge of the B team". Tommy Howarth, a top man, was one of the assistant coaches at Blackburn Rovers. On Friday afternoons I'd finish work early at the Town Hall and go down to the club and ring round players. Some we'd notified on the Thursday. All the players were notified in those days. The A and B teams played on a Saturday afternoon as did the first team and the reserve team. A lot of work was involved on Friday and Saturday.

I would be dashing out with the A team to Stockport, Blackpool, Preston etc., Tom Howarth would be doing likewise, going to Crewe, Chester etc. The first team would be away or at home with Ken Furphy. The work that was carried out was phenomenal. Also Richard Dinnis was with the reserve team. It was a godsend later on when the central league became a mid-week fixture. When the A and B team had games played on Saturday mornings that eased the load of the work on the footballing staff.

Ken Furphy rang me up one particular night. He was going up to Carlisle. "Fred, I'd like you to meet me at the Trafalgar Hotel". In those days it was called the Five Barred Gate Pub at Samlesbury. He had a big Rover car and I had a small Mini or something. I met him there at 6 o'clock and we were on the ground there at Carlisle at 7.20 p.m. We absolutely flew. He frightened me to death.

There I was to meet Jack Charlton and other managers, though Jack Charlton would probably not remember me because I never spoke. I was impressed by Charlton's knowledge of players, the depth of knowledge that he had of the game. I listened to Ken Furphy and Jack Charlton speaking to one another, with a great kind of bondship between them, even though I don't think that they'd ever played together. They probably played against one another. I really enjoyed all this wonderment at being involved in football. I was very happy at Blackburn Rovers. Ken and I got on well together along with Jack Marshall, the club physio. It was a happy club.

Ex-Chief Scout, Harold Readett wasn't too happy with the set up, and, as I expected he resigned. Jimmy Baldwin kept on for a short while after, then he too was to finish at the club. Ken Furphy, I felt, was hoping to go onto bigger things. Rovers Reserves played Sheffield United Reserves on one particular night. He spoke to John Harris, who was manager at Sheffield United. "John", he said, "Isn't it about time you were moving upstairs?"

I got the gist of it, that Ken wanted to manage a big Yorkshire side. He was a Yorkshire man, a smashing bloke was Ken Furphy. With his knowledge of the game and his managerial skills, he was a complete manager really. He'd a bit of education to back this up. He moved on to Sheffield United and became the manager there taking Tony Field, the Rovers striker with him.

By this time I had introduced the Report Expense Sheet to the delight of cash starved Rovers and to the delight of a certain Mr. 'Big Al' Fryars.

I've kept in touch with Ken over all these years. It's a nice feeling.

Ken Furphy leads out the team at Ewood

Tony Parkes, midfield foil for Metcalfe

BLACKBURN ROVERS FC

CHIEF SCOUTS LIST 1974-5-6

Scouts	Area	Remarks
J. Baldwin	Blackburn	Scout & Assessor
J. Birkett	Rishton	Combination Scout
A. Haley	Leeds	Leeds Scout
I. Hanson	Blackburn	Assistant to Chief Scout. S/Boys
J. Mooney	Liverpool	Scout
R. Mooney	Tydlesley	Scout
F. O'Donoghue	Preston	Chief Scout/Part time
M. McGrath	Blackburn	Scout. S/Boy Selector Coach
G. Smith	Manchester	League Scout & S/Boys
J. Williams	Liverpool	Liverpool Scout
J. Campbell	Darwen	Scout & Assessor (Ex-Rovers player Sponge man for Reserves)
T. White	ex-Blackpool Director	Scout
J. Vine	London	Scout
P. Aimson	Dorset	Scout
A. Wilkinson	Barnsley	Scout

(Scouts Director) Board Member
Arthur Langdale Fryars

Gordon Lee - Success for the Rovers

There was a search for an appointment to succeed Ken Furphy and the choice was good. I don't know where Mr. Bancroft or Mr. Keighley had got the information from, but this manager came in. A direct sort of man, Gordon Lee, a tall lad, who had been at Port Vale for a while. Gordon got hold of the 1st Team Squad. I was still acting as Chief Scout at that time and after a few weeks I realised that he knew the Third Division inside out. He knew the players, and the teams and many senior contacts in the game.

Arriving in his office he said, "Fred, have you a minute? I would like to have a word with you". He said simply, "I've heard all about you Fred. The directors have spoken to me, and different people in the game. Richard Dinnis has spoken of you doing a hell of a good job, particularly on the youth side of this club. I don't want to interfere in any way, shape or form. You carry on as you are doing and I'll be happy with that. As far as I'm concerned I'll get on with the first team and that's what I'm going to concentrate on. I'm not going to get involved with the junior squads but if I can help you in any way, I will do. By that I mean coaching or sponsorship, visiting parents or schools, or whatever it is. Don't be frightened of coming to me. If you've a problem with players or apprentices," (there were three or four apprentices there at that time), "don't be frightened of coming to me".

I said, "Fair enough Gordon," and so began my relationship with Gordon Lee which was very warm indeed and has continued over the past twenty five years.

John Butcher came on the scene, a goalkeeper from Newcastle that I brought through after some trials. John Bailey from Liverpool and three or four more apprentices lived in the houses in Nuttall Street. They more or less looked after themselves in those days. They had no hostel at Blackburn Rovers, they just had two houses that we put the lads in, looked after by local housewives. It wasn't an ideal situation for lads, left on their own in the houses. I continually battled for a Youth Hostel. No joy, no money, with 'Big Al' breathing down my neck..

Gordon Lee was very successful indeed. He won the Third Division 1975 League Championship, I remember, there were only a few of us there, i.e. Gordon Lee, Richard Dinnis reserve team manager, Jack 'Nudger' Cambell, Sponge man Jack Marshall, John Howarth, Tom Howarth and myself, of course, were all that looked after all the playing (staff) side of the Rovers.

I spent a lot of time at Blackburn Rovers, - dinner-time, night-time, going to different games. Sometimes Gordon would ring me up at the Town Hall. "Fred would you bring some fish and chips when you're coming down at lunch?"

The training ground was up at Altham in those days. It was just a big muddy pile really. I've seen Gordon and Richard Dinnis when I've gone up there with young trialists. Gordon would be absolutely full of sludge from head to toe. If there was ever a track suit manager it was him. I've watched him work up at Altham. His effort was tremendous. He acquired some good players, probably Graham Hawkins was one of his best lads. There was Andy Burgin and Mick Heaton (now sadly deceased) and others. Yes it was a very, very successful Blackburn Rovers centenary team that gained promotion in 1975.

Scouting Anecdote

One dark November, a very chilly night, John Howarth had put a ticket on for me at the Bury ground. Bury were playing Rochdale in a night game and it was one where there were one or two Bury players who were doing quite well. Some of the other local clubs like my own club, Blackburn, were showing great interest in one or two of the players. When I arrived at the ground, the scouts were put in what they call the chairs, - the chairs being a section of the ground for free tickets and complimentaries for scouts.

That particular night there was the usual posse of scouts there like Nat Lofthouse, (Bolton Wanderers), Harry Woodhouse from Arsenal, and Johnny Walton. I think he was working for Leicester at the time. He died some time ago. He was a good scout. The same chap also played as a young fellow for Blackburn Rovers. There was Tony Collins from Manchester United, and several other scouts that were well known in the area. I think Eddie Quigley was there, myself of course and a chap called Verdy Godwin, who is a right big scouting character in North West football. As a player, I think, he's had more clubs and scouted for more clubs than anyone I know. He's been at Wimbledon, Plymouth and Liverpool etc. He was at Liverpool when I was there. Actually, he was at Liverpool before Director Tom Saunders, who came as the youth development officer. Verdy Godwin, 'wow'. He can sing, he can dance, play the spoons. (As a matter of fact he played the spoons and sang for me in my Testimonial Year in 1985.) Verdy, I think you're great!! Let me continue with the story - I do get carried away.

Scouting at Bury
1974

On this particular match night scouts got their envelopes at the Bury ticket office from the Secretary who gave you the tickets. I said, "Blackburn Rovers". There was a ticket inside for tea at half-time and you would go down from the seats to the gateman, give him the ticket and go into the tearoom along with all the other scouts. There is quite a bit of business done in these places that punters never see. The switching of information and cross-referencing of people and players and places. It's quite valuable for clubs to send scouts to other matches and meet other scouts from other clubs. "The circuit" as it is called, is so useful to all.

When it got to half-time we all trooped down to the gateman, and Nat Lofthouse didn't have a tea ticket in his envelope. The chap on the gate with a flat cap and a muffler, probably had a Woodbine in his mouth, asked, "Have you got your ticket?"

Nat opened his envelope and there was no ticket, so the gateman said, "Sorry tha' can't come in here".

Nat said, "Well they must have forgot to put one in my envelope".

He said, "Well I don't care. I've got mi' orders and tha' can't come in here".

Nat walked away. Behind him was Verdy Godwin, who said, "You what? You what? Do you know who you were speaking to?".

I was stood behind Verdy listening to all this.

"I don't care", said the bloke beside the gate.

"That was Nat Lofthouse, the Lion of Vienna. Cheered by the English troops right round Vienna and who scored that vital goal against that Jeerman fella, them Jeermans, that vital goal. He put England back on the map after the war. You can't give him a cup of tea. What a bloody carry on this is. Never mind anyway, he can take my ticket, where is he?"

Nat had gone. All credit to the gateman. He said, "I've gotten me orders and I don't care if he's Queen of England he's not comin' in here".

Verdy was absolutely enraged by all this. Here the Lion of Vienna was being refused a cup of tea. A few of us decided to buzz off like Nat the Lion. It's strange that a man of such high profile like Nat Lofthouse was denied a cup of tea, and this happens quite a lot. It's happened to me several times.

If you read the book that Fred Eyre wrote, where he was talking about Norman Bodell and himself. Norman Bodell was a chief scout for a particular club, and they wouldn't let him in. Fred makes it sound so funny. It's a great book and you must get it, called 'Kicked into Touch'. It's one of the funniest books I've ever read and every credit to Fred. His son signed on schoolboy forms at Rovers for me. Not a bad young player who needed a lucky break, but didn't get one in his tender years. You need the rub of the green now and then. I'm sure you know that.

The name 'Rovers' was given to the Lancashire Club because of the number of grounds they had, before finally settling at Ewood Park. The club was founded basically in 1875 and here Blackburn Rovers were in 1975, third division champions. It was truly a remarkable feat, a club with little or no resources, dependent on private funding particularly from Mr. Bancroft and friends. I've seen the lights and telephones at Ewood Park suddenly being switched off when I've been working in my Ewood office. Mr. Bancroft rushed down to the ground, looked around, wrote cheques out for Norweb or GPO and gave them to John

Howarth the secretary of the club saying, "Here you are. Get rid of this. Get these lights back on". When John came back from Norweb offices he would get hold of him by the arm saying, "Come with me".

One particular day he came round and was really rollicking John Howarth. "Look at this! This light's on and that light's on. Why isn't that switched off? Have we no groundsman?"

Poor John, he used to get the backlash from Mr. Bancroft. I felt sorry for John many times when I've heard the verbal lashings that he'd been given by Mr. Bancroft. But having said that I liked Mr. Bancroft. He was Rovers. He was outspoken, and outrageous in many things that he did. A lot of people didn't like him as the Rovers Chairman, but he, I am sure, probably saved the club from extinction. He probably spent a lot of the money from the shuttle factory that his grandfather, or it may have been his father, started up many years ago for the local cotton industry. But I liked Bancroft, and he was always courteous to me.

When I had my heart attack he rang up and asked about me, and sent me a big card. Mr. Fryars, the youth development officer, came round to see me, as did Derek Fazakerley and Graham Hawkins. Jimmy Smith came of course, walking into hospital with a cigar in his mouth, and was told to leave by the angry Sister, so I didn't see him. Norman Bodell cheekily came in the middle of the afternoon when he shouldn't have done, - charmed the nurses and got in. Well done Norman. It helped me.

Unknown to me "Bald Eagle" was on the wing, winging his way to Ewood. Blackburn Rovers to me was a very happy club. Gordon Lee went on to Newcastle under some kind of contract dispute with Blackburn Rovers Chairman and the Newcastle Board Chairman. As far as I was concerned I was sad that Gordon left. We gelled together.

Left back John Bailey Rovers and Everton

No matter how good a player is, he must get the breaks if he is to reach the top. A bad injury, a loss of form when he is being watched, even an unlucky bounce of the ball can be so important in football. Being in the right place at the right time means so much in his game and a player needs to be lucky to reach the top echelons of soccer.

A fortunate twist of fate has helped many players in their way to rewarding careers. Goalkeepers have been found completely by accident through the regular man not being able to turn out. Many a deputy - some well known ones too - have gone inbetween the posts for a game and spent their careers there. I often think of John

Bailey, the Ex-Blackburn Rovers defender rated at the time in the £200,000 plus class, as a prime example of a player who got the right break just when he needed it. A snap decision, but as it turned out, a correct one - by Rovers Chairman Mr. William Bancroft. It meant that Bailey became a member of the Ewood staff when he could perhaps have drifted away. He had been sent to Blackburn by one of our Merseyside based scouts, Jim Mooney. He was a would-be left winger (thus his flair for attack) and was found a place in our "B" Team at the time and, after some excellent performances at outside left and left back Bailey was moved up to my squad by Tom Howarth, who thought highly of him.

By fluke really, our regular "A" Team left back was out injured, so Bailey filled in and made an immediate impression. I remember an Ex-Rovers stalwart Jack "Nudger" Campbell then scouting for the club - coming to watch one game and asking how Bailey was. "Fifteen", I replied. "We are going to sign him as an apprentice aren't we?" asked Jack. "We ought to," was my immediate reaction, and we both agreed to have a word with Richard Dinnis. Tom Howarth, "B" Team Coach was contacted by me and he also was more enthusiastic about Bailey than anyone at the club. This clinched it. I respected Tom Howarth's opinions highly.

By the time I got round to lobbying Richard he had taken over as Caretaker Manager - Ken Furphy having gone to Sheffield United - and was under the tremendous pressure of management for the first time. He naturally had other things on his mind and I couldn't seem to get through to him that here was an obvious apprentice. Though I am sure Richard knew that, if only he had time to think about it. I do know he would have agreed with Tom Howarth, Jack Campbell and Myself.

To cut along story short, Jack and I were at Ewood one Saturday morning before leaving for our respective matches when the chairman arrived. Jack gave me the famous "nudge" and whispered "Bailey". I thought why not, and I asked the chairman if I could have a word with him. I explained all about John Bailey and why I felt we should have him as an apprentice. Mr Bancroft's reply was typically brief and precise but to the point. He told me that if I thought that highly of the lad then we had better get him signed on. 'be it on your own head," he said in strident tones.

The following Monday, Richard Dinnis stopped me, told me he was signing John Bailey on apprentice forms and, quite rightly I suppose, gave me rare old rollicking for going over his head to the chairman. He was most upset but the fact remained that the chairman had given the go ahead and John Bailey became a Rovers player. Richard forgave me my indiscretion and said not to do it again. I never did. After that I always spoke to my immediate superior.

John Bailey the developed into one of the most exciting young defenders in the country and it is very satisfying to know you have played a part, no matter how small, in helping a player on his way. But it would have been to no avail without that little bit of luck. The chairman could have said no... but he didn't and Blackburn Rovers gained a star of the future, and a player that made it to the very top with Everton Football Club. Thanks for the "Nudge" Jack Campbell.

I must add quickly, however, that it was through the efforts of Ewood Park coaching staff, who worked very hard to bring out the best in him, that John Bailey was able to achieve what he has done. That goes for all players who make the grade - or 99.9 per cent of them. The coaches in this country are often all to easily maligned.

Along with scouts, managers, club secretaries etc... they help provide the end product of English League Football.

Finding talent and developing it is not merely a one-man job, it's a combined effort. The scout is simply a cog in a very large wheel but without this rather anonymous yet colourful breed of men, the soccer scene both national and international would be much poorer.

Mr. Bancroft on the odd occasion would ask how things were going, especially when we wanted to sign John Bailey on a pro-contract and the other young apprentices I fancied as young professionals. He often said to me, he wished he could have spent more time at the grass roots of the game. After my first puny attempt at this book he sent me the letter. (Illustrated).

William H Bancroft

Mr F O'Donoghue
1 Wadham Road
Frenchwood Road
PRESTON   12th July 1978

Dear Mr O'Donoghue

I have read with pleasure your effort at producing a book on "The Art of Soccer Scouting". I have no objection whatsoever to you carrying on with this project. To prove to you that I have taken time out to read all of it I comment as follows:-

i)   I have altered the sentence regarding the fee for Paul Bradshaw, and it now reads correctly in every way.

ii)   Always being a stickler for the correct use of the English language I would point out there are far too many "gets" and "gots". Two slang words in the English language which can on every conceivable occasion be changed.

iii)   Paul Mariner - did we, or did we not, nearly sign this player?

iv)   I would suggest you leave out your remarks regarding Don Revie, because this man is now "bad news".

v)   Your reference to Mr. David Pickles does not appear to me to be in very good taste.

vi)   Colin McDonald - too many "bloodies" about the place.

The above remarks are in no way intended to be critical. They are purely my observations in an effort to help you with this project.

Yours sincerely

William Bancroft

Fred O'Donoghue

In 1974 I made my first step on the managerial ladder after five great years at Port Vale. I joined Blackburn Rovers in the Third Division, a town full of passion and pride, especially in local players.

My complete staff was Jack Marshall who looked after injuries, Richard Dinnis was coach and Fred O'Donoghue looked after the local scouting, which I felt was very important.

We all pulled together and won the Third Division Championship.

Talking of Fred O'Donoghue, I have known him for many years, scouting for local talent. He certainly did a good job at Blackburn Rovers. I remember him bringing in John Butcher, a goalkeeper, and particularly John Bailey who later played for me at Everton. Fred was very dedicated looking for local talent at all times and in all weathers, determined to find a "Bryan Douglas". Fred's attitude was that skill in a young player would always surface and he wanted to be the first to spot it. He was also very good at discussing football with parents and teachers, which is vital when scouting for juniors.

Gordon Lee

Rovers Boardroom, May 1975.
L/R FOD, Chief Scout, Gordon Lee, Manager, John Marshall, Physio,
John Howarth, Secretary

Blackburn FC, Division Three Champions 1974-75.
Champagne celebrations in the dressing room.

April 1975, The word says it all

The supporters respond

Physio at the time Jolly Jack Marshall

Chapter Five

Blackburn Rovers FC

Jimmy Smith - Bald Eagle

Further changes came for me at Blackburn. In the Town Hall, extension 322 rang. It was John Howarth, Rovers' secretary.

"Fred, can you go down and pick up Jimmy Smith ? He'll be at Preston station at two o'clock this afternoon. He's coming up on a London train. He's coming from Colchester."

I said, "Yeah, what's he like?"

"You can't miss him. He's got a bald head, unless he's wearing a hat. Anyway, he'll be stood at the door at the Butler Street exit."

So I made my excuses at the Town Hall to my boss, Leo Seed, and jumped in my car. Of course, the reason why John asked me to go to Preston was that, being a Prestonian, I knew the one-way system. I know that Blackburn had a nightmare of a one-way system, but so had Preston. But I knew the way to the railway station to pick up Jimmy Smith.

I drove down to Butler Street and approached the taxi-rank, and there was Jimmy, with a battered suitcase, a couple of hairs on his head blowing in the wind, a mac' over his arm, and a scruffy one at that, - he looked every inch like TV detective, Columbo. I pulled up.

"Jimmy Smith?"

"Yes".

"Fred O'Donoghue?"

"Yes."

And there, strangely, I could feel an immediate response of friendship, of comradeship and affability. Jimmy Smith and I from that moment got on really well together.

Jimmy jumped into the car and I whipped him up to the hotel where he was staying in Blackburn. I just had a drink with him and then went back to my home on Revidge Road, feeling much happier at the first meeting with my new boss.

Jimmy Smith got me deeply involved at Blackburn Rovers. I was scouting far and wide. I was doing coaching. I did pre-season training with Norman Bodell and John Pickering. Jimmy involved me in everything.

He also invited me to the Christmas dinners and the different parties. I used to go down to his house on Preston New Road, where his family, my family, his wife

FOD and Jimmy Smith/Bald Eagle.
At the old Ewood Park, I knew and loved.

Yvonne and their three girls all got on like a house on fire.

At Ewood Park the club really got going under Jimmy Smith. We had a good youth policy at that time. I enjoyed working with the youth players and it was all working a treat. Simon Garner was coming into the ranks, along with Paul Round and a lot of good young players that we'd brought through.

Jimmy encouraged me all the way. I was going far beyond the normal realms of work. There just weren't enough hours in the day. Instead of twenty-four hours I was looking to put in twenty-six! I was driving here, there and everywhere, smoking heavily, eating all the wrong foods and drinking most nights.

One of the trips where I felt really under the weather was when Jimmy Smith sent me to watch Sheffield United and a player called Steven Cammack. Jimmy was looking for a flank player, but he was also looking at front players - Steven Kindon and Bobby Svarc. In the end Jimmy decided the player he really wanted was Steve Kindon, the ex-Burnley and Wolves flanker. I think the fee was £70,000 but the Rovers board was unable to back him on this occasion.

I pointed out to Jimmy that his signings must be good ones. He had to get it right. A lot depended on him making good signings, and not paying out thousands of pounds for bad players and creating problems for himself.

It was no surprise when Jimmy rang me at the town hall. "Can you do me a favour tonight, Fred? I want Steve Cammack to go back to Sheffield."

"Certainly", I said. I didn't know how to say no to Jimmy Smith, particularly in this case as he had lost his licence on a drink-driving offence at that particular time. Jim was unlucky. It was something which in those days could have happened to me a few times!

This particular night I drove down to the ground at five o'clock straight from work. Steve got into the car and we drove off to Sheffield City Centre where I dropped him off and drove straight back. It's a long way.

On the way home I could feel some terrible pains in my chest and down my arms, but kept it to myself. It passed off and I never told anyone. It was stupid of me but I didn't say anything about it. Later, of course, I was to discover that I had serious complications of the heart's functions, but didn't realise it at that time.

On 22nd March 1976, I had a terrible heart attack. Fortunately for me, Cathy, my wife rang for an ambulance without delay and I was taken to hospital and placed in intensive care for four days followed by a further nine or ten days on the ward. The hospital staff at Preston Sharoe Green Hospital were brilliant.

People from Blackburn Rovers rallied round me, as also did my family. Everyone was marvellous and kind. The Town Hall staff produced a terrific "Get Well" card.

Jimmy Smith strolled into intensive care, smoking a cigar, but Sister chased him out of the ward! Later Normal Bodell and Graham Hawkins came round to the house along with Derek Fazakerley and Mr. Fryars. I had about twenty-odd cards from the Ewood staff - from Simon Garner and all the lads. They really went out of their way to help my recovery.

I mustn't forget the Town Hall staff at Blackburn, including Leo Seed, my boss, and many others. They were wonderful people at that time.

Cathy overlooked the whole affair with firmness, love and affection. She had saved my life with the direct phone call she made.

It had been a period during which Jimmy Smith was "top of the pops" for me, and I have kept in touch with him over the years and value his friendship highly. I liked to sing "La Donna Mobile" over the phone to him. He screams with laughter at my very bad Italian accent.

Jimmy Smith sadly moved on to bigger things at Birmingham City. More changes were in the pipe-line for the Ewood Club.

Help from Jolly Jack Marshall - sadly deceased

Heart Attack - (and after)

I was absent from my job at Blackburn Town Hall for about twelve or thirteen weeks, going back on the Monday of the fourteenth week. I was a little bit more subdued, not as high-flying as I had been. I was slowing down, or trying to. It has never been in my nature to be slow moving, slow walking or slow thinking. I have always been in a kind of hurry. My illness taught me one thing; that I must take my time, and that I must try to eat correctly, and that I must certainly finish smoking. I had smoked very heavily - twenty to thirty cigarettes a day.

For many years Blackburn Rovers had a physiotherapist called Jack Marshall, known as Jolly Jack to the lads in the game and a real personality. He had been a good player himself and also a top manager at Sheffield Wednesday. In fact, Jack had been right through all the levels in football from apprenticeship, player, manager, to being physio at Blackburn. He had also attended to the MCC Cricket Team when they visited Old Trafford. Jack was a marvellous chap in every way.

He would call me into the treatment room at Ewood, sit me down and listen patiently while I had a very, very long talk about this heart attack. Everyday at that time I went to see Jack - he helped me enormously.

He knew also that I voted Labour and he always used to wind me up about the Labour Party. What about all the strikes that were going on at that time? What about the miners, the transport workers, the postal workers and the teachers. He would talk about the disruption and the hours lost. I would respond about the welfare state, created by a Labour government, and about the greedy capitalists. It was always a right ding-dong affair, but with great respect for one another.

At one particular time when quite a number of the lads and manager Gordon Lee were struck down with 'flu', Jack Marshall and myself went over to Leeds United with a Rovers Reserve team. Jack was acting-manager, and I was the sponge man with the squad.

We arrived at Leeds and of course got hammered 6-1. We had John Butcher in goal. No disrespect to John, as he was only a young lad at the time. John Bailey, Paul Round and Simon Garner were three other very young kids facing a very good Leeds squad.

Les Cocker (an old pal of Jolly Jack's) and the well-known Don Revie were there to see Leeds really take us apart. But it was all part of learning about the game, the different systems, and the qualities of the players. It was good to see how Jack Marshall went out of his way to help our young lads after such defeat.

He also arranged a special meeting for me with Harry Catterick, who was the manager at Preston North End at that time. I went down to see Harry, and was made very welcome.

"Hello, Fred! Come in," he said, and went on to tell me about the time he had a serious heart attack, and had been lucky to get away with it. Oddly enough, he had also been driving over from Sheffield on the moors by Hazel Grove coming into Stockport, when he felt a terrible pain. He was right out on the moors and could see some houses two or three miles away. He drove up to a house, managed to struggle out of the car and knock on the door before falling into a heap. A lady came to the door and he explained his plight. By an amazing chance she happened to be the district nurse. It was a coincidence which saved his life. Within the hour he was in hospital receiving treatment.

Harry taught me a lot about how to pace things out. His odd phone call was always appreciated at Ewood Park by me, where the company of Jack Marshall was a further tonic. Every lunchtime Jack would eat a piece of cheese and an apple, and that was his strict diet. Jack had quite a lot of problems of his own. His wife was disabled and confined to a wheelchair, but Jack was always cheerful. He usually had a joke with you, or he would try to pull your leg. He could weigh players up at once, and see through those who were trying to pull his leg. He'd seen it all and heard it all - no fool was Jolly Jack.

I had several happy years with him during which he helped me tremendously to sign different schoolboys. One example was Mark Patterson.

Mark was at Ewood Park watching a first team game. I said to Jack, "If Mark Patterson goes outside this ground today, I'll lose him. He's from Darwen Vale High School, just up the road, but other clubs are queuing up to sign him."

"Well, bring him down here," Jack said, "and I'll talk to him while you go and find his dad."

I left Mark in the physio room and searched for his dad who was also watching the match.

So we signed Mark Patterson and I still think he was one of the best young players around at that particular time. He played over a hundred first team games for Rovers, before continuing with Preston, Bury and Bolton.

Mark was with Preston when I was working there a few years later. He could be a hot-tempered sort of lad, but always affable and friendly with me, and I never had to reprimand him. We got on really well.

Jack Marshall was again very instrumental in helping me sign other young lads like Paul Round, and others, whom I had brought down to the club. He made all the lads feel very welcome and always took trouble and patience to get them fit, if they had injuries. He would look after their ligaments, tendons and muscle strains etc.

I must say my life was enriched by meeting and making friends with Jolly Jack Marshall and I'm sure a lot of players in the game today, and a lot of managers, one in particular, Lawrie McMenemy, will remember Jack Marshall now sadly deceased.

Jack died recently, so sad when good old friends pass on.

So work continued at Blackburn Rovers with caretaker-manager John Pickering, with whom I became firm friends. My wife, Cathy, and I used to visit his family and have tea together when living in Blackburn. Nice people.

On one occasion, during the close season I was taking part in a show at the Charter Theatre in Preston as a member of the local Gilbert and Sullivan Society. John and his wife came over to see me in 'Trial by Jury' and how they enjoyed it. He couldn't believe how I'd found the time to learn the tenor part in 'Trial by Jury' whilst having such a busy life.

Life was certainly busy, but I was living it to the full, and very happy to be working, scouting and, of course, singing. They were golden days. I was also singing with the Exiles Group, the Kennedy Sisters and Leyland Motors Brass Band when I could spare the time.

At other times I was playing the odd charity game with Les Rigby (sadly deceased), Sammy Taylor, Joe Dunn, Willy Cunningham, Brian Pilkington, Roy Gratrix and a host of other ex-stars.

Meanwhile, on the family side of things, our daughter Helen won a place at Lancaster University, our son Stewart a place at Salford University and Rosemary was at Blackpool College of Technology. It certainly was a busy time, especially on Sunday evenings in term time, driving them to Lancaster, Blackpool and Salford, dropping youngsters and their gear, their laundry etc. at the various colleges.

Jimmy Smith

Returning to the period after my heart attack, Jimmy Smith then appointed Norman Bodell as Chief Scout in charge of administration. I continued in a secondary role, not doing as much work at the club. I was engaged as a scout in my own area, Higher Walton, Preston and Blackpool at youth level.

I remember seeing Norman Bodell and Jimmy Smith spending hours with John Bailey, who went on to fame with Everton. Countless hours were devoted to Paul round and Simon Garner and others, showing them how to use and improve the skills they had. They also had able assistance from John Pickering, which all enabled these lads to go on to become very good players.

Smith, Bodell and Pickering - I thought that was a good combination, offering experience, coaching skill and patience. It was a good outfit, and in the background I was able to supply a number of lads from local schools coming into the club.

Jimmy goes Bananas!

Jimmy Smith certainly had a lot of patience, but he also had a ferocious temper at times.

A particular match was when Rovers were playing Burnley. It was a traditional Boxing Day fixture at Ewood Park. If you know anything about Blackburn and Burnley, it's a real Lancashire hotpot. On this day it proved to be a red-hot hotpot! Burnley were the dreaded enemy.

It was towards the end of the game and the scores were level. I can see the situation vividly.

The referee awards a direct free-kick to Burnley just outside the box. Blackburn set up a defensive wall. Steve Kindon is shaping to take the kick and John Bailey is in the wall. Now John Bailey had done a bit of boxing in the Boys' Club in Bootle and he'd learnt how to duck out of the way of a punch. Anyway, Burnley take the free-kick, with Kindon blasting it into the wall. Bailey ducks his head down and the ball screams into the net! Goal!

Burnley won the game. Their fans went wild in the Darwen stand, the Rovers' fans groaned with dismay.

After the final whistle all hell broke loose. In those days the tunnel led straight towards the physio room, with the home dressing room next to it.

Lo and behold, Jimmy got hold of John Bailey by the neck, intent on strangling him. We literally had to pull him off.

Jimmy had really flipped his lid. He started swearing; "You fluffy bloody thing!" He was calling him, Bails, Bailey, all sorts of names. It took Normal Bodell, myself and one or two players to pull him off.

Nevertheless we all liked Jimmy. It was just the emotion of the moment. He lost control, but it soon passed. Jimmy never held a grudge. All was forgotten the day after. I think Jim was a very good manager for Blackburn Rovers, with ambitions for the club and for himself.

As for John Bailey, he came to no harm, developing into a very good professional at the top level.

Signing striker Bobby Svarc was a bold decision on Jimmy's part. Bob had knee problems but Jim stood by his decision and signed him on despite the club doctor's reservations.

Jimmy also had shrewd ideas off the pitch. He bought a house from Mr. Brown, one of the Directors at Rovers, and he spent a bit of time doing repairs and painting it up. I'd helped on odd occasions, collecting paint, or showing Jim where the big Blackburn wholesalers were.

We were good colleagues and I was sad when Jimmy decided to move on and go for bigger things with bigger clubs.

At Christmas parties he always asked me to get up and sing. He knew I'd done a bit of concert work, so I usually obliged. He liked 'Ave Maria', but one of his special favourites was my Italian version of 'La Donna Mobile' - Pavarotti style!

When I had my benefit year in 1985, Jimmy wrote a humourous note in the match programme, in which he said that I was probably better at singing than scouting. I always knew that I was not a 'chief scout' in the sense of the words. I knew that I was scouting for schoolboys and that my strength was with young players, coaching youth players and organising games and other scouts at ground level. But the top echelons in scouting are men who have gone right through the game. I certainly knew my place within the club, and it wasn't at that top level. Youth scouting was my "forte".

So, when Jimmy wrote in the programme that I was probably better at singing than scouting, in a way he was right. I probably was; I did miss a few lads in my time, to name Paul Mariner and Kevin Keegan as just two, and there were many others. When I think of all the players I've missed I usually have a couple of pints, or a whisky and lemonade. It's like a nightmare. "How the hell did I miss them?" I ask myself. "They must have just had a bad game that day," I tell myself, reassuring my troubled thoughts.

John Pickering was a smashing fellow - a true Yorkshireman who knew his football and always got the best out of his lads. His secret, give your best and demand their best in return. I've said before that John and I were great friends and got on very well. But times were changing. Jimmy Smith had gone, Norman Bodell had gone and John Pickering was soon to follow.

Jim Iley

Jim Iley didn't last long. I never understood what happened there. I didn't really get to know Jim Iley except that I knew that he had played wing-half for Tottenham Hotspur. He brought one lad to the club, a Scots lad, I can't remember his name, but he hadn't ever seen him play. Some managers will spend a lot of time going into great depth, looking at players, not only themselves but getting three or four other scouts to submit reports , as well as making personal inquiries with colleagues. Whatever else, managers should always go and see for themselves.

However, Jim Iley said, "Fred, I've not seen him play, but his record is good enough." I didn't reply, but it saddened me that the player didn't do anything.

Jim wasn't there long after that. Board and management didn't gel. He later worked at Bury with Wilf McGuiness, ex-Manchester United player and manager. Jim certainly had immense knowledge of the game and I'm sure he is currently scouting for some football club.

So it was time for change again at Blackburn Rovers. The number of managers they had over those years was phenomenal, to say the least. When Jim Iley went, I was back in the breach again, doing a lot of work for the club - administrative work, looking after the accommodation in Nuttall Street, the two houses that Rovers owned; looking after the apprentices and signing schoolboys on. My workload was also back to what it had been before my heart attack.

John Howarth, the club Secretary, was helping me a lot in his own special way. John, at that time, was very young for his very responsible job, but he did it very well.

Rovers Youth - Groningen, Holland
European Youth Cup - Winners

Blackburn Rovers under-18 squad took part in the Dutch European International Tournament in 1978. We had some very good young players at Ewood at that particular time. Simon Garner, Paul Round, Duncan Clarke, Brian Moran, Ginger Robinson, Brian Morley, and, of course, Russell Coughlin, probably the most experienced player of them all - and a good player too.

Held annually, the Groningen tournament is very famous, with a number of quality clubs taking part, like Ajax, Benfica, Hamburg SV, Feynoord, Valencia, Roma and many others.

To win this prestigious event is a fabulous experience for any English League Club.

**Mrs Thatcher at Ewood in 1977, chats to coach Norman
Bodell, with Tony Parkes and Bobby Mitchell**

Rovers Squad for Groningen

The team was made up of John Pickering (Team manager), Mr. Al Fryars (Director in Charge/Finance), Tom Howarth (Assistant Coach/Sponge Man). I myself was Tour Manager/Organiser and Scout with an under-18 squad of sixteen players.

We just about had time to have a team photograph before taking the coach to Manchester Airport. We flew to Schipol, then took the train to Groningen. The boys were warmly greeted by lots of Dutch people who met them with smiles and friendly 'hellos'. They took our lads into their homes for the duration of the four day event - Dutch hospitality at its impressive best.

Clearly the British were very popular in Holland, partly due to the heroic efforts of our troops in the Second World War, particularly at Arnhem in 1943.

The adult accommodation had been arranged at the Londres Hotel in the centre of

1977/78 Under 18's Rovers, L.F.A. Cup Winners.
Back Row, Tom Howarth, FOD, John Pickering.

Groningen, quite near the 'red light' district. I was quite relieved that the lads were staying with Dutch families outside the town centre. Mr. Fryars stayed in the hotel for a quiet drink, whilst John Pick, Tom Howarth and myself took a walk round the neighbourhood to make sure none of our lads were out and about! What a way to make a living - those poor girls.

We had a float of £200 for any emergency expenses - medical, transport, sundry requirements etc. Mr. Fryars held the purse strings and he had a unique method of concealing the cash. He hid the money in a brown envelope and stuck it to the bedroom wall behind a copy of a Vermeer painting with tape.

I was sharing the room with Mr. Fryars and every time he came in the room he promptly checked behind the Vermeer print.

Now I had become interested in Vermeer paintings as a young lad. I had seen similar copies of his work in St. Augustine's Presbytery Church Library. Father Geoghan was a keen art-loving priest who loved Vermeer's work. It was 'Lady at the Casement' that concealed the Rover's cash. In the bedroom there were two other Vermeer prints; the famous 'Letter' and 'Woman Reading'.

I could hear again the voice of Father Geoghan saying that through all Vermeer's work you will find lemon and all shades of blue. Vermeer loved soft pastel colours in his later life. I loved that Hotel Londres bedroom because it reminded me of home, church, and old Father Geoghan.

In the tournament the lads played some very good teams and did very well to win them all, to reach the final versus Feynoord, the Dutch Youth Champions.

During the final there was a dramatic incident which could have been tragic but for the skill and awareness of our physio Tom Howarth. Paul Comstive had swallowed his tongue when he collided with the Dutch goalkeeper's knee-cap. Tom was soon on the spot and promptly tilted Paul's head right back in deft medical fashion, and in so doing, undoubtedly saved the young player's life. The ambulance drove right onto the pitch to transfer Paul to the local hospital. In addition to other emergency treatment, he had five teeth removed as a result of the collision, but he was able to travel back with us to the UK, very sore and with a rather toothless grin to boot!

The final was tied at 2 - 2 after 90 minutes, with no further scoring in extra-time. Rovers then went on to win the penalty shoot-out by 5 -4. The cup was ours. We were the champions, and I was just as overcome as everyone else with the joy and emotion of it.

We took all the lads back to the hotel with the cup for a celebration drink, where the team manager John Pick unwittingly ordered ten bottles of Moet champagne - the magnum size!

We were having a great time, giving it everything: "We are the champions! We are the champions!" Even Big Al Fryars was laughing and singing. But not for long!

A solemn, poker-faced Dutch waiter slipped John Pick the bill for the champagne. Glancing at him I saw his red, ruddy face turn white.

"Fred, Fred," came a trembling voice, "520 gilders! 520 gilders!"

Mr. Fryars had caught the tail end of it and asked what he had said. John repeated quietly, "520 gilders." Big Al blew his top. "You stupid buggers! You are the worst manager and tour manager," (pointing at me), "that the club has ever had the misfortune to employ. Do you realise that represents £240. Get upstairs Fred and bring me that brown envelope down from behind the bloody Vermeer you keep going on about."

I did what I was told, right sharp. He opened the envelope to discover that there was just £25 left of the float. Poor Al Fryars! Writing a cheque of his own money didn't go down well with him at all. Jimmy Smith later told me that Big Al had put an expense sheet in to the club, via secretary John Howarth, to recoup his money.

But there was further trouble for FOD. The winner's trophy was a large silver cup with lid and a figurine attached to it. On our way back to the UK I somehow managed to unscrew the figurine off the lid. Big Al's voice rattled out at me, "What the bloody hell are you doing?"

I stuttered and stammered with the lid in one hand and the lone figurine footballer in the other. Timidly I said, "It's come off." This was witnessed by a train compartment full of Dutch people going to Schipol Airport in Amsterdam. I got a further blast of language from the furious Tour Director. "You'll bloody pay for it," he said, "out of your own pocket, not mine. I'll see to that."

I noticed John Pick and Tom Howarth grinning at me behind his back. You sods, I thought - no help from the pair of you, with the Dutch passengers looking at me in amazement.

I went red - blood red, then scarlet, and retreated from the battle scene to a rattling, noisy train's toilet compartment - for a bit of peace and quiet.

But really Mr. Arthur Fryars was all right to deal with. He certainly watched every penny and saw things were done in the correct manner. Payslips and accounts were handled in a proper businesslike fashion.

Those were happy days with John Pick, Tom Howarth and Big Al. But I must not overlook the contribution of Jim Mooney and Ian Hanson to the Rovers cause at that time. I would certainly have liked Ian Hanson to travel to Holland with us. I tried to arrange it, but was unsuccessful. Jim Mooney bringing star player John Bailey to my attention and the club.

The Youth Trophy took pride of place in the old Rovers Board Room, with the figurine firmly screwed to the lid. I sincerely hope that the present day Rovers' Board will see it safely transferred to another place of honour alongside other important trophies in the new Board Room.

A lot of passion is tied up within that cup - including a screwed -on figurine (paid for by me), ten bottles of Moet champagne, and Paul Comstive's five missing teeth!

My wages and petrol expenses remained the same despite our success in Holland. I often called my cheque or payment "Mickey Mouse Money" - IF AND WHEN I GOT IT.

There are some things money can't buy; enthusiasm, love, friendship, a man's pride, dignity and a passion for the game. A scout often knows that he is being used by certain club officials. I certainly did.

But there are also a number of things a scout can earn which are beyond monetary value - the greatest being: other people's appreciation of what he has achieved. And that is not usually the club's directors, but ordinary working-class people who love their club and support this great national game of ours. In my case I was lucky some of Rovers Directors did around 1985 (my Testimonial).

An Anecdote

JIMMY SMITH
Southport's Bobby Gough and Jimmy Smith

In the local North West Premier League, Bobby Gough had been knocking in a few goals for the Sandpipers at Haigh Avenue, Southport. Harry Boyle, the Lancashire FA coach, who also did a bit of scouting for me at Blackburn Rovers, rang me up to come and have a look at Bobby Gough.

I duly attended three or four games in which Bobby Gough was playing and he did well in all the games. Eventually I got Jimmy Smith, the manager at Blackburn Rovers to come with me to Haigh Avenue. Again the boy did well. He played a good game and scored a cracking goal. After the match Jimmy and I were asked to go for a drink in the boardroom. Jimmy who liked a drop, as did I, went with the Southport official.

The Board of Directors started talking about this and that, and good local players in the non-league sides. The conversation eventually came on to Bobby Gough, striker. His abilities, his attributes, were all dramatically highlighted by the then Southport Chairman and his entourage.

Jimmy, winking at me, delicately tried to pose the questions to Mr Chairman. Was he brave, had he a good attitude? Before he could continue his line of questioning, Mr Chairman, his voice rising, said "Brave! Brave!....Attitude! Attitude!"

God, I thought I was listening to the Shakespearian actors Sir John Gielgud or Laurence Olivier. It sounded like something from Hamlet. "He is the most brave player I have ever known, crippled with arthritis, he is under great, and I mean, great pain. Do you realise, Jim, he spends as much as twenty minutes to get his football boots on his feet - Brave! Attitude! bloody hell Jim, they don't come any braver!"

Now Verdi Godwin, the scout of fame, was stood near to me. We could not keep our faces straight. I had to disappear to the toilet to escape the hilarity of it all. Jimmy Smith, Verdi and myself have often recalled that night with the Haig Avenue outfit.

To his credit, Bobby Gough went on to play for Fourth Division Colchester, with great distinction, scoring a lot of goals for them.

Cut Throat Competition

One young player emerged from the Rossendale Area, a certain Danny Keough, a very skilful schoolboy who attended St. Mary's College, Blackburn. His skills were obvious for all to see. Mick McGrath the old Rover's Cup Star, told me ."We've got to sign this young 14 year old lad". I had seen him four or five times and I must say I agreed. His skills, his dedication were especially impressive. Danny had, to my mind, everything required to become a professional footballer.

My approach to his father was made with his 14th birthday about three or four days away, when I visited his home in Rossendale. I told him of the opportunities at Blackburn Rovers, and with Mick McGrath's and Tommy Howarth's coaching, he had every chance of an apprenticeship with Rovers. Danny and his father signed the schoolboy forms for me to save a journey.

A week later I had a phone call from Danny Keough's father. Scout Joe Brown had called round from Manchester United. He had said Fred O'Donoghue was out of order signing Danny before his 14th birthday, and that Danny and his father had second thoughts about joining Rovers. Whatever Joe Brown said to Danny Keough and his father I'll never know, but Danny and his father had now (sadly for me) signed forms for Manchester United. I told him to send my forms he had previously signed back to me at Ewood Park. He did. I could not believe a change of mind over five days. I have often wondered the true story of such an event with Joe Brown and the Keoughs. Some you win, some you lose.

Danny got his apprenticeship at Manchester United, and I was devastated when I heard of his serious spine injury with the United set up. I often think of the Keough's change of mind and think of If! If! I wonder if he had kept his word and joined the Rovers!! Mick McGrath was upset and believe me so was I. His dad later rang me when Danny was at Exeter but then his chance and opportunity had gone.

Football is so fickle. Lady luck often, sadly, reigns supreme. In Danny's case it didn't work out. Danny and his father did what they thought was best. "It's a funny old game," says Jimmy Greaves. How right Jimmy is. So is scouting.

Blackburn Rovers Football & Athletic plc

Dear Sir

Scouting Appointment Season 1973/74

Your appointment as a football scout for the company is confirmed on the following terms:-

1) You will be paid expenses only on a monthly basis as follows:-
   7p first 100 miles - 5p after
   Stamps, telephone and meals as pay sheets

2) If during the period when you are employed by the company a player recommended to the company by you

   (i) is signed as an apprentice footballer you receiver a bonus of £25.

   (ii) is signed as a full time league professional you will receive a bonus of £50.

   (iii) plays 10 full games in the company's first team during any of the first three football seasons after being signed as a full time professional you will receive a bonus of £100.

   (iv) 2% of any transfer over £25,000.

3) Your appointment may be terminated on one week's notice given in writing by either party to the other.

4) No further claims on the company (after termination with the company) will be paid.

Please sign the agreement and return to Mr J M Smith. Copy for your reference. Please note agreement with the club, other than this, are now terminated.

Yours faithfully
for Blackburn Rovers Football & Athletic Club Co. Limited

J M Smith
Manager

Blackburn Rovers - Howard Kendall

The phone extension 322 buzzed again at the Town Hall in Blackburn. It was John Howarth

"Fred, Mr. Bancroft's been on to me. He wants to know if you could pick Howard Kendall up this afternoon at two o'clock at Preston Railway Station".

I thought, "Here I go again!"

"Howard Kendall?"

"Yes", came the reply. "Our new manager. He's been assistant manager at Stoke. He's come with very good references."

Being a Prestonian I knew about Howard Kendall - the youngest player in a cup final - and what a good player he was. I remember seeing him play and I remember him going on to bigger things at Everton.

I duly went to Preston Station, driving down New Hall Lane, via Queen Street, Winckley Square, Fishergate and into Butler Street. Howard Kendal was standing there in just the same place that Jimmy Smith had stood. He'd come from somewhere in the Midlands.

I pulled up. "Howard Kendall?"

He smiled. "Fred O'Donoghue?"

"Correct."

He got into the car. He was different from Jimmy smith, who had a kind of immediate warmth. Howard wasn't really friendly. He was alright, but I didn't feel as comfortable as I had been with Jimmy Smith.

We drove off to Blackburn and went to the accommodation. That particular night there was a function at Preston North End in the Sports Club in Deepdale Road. I don't recall what the event was but they'd asked Howard to attend, and I accompanied him. We had a fair night, enjoying a couple of drinks and some good company. Everyone knew him.

While driving back to his hotel in Blackburn he asked me how much I thought we could get for FAZ - Derek Fazakerley.

I replied "I wouldn't sell. We need him"

Howard soon got into the swing of things at Blackburn Rovers. It was a very astute appointment. He was not just the manager. He was also playing for the club, and very good in both roles.

That particular season Howard played regularly and was able to encourage the young players around him. He did very well and you could see the side's improvement from his experience , his skills and his maturity on the ball. By his example the team played with tremendous passion and flair, and Rovers finished a whisker of a decimal point off promotion to the First Division during his time at Ewood.

Eddie Quigley - Howard Kendall - Mick Heaton

When Howard Kendall joined Blackburn Rovers it was on the agenda to recruit a big name chief scout. Quite soon I met Jimmy Armfield at the club.

"Hi, Fred," he said. "I've been tapping up Eddie Quigley, the old Rovers and Preston player, to come here as Chief Scout." I thought that was wonderful. Eddie Quigley had great skills as a player, and had been one of my idols when young. I told Howard Kendall that it was great news. I could work with Eddie Quigley. I was confident of this, even though I had not met the man in person.

But alas, Eddie Quigley and Howard Kendall were not really compatible. I always felt that there was a strained relationship between them. Nothing was ever said and I certainly never heard a bad word uttered, but I could tell there was something there.

Howard Kendall cooled off towards me as well because of Eddie. I had helped Eddie when he first came to Blackburn Rovers with all the addresses of the schools, the names of the teachers, the phone numbers of all the boys and most of my connections. He brought along a scout with him called Ted Taylor who was to prove one of the best scouts Blackburn Rovers ever had.

Ted Taylor was a headmaster at a school in Bury and Eddie used to use him for getting the best schoolboys in his area for the Ewood club. I can't praise Ted Taylor too highly. I still ring him up on a regular basis. He used to love my singing of G. and S. ballads on scouting trips and at other functions we attended together.

Eddie Quigley was a gentleman, with a lot of dignity and charm. He wasn't bossy or foul-mouthed or anything like that. I rated him very highly and it was great to be part of a team with him.

There were loads of good players coming through the youth policy at this time, such as Mark Patterson and Simon Barker. Ted Taylor and I really started the Rovers production line of good players, which brought in millions for Rovers in transfer fees. One of the most recent has been the £3.5 million move of David May to Manchester United. Well done Ted Taylor.

The time Eddie and I clashed with Howard Kendall was when the commercial manager, Joe Witherington, asked me for some kind of story about youth policies, with some notes of advice for would-be schoolboys joining the club, to be printed in the programme.

One of the parents had taken a photograph of Eddie Quigley and myself on the

Crown Wallpaper ground in Darwen. Beneath the photo we printed a list of do's and don'ts for signing schoolboys. And if a boy wanted to join Blackburn Rovers we included all the good advice we got from the P.F.A., the English Schools' F.A., the Football Association, and the Football League.

The programme editor put the photograph of Eddie and myself with all the advice and rules underneath.

Mick Heaton by this time had become a very firm friend of Howard Kendall and they would share the odd bottle of wine, or two, at lunchtimes. They were like two peas in a pod at that time and Mick Heaton became first team coach helping Howard Kendall.

I always felt that the manager and Mick Heaton considered Eddie Quigley and myself were some kind of threat. Perhaps it was something to do with the fact that Eddie was quite popular with the board. I may be wrong about all this I hope I am, but I felt a bit under pressure from the pair of them.

When Howard Kendall saw the item in the match programme he sent for me and gave me a telling off about it. In future, I had to go through him. He was the man who decided what went into the programme, not Eddie Quigley, not me, and if it happened again I was down the road.

This really upset me. When I approached Mick Heaton he more or less said exactly the same about me and Eddie. I thought it was all a bit silly really, because I myself had no ambitions to be anything but what I was - a scout, a humble scout, the lowest of jobs in the footballing world.

It may be the last job in the line, but to me it can also be the main job. A football scout is usually a chap who has no other avenue into the game. I was quite concerned about the whole matter of the programme notes, a copy of which is reproduced in this book. *(See page 135)*

Football management is a delicate job, to say the least. Back-stabbing is often rife; suspicion a constant disease. It is all about opinions, and 'yes-men' abound in some not-too-happy clubs. It affects the directors as well. As John McGrath used to say - "There's them and us!" John was so right in his observations about our national game.

Having said that, Howard Kendall did great things for Blackburn Rovers, make no mistake. Sadly for Rovers, he was very ambitious and went on to fame with bigger clubs such as Everton, the Spanish side, Sociedad, Manchester City, Sheffield United and Everton, recently returned to Greece.

He was a high-flying manager, a very good player and quite an affable bloke at times. And yet at other times I felt he didn't really like me. But I wish him success wherever he goes. He gives the best pre-match talk to players I have ever heard.

Howard Kendall left Rovers, taking Mick Heaton with him.

Again time for change at Ewood with Howard Kendall moving on.

Blackburn Rovers
Bob Saxton - Jim Furnell

Out of the blue from Plymouth, six foot plus, barn-storming in, came a chap called Bob Saxton, and alongside him, Jim Furnell, to take over the reins at Blackburn Rovers. Bob Saxton was a dour Yorkshireman and a big guy.. Brian Clough once described him as a man of steel. But he was a quiet man of few words, and very studious. Jim Furnell was appointed assistant manager. Later, he became Youth Development Officer - my old position. The new team took charge - Bob Saxton and Tony Parkes with the first team; Jim Furnell and myself helping out with the reserves, youth development section, youth teams and the schoolboys.

Again I had returned to what I enjoyed most, signing good schoolboys and several names come to mind: Mick Salmon, Paul Comstive, Jason Wilcox, Franz Carr, Leonard Johnrose etc.

The development of Micky Salmon was very interesting. He came to us from a Leyland school and went on to play in various teams for Rovers. The last time I saw him he was playing for Charlton Athletic in the 1993-94 season, and what an amazing game he had. He must have felt ten feet tall as he faced Blackburn Rovers after having been released by Bob Saxton. Now he was back defying the million pound team assembled by Kenny Dalglish and Jack Walker. This is strange, but I can never ever remember seeing or meeting Jack Walker in all the years I worked at Ewood.

Another signing was Franz Carr, who had a brilliant schoolboy career. I was helped very much by Steve Done, the P.E. teacher at Our Lady's High School, in Preston, in our desire to keep him out of the hands of the bigger clubs. I was very, very lucky, as a number of clubs were after Franz, Leeds United in particular making a big push at that time.

Then there was Jason Wilcox, the boy from Bolton St. Bede's who couldn't get into the Town team. But I was lucky enough to see him play and I invited him down on Sunday mornings to Witton Park with his dad in close attention. We had an all-weather pitch there, and he developed well with Jim Furnell and Tony Parkes helping him along. You could see that this boy was going to become a good player and I signed him in the bedroom at 112 Nuttall Street, which was my office, with his parents in attendance. Jason has proved to be possibly one of my better finds over the years. His mother recently sent me a photograph of Jason and his baby. Happy days for Jason and family! Jason used to keep in touch and always sent a Christmas Card.

Paul Comstive - Lucky Strike

It was a rainy Saturday afternoon when most of the games were off. It was probably February or March of that particular year that I watched Paul Comstive play on a local park in Eccleston. I'd been to two or three games that had been called off this particular day. It was pouring down and I was passing through Eccleston when I saw this game on. It was Chorley boys against Eccleston boys in an under-sixteen game.

I had been watching for a short while standing next to another spectator. The outside left was a big, strong, fast-running, left-foot sixteen year old and I liked what I saw. He had strength and determination as well.

I just happened to say to the chap stood next to me, "I like this outside-left. You don't know who he is?" I was trying to get his name without attracting the attention of the team manager. "Yeah", he replied. "It's my lad. I'm Tom Comstive."

"Oh," I said. "I'm Fred O'Donoghue of Blackburn Rovers."

"I've heard of you", he replied, and I told him how impressed I was with his son.

I got Paul to come down to Blackburn Rovers, after ringing his club and getting the secretary's permission. He was still an amateur and we could have served a seven day notice but we didn't. The Chorley club were very good and Paul went down to Blackburn Rovers on trial. Sure enough he went on to become a professional and made a bob or two out of the game.

The last time I saw him he was playing for Brian Kettle at Southport F.C., with his dad, mum and family in close attention. He recently retired.

Paul Comstive was a lucky strike for Blackburn Rovers. He became an apprentice and graduated to the first team. He later played for Bolton, Chester and Wigan Athletic. It was just the luck of the draw for Paul that his father was stood next to me, and also the luck of the draw that I was in Eccleston on a day when all other games were called off. Obviously there is a great amount of luck in this game when it comes to being spotted by a scout. It's not so bad nowadays as all the main school games are meticulously watched by all the top clubs. But that was one occasion where it was the rub of the green with Lady Luck helping you out.

The Big Lads - Steve Galliers : David Lee

Two players that Blackburn Rovers did not take on as apprentices really upset me, especially little Stephen Galliers. So much so that I nearly walked out on the club. Jimmy Smith and Mr. Fryars were responsible for Stevie Galliers, the boy from Eccleston, not being taken on.

He went on to play for Wimbledon, throughout their meteoric rise from the lower divisions. He was a great little player and I was most upset that he wasn't taken on.

Mr. Fryars told me that if I didn't shut up about 'Gallies (the Shrimp)' I could bugger off. Jimmy Smith didn't help me on this occasion.

David Lee was another small lad that Fryars said was too small, a view I didn't share, as with the opinions of both Bob Saxton and Jim Furnell about Micky Salmon, the keeper from Leyland. I really rated this young keeper. It's a game of opinions.

One of the first things that Bob Saxton did when he came to Blackburn Rovers was to sack Eddie Quigley. I just couldn't believe it at first. I was astonished that they could sack Eddie, but I always thought that they felt that he was some kind of threat. I will not go into details or name names, but it was surprising how many contacts Bob Saxton lost at that time as a result of this action.

The Chairman, Bill Fox, together with Bob Saxton arranged a meeting for myself and Tom Howarth. I received a phone call from the Club Secretary, John Howarth saying, "The Chairman wants to see you Fred."

I knew Bill Fox very well. He had delivered potatoes to my off-licence when we lived in Randall Street in Blackburn. I knew him as a business associate, but we were also great friends. The meeting took place at 112 Nuttall Street, which I attended with Tom Howarth, the 'B' team coach.

Chairman Fox said, "Now listen. You know that Eddie Quigley's gone. The Youth policy at this club is going to be radically altered. First of all, we haven't got the money that we need to set up a proper youth programme. But there's no reason to worry about your positions with the club."

He looked straight at me with his steel-blue stare. His ginger hair seemed to be on fire with Bobby Saxton looking on. He went on, "We want you and Tom to look after the youth side of the club. You go out and bring them in Fred, just like you have been doing for so many years. We'll see to your petrol and we'll give you a pound or two. You can go on club trips and the facilities of the club are all yours. Just get on with it. I'm sure you'll do a good job, the both of you."

I mumbled something like. "Aye, all right!", but it didn't really sink in. Tommy

Howarth just mumbled "OK, Mr. Chairman." Both of us, however, were not really happy at losing some of our pals.

Here I was, having just lost my mentor and friend, Eddie Quigley, who was a very astute fellow. He knew his football and that was it. He was most upset, of course, at losing his job. He was about 61 or 62, I suppose, and he had four or five years to go to retirement. Sadly, I don't really think that Eddie had made a fortune in football, after earning only £8 or £9 a week when we was a young player.

But these things happen all the time in football and you have to accept it.

I would go in to see Bob Saxton with reports of the players I was watching in the schoolboy games. Now and then he would congratulate me and say, "Well done!" if we signed on new apprentices and those he signed as "Pro's".

But it just wasn't the same - not like it had been with Jimmy Smith. Bob was different from either Jimmy or Gordon Lee. In fact of all the managers at Blackburn, the ones I really liked were Ken Furphy and Gordon Lee, although in my heart my real favourites were Jimmy Smith and John Pickering. These four had equal ambitions to match the others, but they never lost the common touch with club staff members, guys like me.

I must pay a special tribute to Bob Saxton. I thank him from the bottom of my heart for the testimonial that he arranged with Chairman Fox. He allowed me to set up a twelve-month testimonial fund, with £7,000 ringing up on the till at the end.

They were the Rovers' managers I liked best of all, but I never really felt in close contact with Bob Saxton, compared to some of the other managers I had known. But I had total respect for him and will always be grateful to him for settling-up my house mortgage with his kind gesture. I could actually say that I own my home, which was more than my father did at my age.

My time at the Town Hall was coming to an end, and I was offered early retirement at the age of fifty-eight and a bit. I realised that I was again trying to do too much. I was trying to combine Town Hall draughtsmanship in the traffic section, whilst at the same time helping to run Blackburn Rovers youth policy. I was forever attending matches, seeing parents, whizzing around all the different connections.

So, I decided to take early retirement in June 1985. I thought, quite wrongly, actually, that I would get some kind of a job at Ewood Park. I went to see Bob Saxton.

"Boss, I'm taking an early retirement".

He said, "Well, I don't blame you. You're doing a bit too much".

Blackburn Rovers were struggling financially at that particular time. Well they told me they were, anyway - Bill Fox, Mr. Brown and Mr. Fryars, in unison. They were always hard up, to hear Mr. Fryars talk. I said to Bob Saxton, "Do you want me to come down?" He said, "Oh yeah, come on. You've got your little desk there. You'll be opposite Jim, in the little office in Nuttall Street." (The front upstairs bedroom).

"Well will there be some, like, remuneration for me working?" I inquired nervously.

His craggy face knotted, "Wait a minute," he said, "I can't get nowt for myself. We've no money. No. You'll just get your petrol expense like you have been doing."

I said, "But Bob, if I'm coming down here during the day, I'm going to take some of the administration side off Jim and lots of other things besides."

Jim Furnell was far, far overloaded. That night Jim and I met at the Five Barred Gate Pub, unknown to anyone. We had a long talk and I decided to stick out for some money - £10 or £20, something silly, but I wasn't going to go down to the ground everyday for nowt.

Bob Saxton was adamant. "No." I didn't approach Chairman Fox because the Chairman always has to back his manager, and you just don't go over the boss's head, or else! You just don't start talking to Directors about finance. Some people do, but I never did. I always went through the manager, but steely Bob was adamant that he wasn't going to give me anything.

"Nay," he said, "tha must be joking. Tha's only scout in England that's had a bloody testimonial off us!" I said, "Well, that may be, Bob, but I'm only 58. I've another seven years to work. Are you wanting me to work for nothing for another seven years until I'm 65, or whenever I decide to finish at the club?"

He still wouldn't budge. Most upset, I wrote out my resignation, in simple terms, and before Bob Saxton had a chance to call me in, I sent everybody on the Board of Directors a copy of it. Mr. Fryars, Youth Director; Bill Fox; Bob Coar; all the Board received it. John Howarth, the club secretary, read it, of course, as did my colleague Tony Parkes.

I had worked closely with Tony Parkes for many years. At odd times we'd go for lunch between 1 and 2 p.m. for meat pie and chips, or whatever, at a little cafe on Bolton Road. Tony Parkes was a great character and fine servant at the club and still is.

However, I resigned from the club. It was a very sad time for me but that was the end of my term at Blackburn Rovers.

During my spell at the Rovers, covering fourteen or fifteen years, we certainly had our ups and downs, some happy times and some sad ones. The most rewarding were the recollections of boys you'd seen on school pitches: Wilcox, Salmon, Carr, Johnrose, Patterson, and a host of others that just didn't quite make it to the big time.

It is a very, very rewarding job, but I wasn't going to work for nothing. "A labourer is worthy of his hire," so the Bible says.

P.F.A's Gordon Taylor was most upset with my decision, and I suspected Bill Fox had been talking to him to try and change my mind.

Looking back, I've been richly rewarded by the loyalty of many of the Rovers' players, and their parents, that I met in the game, and not forgetting all the scouts and coaches of other clubs. A host of genuine, life-long friends.

Having won the Manx Cup in 1983, Rovers do
their bit to promote tourism

Simon Garner

Chapter Six

The Testimonial

I don't know of any other scout who has been granted a full year's testimonial and it came about for me in a very strange way.

Blackburn Rovers were only paying me petrol expenses at this particular time from 1980 to 1985. Bob Saxton and Bill Fox had arranged to see me about cutting costs as a money-saving move involving the sacking of Eddie Quigley and a reduction in scouts' expenses.

On this particular night I was on duty with Rovers Reserves. Bob Saxton, Jim Furnell and myself boarded the bus with the reserve squad and set out to play Huddersfield Reserves. Traffic was very favourable to us and we arrived very early at the ground, around 6 p.m. for a 7.30 p.m. kick-off. We had loads of time to kill.

The manager let Jim sort out the team, their positions, set-pieces, free-kicks etc. Bob turned to me saying, "Fred, we'll go for a drink."

We came out of the Huddersfield Town ground, walked a short distance up Leeds Road and found this pub on the left. I think it was called The Dog and Partridge.

"What you having Bob?" I asked.

"A pint of bitter," he replied. We were chatting about this and that, when suddenly he said, "How long have you been in local government, Fred?"

I said, "Oh, twenty-odd years or so."

"Have you paid for your own house yet?"

I said, "No, I think I owe about three or four thousand. It seems to have taken me a long time."

The questions continued, "How old are you?"

"Fifty-seven".

"How long have you been with the club?"

"Well, a long time. Longer than I care to remember."

"Did you ever really get anything, like off the club, off the managers?"

I said, "Yeah, when I first started with the club I got £10 a week and my petrol expenses. Later Jimmy Smith gave me £10 a week, petrol expenses, 2% of any transfer, plus £25 for any schoolboy that was signed as an apprentice, £50 if he turned pro and £100 when a boy made it into the first team."

Jimmy Smith had probably been the most generous of the lot.

I went on, "But of course, if you remember Bob, when you came along, this contract we had, which I've still got a copy of, you kicked into touch. You kicked all the contracts into touch."

"Has nobody ever been paid money?"

"The only chap that got any money," I explained, "was Jim Mooney when we sold John Bailey to Everton. He got £500 in cash that Eddie Quigley managed to scrounge off the Board. Apart from that I never knew of any scout, in my time, who had monetary gain."

"That's terrible, Fred," he said. "Tha's been there all these years and fetched all them players." He started rhyming some of the players that came through me. "You've been 'A' team coach, Youth Development Officer, Chief Scout, Accommodation Officer and General Factotum for everybody really. I'll try to get you a testimonial."

Around the same time there was a player called Norman Bell, who was a centre-forward who had broken his leg after being at the club about eighteen months or two years. The Board, through Bob, decided to give Norman a full testimonial year to help him financially. This I could understand, and I think his testimonial was started at the end of that season in 1984, so mine started 1985/86 from New Year to New Year.

The actual events I have detailed elsewhere for the reader to peruse, but there's only one chap that I must single out who was absolutely outstanding for me, and that was Marshall Pickup, the treasurer for my testimonial.

He also did a bit of scouting for Blackburn Rovers and I always thought a lot of him. He gave me a lot of help and good advice. As we got stuck into the work he was unbelievable. I never realised just how much work is involved in organising a testimonial.

Another stalwart helper was George Turner, a quiz-master who spent a lot of time with me and did a great job with Quiz Nights.

There were difficulties but I was lucky to enjoy a lot of co-operation. My day job suffered a little bit at the Town Hall, as did my scouting duties at Blackburn Rovers.

I wasn't so lucky, however, for when I contacted the big clubs for a benefit match with Blackburn Rovers, I was only a small fry in the eyes of Ron Atkinson, Howard Kendall and others. They didn't really want to know me.

One Friday night at Tranmere, watching a league game, I met Billy Bingham, the Northern Ireland manager.

"Bill, I'm having a testimonial and I haven't got anybody to play", I said. "How about coming up to Ewood Park at the end of May?"

He thought about it. "Hey, that doesn't sound a bad idea. I can look at one or two players in the North West like Noel Brotherston at Rovers. Also there's Quinn and a couple at Burnley."

I was over the moon. He finally arranged to come on May 12th or 13th, finally fixed for the 12th - my very own testimonial match.

That day dawned, and what a day. The heavens opened. Talk about bad luck - it was rain, rain and more rain.

My pal, Jim Furnell had rushed over to Stockport to collect the Northern Ireland kit, whilst Tony Parkes also drove to Manchester to pick up two of the Irish Queen's Park Rangers players, who were arriving by aeroplane.

But the rain never abated from morning to night. Ewood Park was like a swimming pool, totally unplayable.

Fate decreed however, and everything had been pre-arranged - the meals, the dinners, the Mayor, Tom Finney, Gordon Taylor, Peter Doherty and all the VIP's I could think of at that time. They'd all been invited to attend.

Due to the appalling weather it was a dead loss at the turnstile. The gate just about balanced the expenses incurred. Where I did make some money was from sponsorships such as British Telecom and other firms like Whitbread's that came in and helped me out.

I owed a great debt to those organisations, without whom I could have been owing money to various suppliers, caterers, printers etc.

At the end of 1985 I concluded the programme with a final night at the John Lewis complex. My old friend Bill Fox handed me a cheque for just over £7,000, for which I was most grateful. I was able to settle my house mortgage with the Halifax Building Society. It was the culmination of a year of very hard work, which enabled me to obtain the deeds of my own home.

I had a lot to thank Bob Saxton for, following that little chat over a pint in the Dog and Partridge on Leeds Road in Huddersfield.

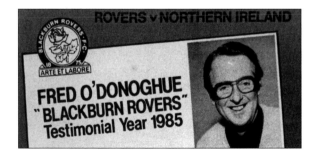

Fred O'Donoghue Testimonial Fund
Receipts & Payments A/C as at 8/1/86

Receipts

RACENIGHT (Blackburn, Ewood)	£	326.24
PEPPERMINT PLACE (Blackburn) - Miss Blackburn Rovers	£	401.71
MULLARDS SPORTS QUIZ (Blackburn)	£	74.00
FARMERS ARMS (Higher Walton)	£	146.00
CHERRY TREE C.C. (Blackburn)	£	72.50
DOG INN QUIZ NIGHT	£	111.24
LANCS & YORKS INN (Bamber Bridge)	£	90.00
ROVERS V NORTHERN IRELAND MATCH	£	2,615.67
GRAND RAFFLE	£	1,272.34
STAG NIGHT (Rugby Club, Blackburn)	£	150.03
GOLDEN GOAL (Various Pubs in Blackburn & District)	£	338.25
CHORLEY S.Q. QUIZ (Chorley Football Club)	£	52.19
SWAN INN QUIZ (Higher Walton)	£	52.00
HOSPITAL INN QUIZ (Hoghton)	£	46.90
HYDE PARK S.Q. QUIZ (Preston)	£	35.00
PADIHAM C.C. (Cricket Match) - All Stars (Jim Kenyon)	£	25.50
SPORTSMAN'S DINNER (Blackburn)	£	376.48
TROPHY DONATIONS (Various Firms)	£	255.00
ROEBUCK HOTEL (Leyland)	£	15.00
FURTHERGATE CLUB (Blackburn)	£	40.19
ACCRINGTON STANLEY QUIZ (Football Club)	£	65.00
CHORLEY V ROVER MATCH (Chorley Motors)	£	30.00
PADIHAM WANDERERS QUIZ (Accrington District)	£	55.00
VOLUNTEER ARMS QUIZ (Accrington District)	£	57.00
FARMERS ARMS QUIZ (Blackburn)	£	64.48
100 CLUB RAFFLE QUIZ (Blackburn)	£	47.85
NALGO QUIZ NIGHT (Blackburn)	£	108.44
HARVEYS SOCIAL QUIZ/DANCE (Blackburn)	£	50.55
ANCHOR HOTEL QUIZ (Darwen)	£	70.61
SHEAR BANK HOTEL QUIZ (Blackburn)	£	88.49
GRAND QUIZ (Ewood Park)	£	157.04
BANK INTEREST UP TO 31/12/85	£	215.67
	£	**7,506.37**

Less Payments

GAMING LICENCE	£	20.00
FOOTBALLS FOR RAFFLES	£	55.00
LETTERHEADS	£	72.22
SPORTS QUIZ - BROWNEDGE (PRINTING)	£	17.82
MEDALS FOR QUIZ'S	£	25.06
EXPENSES FOR RAFFLES & QUIZ'S (1)	£	140.00
EXPENSES FOR RAFFLES & QUIZ'S (2)	£	45.00
SUNDRY EXPENSES	£	2.99
	£	**478.09**

PROFIT   **£ 7,028.28**

Prepared by Marshall Pickup

Rover's V Northern Ireland Match

Receipts

Sponsors	£	2,362.50
'A' Box	£	460.00
Stand Tickets	£	90.50
Raffle	£	63.90
Sale of Programmes	£	138.87
Gate Receipts	£	2,359.50
Cash Over from John Howarth	£	5.50
Billy Bingham Donation	£	89.00
	£	**5,560.77**

Payments

Telephone Expenses - Secretary	£	7.50
Expenses - Players	£	531.72
Disco	£	25.00
Footballs	£	47.33
Insurance	£	50.00
Tax	£	50.00
Len/100 club	£	69.19
Stamps/Envelopes	£	22.36
Printing Tickets and Posters	£	16.00
Advertising	£	389.85
Drinks in Sponsors Lounge	£	48.90
Buffet	£	747.00
Expenses - Petrol Jim Furnell & Tony Parkes	£	30.00
Players Gifts	£	293.25
Printing Programmes	£	350.00
Gatemen's Expenses	£	267.00
	£	2,945.10
PROFIT	**£**	**2,615.67**

Fred O'Donoghue
"Blackburn Rovers Testimonial Year 1985"

31 January 1986

Dear Mr Chairman

On behalf of my family and myself may I thank you and the Manager along with the board of Directors for granting the past year's testimonial on my behalf. As you are aware, I have held a variety of positions at the club (in my part time capacity).

At our last meeting you asked me for a track record of my efforts for the Club, i.e. League players that I have been connected with.

Please note there are also other scouts involved Mr Chairman

Messrs Jim Mooney - Scout Liverpool

Tom Howarth - Scout and Coach (Local)

Eddie Quigley - Chief Scout, Ex PNE/Rovers

Ian Hanson - Local Scout

Steve Done - Schoolteacher at Preston

The above team did very well for the Rovers, and helped me out a lot in signing these young players, who have all played at league club levels, and there are lots more that just didn't make it.

Name of Player		Team
1.	John Waddington	Rovers
2.	John Butcher	Rovers
3.	John Bailey	Rovers
4.	Paul Round	Rovers
5.	Tim Parkin	Rovers
6.	Mickey Salmon	Rovers
7.	Mark Patterson	Rovers
8.	Simon Garner	Rovers
9.	Franz Carr	Rovers
10.	David Lee	Bolton

11.	Stephen Galliers	Wimbledon
12.	Jason Wilcox	Rovers
13.	Jimmy Willis	Leicester
14.	Paul Comstive	Rovers
15.	Peter Devine	Rovers
16.	Darren Donnelly	Rovers
17.	Leonard Johnrose	Rovers

Further Notes

Re: Simon Garner - Sent to Rovers from Boston by J Smith's scout. Jim and myself rubber stamped his apprenticeship with the club.

Positions held at the club:- 1. Chief Scout. 2. Youth Liaison Officer. 3. Assistant Chief Scout. 4. 'A' Team and 'B' Team Coach. 5. Assistant Coach to Youth Squad. 6. Tours Manager and Organiser. 7. Accommodation Officer. 8. Town Hall Liaison Person.

Yours faithfully
Fred O'Donoghue

Testimonial Presentation Night, Cheque from Bill Fox for £7,028.80.
L/R Bill Fox, Wilf McGuiness, Ian Baldwin, Fred Eyre, David Jones, Marshall Pickup, The FOD

Get Well card from my friends at the Town Hall and Ewood
March 26th 1976, 1st Heart attack

Chapter Seven

Preston North End
The start at Deepdale

North End Director, Barney Campbell, had taken note of a letter from me to Gordon Lee, who was manager at the Deepdale Club at that time. It must have occurred to him that it was strange for a Preston lad to be working for the Rovers. Why did he not have a yearning to work at his home town club? So it was that Barney made the initial inquiry for my services.

He was a well-known local landlord and caravan tycoon. Barney (Conman) Campbell of Lostock Hall manufactured and sold vast numbers of caravans to the public.

His glasses glinted at me as he spoke in the Guild Club at the Deepdale Ground. "What about joining your home town club?" he said, getting hold of my arm and steering me towards the bar. "Two whiskies, please, with a touch of lemon. I've had you in mind for a long time," he said in his soft, persuasive voice.

I had just been given a testimonial year at Blackburn (1985) and I must say, I felt a little guilty in the face of his audacious approach. But as I was soon going to resign from the Rovers, the thought of it began to gain credibility in my mind.

Barney arranged to meet me at the Leyland Resort Hotel for an 8.30 a.m. breakfast. He duly arrived, half an hour late, puffing a cigarette, saying, "Do you know, Fred, I nearly forgot this meeting!"

"Oh!", I said, "Do you not keep a diary of your appointments?"

He replied, again in that soft, subtle-toned voice, with his glasses glinting, "I never keep a diary. I never did."

And then, unexpectedly from him, he came out with a quotation from one of Kipling's poems: "If you can keep you head when all about are losing theirs and blaming it on you...."

A piece of crispy bacon I was munching stuck in my throat. I started to choke and laugh at the same time. After I had settled down, he arranged a further meeting with his co-directors, again at the Leyland Hotel.

I recall Chairman, Mr. Leeming, Mr. Garratt, Mr. M Woodhouse, Mr. J Francis and Conman Barney, of course. I can't remember who else. Brian Kidd, whom I had met at the club, was courtesy itself to me. I liked him, but I was not happy at leaving Rovers so quickly, and I gave backword to Barney.

The friendly Brian Kidd, a few weeks later, left the club and didn't have very nice things to say about PNE

It was some time later that I learned that the Board had turned down Barney Campbell's protÈgÈ, (that being me), for a position with the club.

A few months later, after I had resigned from Rovers, Barney approached me again, and we had several meetings. John (the Madman) McGrath had been appointed manager with Les Chapman as his assistant and Walter Joyce as Youth Development Officer.

Suddenly, there were three jobs to hand.

The first - one of my best friends, Gordon Taylor, a good player at the Rovers and now PFA Chief Executive, had hinted at a place for me at Deepdale on the Community programme with Mick Baxter, now sadly deceased. Gordon had been upset at my resigning from the Rovers and told me so in no uncertain terms. Bill Fox had joined in, and I was also unpopular with solicitor Terry Ibbitson, who also had a go at me.

The second job in the offing was with Brian Hall, the ex-Liverpool FC player who was looking for selected staff for the stadium pitch at Deepdale, and a dialogue took place with the Preston Local Authority, but nothing came of it. Brian Hall, of course had been a Liverpool star in his hey-day, and I was later to sign his son Andrew on schoolboy forms. He was a smashing lad who didn't get any breaks in the game. Brian is now back with the Merseyside club, and doing well.

The third approach had both Barney and Walter Joyce having a go at me to join PNE. I agreed to have a meeting with Mr. Keith Leeming, Chairman at Deepdale.

The club was in the financial doldrums, said Mr. Leeming, and could not offer me full-time staff wages. But they could pay me £50 a week for a ten-week trial period (See original copy at end of chapter).

I duly signed, and thus began a six year plus (1960 days) spell, to the date of my resignation from the PNE Club on 11th January 1993.

John McGrath was now managing the club and I could see that I was going to be very busily engaged in the set-up at Deepdale which Walter Joyce was trying to create with his schemes for the youth development side of the club.

At that time Preston North End was doing very well, winning a lot of games and gaining promotion that season with McGrath at the helm.

So I began to work at Preston North End in the field of liaison and scouting. My job covered youth scouting, watching clubs locally and recruiting good schoolboy players. I also arranged programmes in the Centre of Excellence and set up games with other clubs. Walter was doing the coaching with Les Chapman and John McGrath at senior and YT levels.

When I arrived on the first Monday morning, there was John McGrath talking to

Keith Macklin on Red Rose Radio, doing some kind of interview about the previous match. He said, "Hi Fred, come here!"

He was a big powerful man with a character to match. When he entered a room the whole atmosphere changed with his presence. He was such a dynamic sort of person.

"Come on. Come with me at lunch. Just have a look round and then come with me at lunchtime."

We both went up to the Conservative Club in Preston, near the Old Bull and Royal. John McGrath was the lunch-time speaker, and he got a nice little drop in his back pocket for doing so. He was brilliant, quite brilliant - pulling the F.A. to pieces, pulling the game to pieces, blokes he didn't like, blokes he'd kicked.

He was a high-flying man was John. They called him the madman and he calls himself the madman, with some justification, no doubt. When he talked to players he used to peel the paint off the walls. His verbal "command", if that's the right word, was something to marvel at. It was a different ball game to me, just listening to him.

I did almost everything at Preston North End: sponge man for the reserves, coaching, driving the team bus, painting, scouting, admin work. I also stood in at reserve matches with tannoy announcements for a chap called Bernard Ibbison, a retired police officer, with whom I became good friends. When Bernard wasn't doing it, I would go along and do the mid-week matches on the PNE tannoy system.

John McGrath made me feel very uneasy, however, when his temper tantrums displayed themselves time and again, especially with Les Chapman. Poor Les, when he would pick on such little things and start shouting the odds.

I didn't really think I was going to be happy, but Walter Joyce, who was my mainstay at Deepdale said, "Take no notice Fred, it passes."

Les Chapman also, whom I had great respect for, as an affable colleague, helped me through this period. If it had not been for Walter Joyce and Les Chapman I wouldn't have been there. I just couldn't have stayed there with John McGrath, as I will illustrate with the following episode.

Barney Campbell had got hold of me to see if we could do something for the senior citizens. He said, "Why don't we set up a Preston North End Senior Citizens' Club?" Barney suggested I got on with it, so I did. I got Mick Baxter the Community Officer, to help, and we approached all the old people's homes in the area. We produced a Senior Citizens' Card and organised a cabaret concert in the Guild Club, which attracted many local pensioners.

Part of the entertainment was a sing-song with a good little combination outfit comprising Ron, the drummer and an organ player from Lostock Hall St.Gerard's with a bass accompaniment and singer.

They all came along for a really good night - singing, dancing, housey-housey, pies, peas and, of course, pints! How the pensioners loved it.

About two days later I was approached by Bob Saxton, who had come in to help McGrath after having been sacked by Blackburn Rovers. He said, "Fred, the boss wants to see you in Box 12 immediately."

Sitting in the box were Walter Joyce, Les Chapman, Bob Saxton and the madman John McGrath.

"Sit down," he said. "Why are you talking to directors?"

I said, "What do you mean?" I knew he was going to have a go at me.

He repeated the question, "Why are you talking to directors?"

I said, "Which directors?"

"Barney Campbell," he said. "Don't you realise that you are going above my authority." This was about two o'clock in the afternoon. By a quarter to four it was going in one ear and out of the other!

He accused me of conniving and plotting with the Board. According to him, all the secrets that should be kept within that room with Les Chapman and Bob Saxton, I was informing the directors about. I was a mole. He didn't know whether to sack me. I thought at one time he was threatening a good hiding. It was absolutely unbelievable the things he was saying about me.

Eventually, in the end, as Walter Joyce had said to me previously, and as Les Chapman had also said, "Let it go in one ear Fred and out of the other." And that's just what it did. All the language and all the swearing. The man really blew his top about this Senior Citizens' Club and me talking to Barney Campbell. The truth was Barney Campbell came talking to me.

The other problem was that I'd asked for a rise. I'd been there quite some time on £50 a week. I was putting in fifty to sixty hours a week for virtually nothing, and there's this fellow going at me hammer and tongs.

I came out of that box battered and bewildered, thinking what the hell am I doing here?

Bob Saxton didn't help me in any way. He just sat there. So did Walter Joyce and Les Chapman. Nobody said a thing. I thought Walter might have a go at him, but no way!

However, as the afternoon wore on, he went on and on, going into things where I didn't even know what he was talking about. He'd had these meetings in the boardroom. He was going to flatten Barney Campbell. He was going to tell that Woodhouse that he wanted money for Mike Flynn a young centre back he fancied.

This meeting in Box 12 - it wasn't really a meeting at all. It was all the things on John McGrath's mind. And yet there was something about the man that I liked. His coaching, for instance, was par excellence. And he could be very warm, even though he didn't really have a lot to do with me. It was just that he didn't like people talking to the Board or to any of the directors. He had to be the man. They had to see John McGrath and nobody else would do.

I came out of it completely stunned. I went home that night and slept very little. The following morning I came into the ground with the intention of resigning, a letter already written out in my pocket, to give John McGrath.

Les Chapman got hold of me and said, "Come here, Fred, I want a word with you. You are one of the best scouts in the business. You are also one of the most likeable chaps I've met. Don't pack it in." he knew I was thinking of resigning. "He's John McGrath. That's why they call him the madman. He'll probably have forgot all about it today."

This advice from Les stopped me from resigning. Sam Allardyce was a player at the club at the same time. He often recalls that afternoon when McGrath's voice was heard shouting at me, in Blackpool!

Sure enough, as predicted, John came in and said, "Hiya Fred! Let me get the lunch." I felt as though he was saying to me, I went over the top yesterday. With McGrath's money I went out and bought turkey batons from the corner shop on Blackpool Road. But, I've never ever been shouted at like that. I've never ever been in such a position of dumb helplessness. You couldn't answer him back. It was very out of order, but it was also sadly illuminating and enlightening. As a matter of fact I think from then on it did me good. The rage inside me was unbelievable but I kept control of my temper. That was the plus side. That was what John McGrath had produced - control, plus the fact that he was a big man, too big for me to tackle. My common sense prevailed.

I couldn't really like John McGrath, but yet, as I have said before, some of his coaching, particularly his heading sessions in the gymnasium at Deepdale were absolutely brilliant. He could really get players to excel themselves in training sessions.

But he was a strange, very strange man, who despite a lot of success at Deepdale, could also descend into the depths of despair. At other times he was a brilliant after-dinner speaker, with superb oratory and some stories that were stranger than fiction. I am richer in experience through knowing him.

During John McGrath's reign at Deepdale I asked him about taking in a Youth Tour, because by this time we had got some really good young lads - Nathan Peel, Martin James, Lee Ashcroft, all very good players. So Walter and myself agreed that it wouldn't be a bad idea to take these lads on a trip.

John McGrath knew a chap called Rennie Hann, who operated from London. He was really an agent, and a very shrewd operator was this Rennie Hann. We fixed up with him for the Under 18 Squad to visit the Le Croix Tournament in France in 1987. So, we got our team together and paid Rennie Hann for the airfares and a fee for his organisation of it, so we thought!

It turned out to be a story of agents on the make.

We flew out to France from Manchester and in the first game met the Russian side, Moscow Dynamo, who hammered us 6 - 1. By now we had realised just how strong these Under-18 European teams were. In that particular tournament there were some great sides; there was Feynoord, Hamburg SV, the United States, Santiago Youth Squad, (Chile), Benfica, Real Madrid. You could name all the top clubs in Europe and they'd all been in this particular competition.

The Russians were a very strange bunch of lads. They kept to themselves as they all marched into the dining room together, ate their meal, and all marched out together. They didn't smile much and wanted to buy off our lads their jeans and T-shirts when their coach wasn't looking.

As far as the trip was concerned, it was very enjoyable. There was myself, Chairman Mr. Leeming, who was very good company, coach Mick Finn, and Walter Joyce of course, in charge of the team. The team did reasonably well, and came back with a couple of trophies for the best-dressed side, or something like that.

We came back a lot more educated about European trips. Whilst we were there the radio people came in to interview Walter Joyce and Mr. Leeming. I was stood at one side whilst the French interviewer, Armand, said, "Now tell me, Walter, about all the great clubs you've played for. You played in Europe for Burnley and Blackburn Rovers?" He went on pontificating about what Walter had done.

"And you, Mr Chairman, the Chairman of the great club of Preston North End. And tell me Fred, who did you play for?"

I said, "I played for St. Augustine's in the Preston and District Catholic League."

Well, there were howls of laughter from all the people around. They just couldn't stop themselves.

The poor Frenchman was perplexed. "The what, Monsieur?" Again I said, "St. Augustine's in the Preston and District Catholic League. I've also been captain of the Preston and District League team."

Actually, I was belittling myself. I had played in trials for Fleetwood, Lancaster City and for Blackburn Rovers 'A' Team. But it was so funny, all these people name-dropping about teams they'd played for.

From that moment I became friends with the French hierarchy at a stroke, thanks to a bit of humility and a slip of the tongue. The French loved it. I still speak to Armand now and then on the telephone and have kept in touch with him over the years.

Whilst on this trip I'd met the President of the Le Croix International Tournament, a man called Michael Montembaut, who spoke no English. The interpreter, my friend Armand, was excellent. He told Walter, the Chairman and myself all about his time in the Resistance, during the war. He had escaped from the Nazis, reached England and joined the Free French Army. What a smashing fellow.

Talking to him about finance I happened to say, "Well Armand, it has cost us quite a lot to make this trip."

Armand, with a puzzled frown said, "How do you mean, Fred?"

I said, "It's cost the air fares for a start. We took the club minibus to Manchester, got on the plane, flew to Brussels, then took your bus."

He said, "How do you mean? You paid?"

I said, "Well, we bought the tickets off Rennie Hann."

This conversation was at the farewell reception on the final day of the tournament and was later translated to Michael Montembaut. He, in turn, told me, through Armand, that they also had paid Rennie Hann to bring us over. What had actually happened was that Rennie had charged Preston North End for organising this trip and had also charged the French authorities for the organisation. Rennie was on a winner. He was getting two fees for one job. Rennie Hann's explanation was that his fee for arranging club tours was quite normal.

After this experience, PNE dealt directly with the French authorities.

Under 14's and Under 16's - Ireland's Milk Cup

(Goings on) in Northern Ireland - July 1991

PNE - The Milk Cup Competition - 1991 and 1992

For the duration of this tournament we were staying in a boarding house, the name of which I have diplomatically forgotten, but it was in Port Rush. All the games were staged in the various small towns of Northern Ireland - Coleraine, Port Stewart, Port Rush, Limvady.

This particular boarding house was really awful. It was just a simple guest house, but the landlady was really struggling, for every morning while we were there, all that the lads had to eat for breakfast was cornflakes and toast. As much toast as they could eat, some cornflakes, and that was it. Plenty of tea however!

There were several adults in the party, including Bill Holland, father of one of the players, and Ray Linford, the coach driver who had taken the coach from Preston to Stranraer, over on the ferry and then drove us all round Northern Ireland, including trips to Giants's Causeway, and other highspots of the northern coast and the beautiful Antrim countryside.

On this particular morning I had got a bit fed up with toast and cornflakes and as we all sat round the table, I said to the young waitress, "Excuse me, love. Do you think you could ask if I could have a little bit of crispy bacon for my breakfast of a morning?"

She said, "Well, I'll ask," in her lovely Irish soft-toned voice.

She walked away, came back, and said, "Sorry, the grill's been switched off."

Well, all the lads started laughing and just couldn't stop. We had to go out in the morning and buy our breakfast at a local cafe, but it created such a laugh as the lads enjoyed my swift demise.

It was all very sad really but obviously the landlady was struggling to make ends meet. We had paid quite a bit. I think it was £95 per head, and you're talking about sixteen boys and four adults at £95 a head, which came to quite a lot of money actually.

But the football in Ireland was first-class, and the people were wonderful. They made us so welcome in their quaint Irish way.

The second time we went over to Ireland it was with the Under 14's in 1992. Les Chapman had appointed me manager of the team with coaches Steve Grand and a lad called Darryl Woods, both coaching at the Centre of Excellence. It was a very strong and powerful side that we took over in July of that year.

We had a really good team spirit, but a sad incident was when Ian Stanley, the outside-left from Penwortham broke his leg in the second match against Norwich. We lost the game 2 - 1 but on the whole it was a successful tour, and we had possibly one of the best sides that I've dealt with in my time at the club. Most of the lads were on schoolboy forms with PNE.

Ian Stanley had to return home early and Darryl Wood did a sterling job in taking him home by road via Stranraer. It's a long journey by road and no mean achievement.

The 1992 Under-14 Northern Ireland trip was really exciting. I'd met Nobby Stiles the previous year, who managed Man United U/14 Boys. This time I met Harry Gregg - a tremendous fellow, all 6ft 3ins of him, and he's still as bouncy and lively as ever, with his wife, and daughter Karen. They really made us welcome at the Windsor Hotel in Port Stewart. It was a really good Irish welcome. The food was tremendous - ham, eggs and bacon, and as much as you wanted. Harry Gregg, or to be truthful, his wife and daughter, do a really great job at the Windsor Hotel.

Whilst we were there I met Pop Robson and Les Kershaw and all the Manchester United team. Weren't they delighted when we won the Northern Bank Plate in Northern Ireland. Les Kershaw and I became firm friends.

As for Nobby, I'll tell you a little anecdote about him. In the final we were destined to play Stella Maris, whom Manchester United had played in the earlier stages. Stella Maris, a team from the Republic, based in Dublin, had done well to fight their way through to the final, and they had quite a number of good players.

One particular lad that I'd picked out was Desi Baker, whom Manchester United later signed on schoolboy forms. He was the main Stella Maris striker. I'd seen him three or four times and what a good player he was.

Now every night the PNE staff and the Man United staff used to come out of the hotel after settling the lads down in their bedrooms. One of the staff would keep watch whilst the rest of us used to go for a pint. Nobby Stiles, myself, Pop Robson, Man United's Irish Scouts, Les Kershaw, Steve Grand etc., went up the promenade road to a local pub. It was behind a restaurant actually, where we could booze until whatever time we wanted.

Nobby knew we were in the final and he offered me his congratulations. I said, "Nobby, have you a minute?" I took him into a corner.

"What's to do Fred?" he asked.

"We're playing Stella Maris tomorrow."

"I know," said Nobby.

"This striker lad that's up front, Desi Baker," I said.

"I think he's playing out of his skin at the moment," Nobby said. "Track him, Fred. Put somebody on to him and track him. No matter where he goes he's going to score. But just track the lad. Play him tight, he's such a good player on his day. Don't let him turn."

So, come the match, I detailed one of the lads to mark this player, a local Preston lad called Martin Lupton. He did his best but Desi still scored two goals, and we felt it kept him quiet a bit. The match finished 2 - 2 at full-time, so we had to go into sudden-death penalties.

The Coleraine ground was packed, with all the Man United staff, and all our hotel staff supporting us. Lo and behold we managed to win the match after one of their lads missed a penalty. They were heart broken. If ever you saw a bunch of lads crying it was the Stella Maris team in Coleraine. What a sight! Fourteen years of age, the spirit of youth and the desolation of defeat. The other side of the coin saw the joy and triumph of Preston North End Youth.

It was a great day and the climax of a great trip to Northern Ireland as we returned with the Northern Bank Plate trophy which I believe and hope is still in the Preston North End trophy cupboard.

And what joy for all as the Under-14 team returned to Deepdale as heroes with the trophy held high for all the parents to see as they cheered us off the bus at midnight at the Deepdale ground.

These then were the highlights of my trips with Preston North End to Northern Ireland, not forgetting the:

-	Two trips to France with Walter Joyce, Les Chapman and Mr. Leeming.

-	Meeting the people over there, like Armand and the French Tournament president, Michael Montembaut.

-	I would like to record the assistance of ex-police superintendent, and friend, Nigel Webster in Port Stewart, Northern Ireland, with his positive disciplined thinking.

-	Most of all, you remember the boys who were in your care. You had to be a bit strict at times, and pull one or two of them up and threaten to send them back home if they misbehaved. But in the main, with proper control, they were great experiences, and some of my happiest footballing hours.

Preston North End F.C. Ltd

Job Specification

F O'Donoghue, Tech Eng CEI
Full time Liaison Scout

Assistance to Walter Joyce and Manager at all times. To organise the administration side of and the position of scouting activities.

Staff post for at least 13 weeks full time work
1st pay from 8 December to 14 December 1986 (6 days)   £50.00
2nd pay from 15 December to (13 weeks) - weekly pay agreed £50.00
Tax and stamp - Football Club to pay

Signed Fred O'Donoghue

Signed K W Leeming
             Chairman
             Preston North End FC
Dated   16 December 1986

Work by Liason Scout F O'Donoghue   W/E Sun 2 Feb 1987

Mr Chairman: A Typical Week's work to date

	Hours
Monday	
Office 9.20 am/3.00 pm/12 pm. Reserve game at Grimsby	
total hours with PNE (Scouting)	15.00
Tuesday	
9.30 am. Office work, letters, trial lists 6.00 pm Everton v	
Sheffield Res. Home 10.00 pm. Watching players for	
Manager (Scouting)	11.30
Wednesday	
2.30 pm Files, letters, organising games and under 13's	
trial lists. Wednesday Evening PNE Reserves Assignments	
W Joyce. Home at 10.00 pm *(Plastic Pitch Meeting, M Baxter,	
W Dore, Mr Campbell 11.00 am)	11.30
Thursday	
9.30 am Office Mr B Campbell organising Senior Whites	
Club contacting all the concerned artistes. Home 5.00 pm	
Under 13's application forms issued	7.30
Friday	
9.30 am Office Home 5.00 pm. Replies to letters etc.	7.30
Saturday	
am. Scouting Under 16's Lancs 9-12 Youth Level	3.00
pm. Scouting Tranmere v Aldershot Senior	4.00
Sunday	
Writing up Scout reports. Telephoning Artistes for Senior	
Whites	2.00
TOTAL HOURS	**62.00**

Costs Incurred

Car Running Expenses	**£**
12 months Road Tax - 12	8.33 Mthly
Insurance £120.00 (fully comp)	10.00 "
Petrol average over 4 weeks	30.00 "

Telephone Expenses

Outside/Office total for 4 weeks (40)

I am averaging 10 a week duration of call varies (i.e 30p) 12.00

i.e. Youth Managers, parents, artistes, Federation, PFA,

Senior Whites. Difficult to assess

Car Repairs

Tyres, etc. oil. depreciation value   10.00 Mthly

These are average monthly expenses £200.00   Wage

                                 Less   £ 70.00   Incurred costs as above

                             £130.00

Average basic wage per hour 52P

Fred O'Donoghue

A special note: Walter Joyce's PNE Soccer Academy

The academy also consisted of the following persons who contributed so much to the unique success of the PNE Youth Policy at that time. Funds were cleverly acquired by Tom Hasty and Frank Hewitt in having a series of Sportsman's Dinners at various venues in the district. As also did Messrs Jim Dean, Dave Borland, Steve Borwick and Keith Neilson in other federation fund raising events supporting this active successful academy. Other chaps on the PNE Junior Federation included some first class coaches, Peter Warburton, Keith Aspinall (now sadly deceased Ex Headmaster, St Gregory's), Steve Grand, Darryl Wood, Mick Finn, (Jim Parker, Kit Man), Ron Mears, Nigel Webster, Glen Bohanon, Stuart Pilling and Peter Corbett, who by the way did their coaching for the PNE youngsters for no personal fee whatsoever, saving the club thousands of pounds. How much it is costing my old club now I shudder to contemplate. Such a pity the excellent set up was dismantled by ignorance of the facts by certain PNE officials.

1987-Croix Under 18's International in France.
L/R Chairman Leeming, Walter Joyce, The FOD.

The Walter Joyce Soccer Academy

Fred O'Donoghue who was assistant to Walter Joyce, is very well known throughout the North West region in the scouting business and earned his great respect through his sincerity and his undoubted commitment to the job. Although he made a name for himself at Blackburn Rovers, culminating in a well deserved testimonial, he gave as much to the youth policy at Preston North End as anybody.

After resigning at Blackburn, Fred's post at Deepdale was supposed to be 'part-time', but his efforts during the period 1986-1992 when he teamed up with Walter Joyce were unquestionably full-time. Quite a few of the youngsters they had under their wing at Deepdale came through the youth system and played for the first eleven at Football League level. They include Lee Ashcroft, Martin James and Nathan Peel, who when sold brought in around £370,000 to the North End club.

Lee Cartwright is another who should in time play at a higher level and is, at the time of writing, a regular in the present PNE team with more than 100 league appearances behind him.

Ian Nolan, a former PNE YTS who was released by Deepdale has since made his mark in the high flying Sheffield United team, whereas Andy Pilling, after just one game for Preston, went on to make over 100 appearances for Wigan Athletic.

Other players who came through the system when Fred and Walter were at Preston North End and played in league games for the club include Adrian Hughes, Matthew Lambert, Steven Anderton, Jason Kerfoot, David Eaves, David Flitcroft, David Christie, Craig Moylon and Steve Finney who is currently at Swindon FC. The latest player to make money for the club was Chris Holland who signed for Newcastle United for a minimum fee of £200,000. Fred signed Chris on when he was a 14 year old. Initially coaches Peter Warburton and Steve Grand helped Fred and Walter out in coaxing young Chris to join the club.

Two young apprentices already at Deepdale when Fred arrived but still came under the guidance of Walter Joyce were Nigel Jemson, later to make a name for himself at Nottingham Forest and Sheffield Wednesday, and Alan Kelly who made a good profit for Preston with his transfer to Sheffield United, now an Eire International.

When Fred was at Blackburn Rovers he persuaded two Preston born lads to try their luck at Ewood Park, namely Lennie Johnrose who later played for PNE on loan, and Franz Carr who progressed enough to play for England's Under-21 team.

Fred, currently at Blackpool Football Club is a popular, friendly approachable guy who knows the game inside out.

Best of luck with the book Fred.

Yours sincerely

Ian Rigby

PNE Official Historian 1994

Ryan (Wilson) Giggs, Manchester United

One of Walter Joyce's PNE scouts was Terry Griffin, a member, at the time of Salford Football Club. He had told Walter of a certain young player called Ryan Wilson with exceptional skills, for his age of fourteen. Walter told me to arrange for Ryan Wilson to play in the PNE federation youth games held on the plastic pitch at PNE. At that particular time, this I did! Young Ryan arrived at Deepdale limping; he had been hurt with his Sunday team and was obviously unable to play. Walter, Tony, Ryan and myself went up to one of the boxes that overlooked the pitch at Deepdale. Walter then went into great detail about his chances at a club like Preston rather than big city clubs. Ryan went on to say that he was interested in the Preston Club and yet however there was also other clubs interested in him joining them. Not seeing Ryan play, we couldn't really offer him the Schoolboy forms. I kick myself when I think that if I had been more positive and followed this slim chance up the week after, who knows Ryan Wilson the now famous Ryan Giggs, who changed his name the week after his Deepdale visit, could now be playing for Preston North End FC. This player is just another to be added to my very long list of players, I have missed.

A list of boys who made first team places with PNE and/or other league and non-league clubs.

1985-1991 PNE Soccer Academy
Walter Joyce (Youth Officer)and Fred O'Donoghue (Youth Liaison Scout) (PNE Staff)

		Reported Fee
1. Lee Ashcroft	PNE YTS-West Brom Albion	£ 250,000
2. Nathan Peel	PNE YTS-Sheffield United/Burnley	£ 75,000
3. Martin James	PNE YTS-Stockport County	£ 70,000
4. Chris Holland	PNE YTS-Newcastle United	£ 150,000+
5. David Flitcroft	PNE YTS-Chester City	Sell on Clause
6. Adrian Hughes	PNE YTS-Retired with injured knee	-
7. David Eaves	PNE YTS-Morecambe/Bamber Bridge	Free
8. Matt Lambert	PNE YTS-Bury/Morecambe	Free
9. Steven Anderton	PNE YTS-Morecambe	Free
10. Jason Kerfoot	PNE YTS-Bamber Bridge	Free
11. Steve Finney	PNE YTS-Swindon FC	Free
12. David Christie	PNE YTS-Halifax/Hyde United	Free
13. Craig Moylon	PNE YTS-Now at University	Released
14. Andy Gill	PNE YTS-Chorley	Free
15. Chris Hollis	PNE YTS-	Free
16. Jamie Close	PNE YTS-Netherfield	Free
17. Adam Critchley	PNE YTS-Chorley	Free
18. Simon Burton	PNE YTS-PNE Pro	Free
19. Gary McCullough	PNE YTS-Retired with badly broken leg	Free
20. Lee Cartwright	PNE YTS-PNE Pro	-
21. Craig Allardyce	PNE YTS-Blackpool FC	Free
22. Jamie Squires	Under 18 England Trials 1st team pro	
23. Kevin Kilbane	Under 18 England Trials, PNE Reserve games Irish International U/21 Call up trials	
24. John Calligan	PNE Reserves, Eire Republic Trialist u/16Free	
25.Stewart Parkison	YTS PNE now at Lancaster	

Lee Ashcroft played for England Under 21's

Chris Holland played for England Under 18's - Now at Newcastle £150,000

There are also 4 Y.T's in the pipeline for PNE
1.   Paul McKenna - Pro with PNE
2.   Kyle Hayton
3.   Simon Stewart
4.   D Lucas - England u/21 trialist. Pro with PNE
(Jim Price, Rochdale YTS) and (Danny Woods Bury FC)

Quite a list for the Walter Joyce and Fred O'Donoghue PNE's Soccer Academy efforts 1985-1991.

Note:

I reckoned over half a million pounds was gained by PNE with the sale of the players brought to the club, with more to come.

Final Deepdale Days

And so I came to my final days at Deepdale.

To deviate slightly from the main events - previously Derek Allan had left the club in somewhat strange circumstances, very strange circumstances. Derek was a tremendous worker, or to be more accurate, a workaholic. We would be out on the pitch with the boys, on coaching sessions, as late at 9.00 pm, and Derek would be working away in the office

Now, ten games into the 91/92 season, the Manager, Les Chapman, was under great pressure, after struggling the previous season to avoid relegation. Things were coming to a head, as we all sat together in the referee's room at Deepdale - Les, Sam Allardyce, Walter Joyce and myself. But it always comes as a blow when the inevitable happens.

The first ten results in 1991 were not impressive and nearly all the Director's cars were lined up on the nearby parking lot.

The phone rang. Les was wanted in the Board Room. He went upstairs and he was promptly informed that he was sacked.

Sometimes an ex-Manager has to employ a solicitor to get his contract paid up, and, from the ensuing wrangle, lawyers can make a fortune in fees. In smaller clubs it can be particularly difficult for a manger to get hold of his settlement cheque.

But, in sacking Les Chapman, the club actually paid him up as well. In fact he got his pay cheque the same day.

So, he came back downstairs and sat down, totally devastated. Then they sent for Walter Joyce.

Walter had previous managerial experience, and years of coaching behind him. As he left the room he had a wry little smile on his face and I'm sure he felt in all the world that he was going to get the top job. But I didn't think he would. I had the feeling that there was somebody else in the background.

Walter came back. He said that he'd got a job here for life, and the Board wanted him to go back to looking after Youth Development. I could see that he was deflated, from the look on his fact, at not getting the job of manager, or even caretaker-manager.

Next to go upstairs was Sam Allardyce. Now this I did fancy. Sam's a smashing chap and I used to enjoy working with him on the Youth programme. We would go out together, each taking a group of YTS lads. We would go down to Factory Lane in Penwortham, or to different schools, or on to the training ground at Fulwood Barracks. Sam is a smashing coach and it was a joy to work with him. He didn't mess about with the lads. He was a disciplinarian and made it very clear what he wanted, and what he thought.

Sam came back into the room and told us that he'd been appointed Caretaker-manager.

It was very sad to witness Les shaking hands with Sam and saying, "All the best, Sam. I wish you every success and I really hope that you get the job."

Then he shook hands with Walter Joyce, whom he had known for many years, both of them being Oldham boys. He turned to me, saying, "Thanks for everything you've done Fred. Carry on. Do your best for the lads." I said I would do, with a tear in my eye because I really admired and liked Les Chapman. Maybe he's not a director's manager, but he was certainly one of the lads.

But the decision meant that Les was walking out of my life.

After a few minutes I said to Sam, "Well, what's my position now?"

"Just go back to what you're doing. Do what you do best," he replied and that was it. All change, once again, and Sam was in charge for the time being.

However, it seemed clear that there was something going on in the background. There were three characters driving the events along, and each one had a very strong personal agenda. I may have been just a scout, but I saw a lot of things and had my own opinion. They had a perspective which I couldn't sympathise with.

Mr. Woodhouse, for his part, gave the impression that there was very little he didn't know about; motor cars; exhaust pipes; oil; football; talking to managers; using his contacts etc. He gave an air of supreme self-confidence in his own intellect.

Then there was Paul Agnew, an ex-reporter with the Lancashire Evening News. He was a smart man who stayed close to the Chairman. He'd written a very good book about Tom Finney, involving a lot of detailed research. I used to like Paul and I admired his forthright style, but he wasn't really my cup of tea.

Finally there was Derek Shaw, a very wealthy man with a large house, a swimming pool and four or five cars. You couldn't avoid the impression that being on the Board was just a social thing for him.

I may be wrong but I think between the three of them they had already decided that John Beck was the man.

Paul Agnew had a piece in the Evening Post about John Beck. "His track

record is second to none," it informed us. The Board were going for the top man in the field and made it clear they would leave no stone unturned until they appointed a manager with a proven track record.

Sam knew that he was just the manager for the time being. But it was a sorry sight to see how the Board strung him along, with comments like: "We're not quite sure about the managership yet," or "We'll have to have another meeting."

After six weeks I said to him, "Sam, you've no chance. You're not going to get this job. It's going to go to Beck."

Out on a scouting mission I'd bumped into a scout who worked for Cambridge, Glen Bonnell. He told me that John Beck was going to be offered the job. He'd applied for it, but for the moment he was in Tenerife with his girlfriend.

It turned out to be prophetic. I went in one Monday morning and saw Mr. Woodhouse's car outside with two other cars I'd not seen before. I think they were H registered Fords. Clearly something was taking place.

Stepping across the threshold I immediately ran into Mr. Woodhouse with my usual breezy, "Top of the morning to you."

"Is Sam knocking about?" I asked.

It wasn't a question designed to amuse him. He gave me a sour look.

"Oh! Do you not know?" he asked.

"Know what?"

"We have a new manager. Mr. Beck is the manager now." His glasses lit up as he said it.

"Oh, now what about that", I said as I walked past him into my little office under the stand.

So, John Beck arrived on the scene. He was very good at making his feelings clear. He didn't speak to me at all and he hardly spoke to Walter. Obviously we were in the way already. After my years in football I could both see it and sense it.

I felt at that time very low as John Beck came in and the relegation disaster followed soon after. You can't prove a negative, as they say, but it was my view that if Sam Allardyce had been appointed the club would have stayed up, and I am not alone in this opinion.

My resignation letter was already written out. I had already done this two or three weeks after John Beck had taken over. Walter knew about this and said, "Don't hand it in yet, Fred."

I said, "I'm going to hand it in a soon as I get a sense that it's got to be handed in." You have to have a belief, a faith in a certain method of playing this game. I certainly wasn't going to stick around too long with his new grouping and their philosophy.

Then the management, with one member in particular, introduced certain methods of treatment towards the younger players that they wanted to be rid of. It wasn't a style which I could go along with. It didn't exactly match the principles of the P.F.A. either. I saw a lot of unhappy people who could see no future for themselves at the club.

It was not a happy time. It hurts you when you have spent years trying to persuade youngsters to throw their lot in with the club. Now they are coming to you with desperate stories and desperate expressions on their faces.

My advice was, especially to the younger players, always the same: "Stick it out. The club comes first. Carry on and play your best for Preston North End."

One night after coaching at Deepdale, Walter and I, called in at the Yew Tree pub Walton-le-Dale on the way home. We were just enjoying a pint of Boddy's, when who should come walking in but John Beck with his attractive girlfriend. He couldn't avoid us, so he came over with a cold smile and joined us.

I think that was the only time he ever spoke to me socially with Walter. He did his best to be sociable but he didn't find it easy. It was one of those conversations where people talk but nobody hears what's being said. The words just float away into the air like tobacco smoke.

To give him credit, he passionately believed in his style of football and his style of management. I couldn't share his faith in either, but it's a free country. But one question kept popping up in my mind. Something I found very irregular. How is it that a manager can get the sack after being such a resounding success at Cambridge United?

Plenty of food for thought then.

John Beck's style of play did not suit my fellow coaches at PNE either. Steve Grand resigned, - possibly the best u/14 coach I've known, for the quality and range of his techniques, skills and maturity. He was a balanced man with great dignity.

Darryl Woods, another coach, also resigned. He was really effective and great with the lads. He was a good experienced local player himself, but John Beck ignored him.

Then Peter Warburton, Director the School of Excellence, went his own way. What a sad day for my beloved PNE to lose the services of the real top man of coaching in the Preston area.

Final Day - The Last Two Hours

I went in to work that particular morning and I can still see it now. The receptionist, Audrey, came running out.

"Mr Beck wants you Fred. Fred, Fred, Mr Beck wants you right away."

It would be about ten past ten when I arrived. I was late. I thought this is it. I went into my little office to take my coat off. Peters came in.

"The boss wants you upstairs right away," he snapped, in an aggressive manner.

"Hang about a bit. I'll be up there, " I replied, with all the calmness I could muster.

So I got my resignation out, made my way upstairs to Box 6, and knocked on the door. Stepping inside I saw Paul Agnew and John Beck waiting to pounce on me. I was well prepared for it. Before they could open their mouths I said, "Don't say a word. Everything's in here." And with that I slapped down the envelope on to the desk really hard.

I'll never forget the look on their faces. Agnew's eyes and open mouth. Beck's big pop-eyes staring in amazement. Not a word was said. They didn't get the chance. I turned round, walked out of the box, went downstairs, and threw all my gear into a black bin-liner.

Walter came in, all flushed. He started, "I've had a word with the Chairman...."

I could see that he was shocked. "I'm not having a word with the Chairman," I said. But I'll give Woody Woodhouse a call." Or words to that effect.

I felt on top of the world, having spiked their guns - Woody, Beck and Agnew. I picked up the phone.

"Mr Woodhouse It's Fred O'Donoghue speaking."

"What can I do for you?" he asked, in his curt manner.

I said, "I've just resigned from the club."

"You what? You've just resigned from the club?" he echoed. "How have you done that?"

"By letter," I said.

"Letter, letters, which letter?" he asked.

"I got the typist here to type it for me." Actually that was not strictly correct. Jim (PNE) Dean had updated the first draft, and it was his copy that I'd handed in.

Mr Woodhouse said, "You've no right to do that."

I said, "What are you talking about Mr. Woodhouse? Listen, I'm giving you a courtesy call here. Do you understand me? A courtesy call to say I've resigned."

Knowing that I had been lined up for the sack, it gave me great satisfaction to depart with my pride intact. I felt on top of the world, really.

Naturally, I had to forgo any thoughts of redundancy money similar to the settlement negotiated by Walter Joyce through the PFA. On the other hand I felt on top of the world, having spiked the guns of the authority, coupled with relief that an unhappy chapter had been concluded with a clean break.

To keep the record absolutely fair and in proportion, it has to be said that club directors, and Chairmen in particular, are in an impossible situation. Preston North End's directors were no exception. Mr. Woodhouse, with his financial clout, his business and other connections, certainly kept the PNE club alive. His money, I'm sure, paid the wage bill on occasions.

The same is true of Chairman Leeming. He actually confided in me at Croix, on the French trip, that his finance had intervened to keep the club afloat more than once, and that I can certainly believe.

At the same time, they have to stand such a lot of aggro. The Chairman took some dreadful abuse from so-called supporters. "Leeming out," was the chant outside the front entrance after one match. And again at one particular match at Chester I witnessed some terrible scenes with louts wanting to have a go at Keith Leeming. He certainly didn't deserve to be the focus of such ugly scenes and such an outburst of misguided passions.

But, as Shanks put it, football's more than a life or death affair.

So that was the end of my time at Deepdale - a mixture of happy times and bad times. When there was no money it was a question of scrounging paint off Johnston's Paint firm in North Road to decorate the dressing rooms, the washing and drying rooms. It was often a struggle for Sam, Walter and myself to do the decorating that close season, and other jobs besides.

Then there was the tragedy of Harry Hubbick dying on the job - a loyal and uncomplaining servant - an ex-pro who was getting about £35-£40 per week, I was told.

The Youth Director at Preston North End was Ted Griffiths. And after I had left the club, he kept in constant touch with me about his worries for his beloved Deepdale. If ever a man loved the club, it was Ted - a veritable giant of PNE. I felt desperately sad at the thought of losing a good friend, confidante and mentor. It was with great sadness that I learnt of Ted's death about nine months after my resignation. Both he and his good lady were stalwarts of youth.

Let us still hope that my boyhood dreams of PNE winning league and cup come true under the stewardship of whomsoever. I'M STILL A NORTH ENDER. It's still the first result I look for at 5.00 pm every Saturday.

So it was that Walter and I left Deepdale at around 11.30 am on that fateful morning and made our way to the 'King Bill' - its real name being the William the Fourth pub on London Road. We had a drink together and talked about the past and the future.

Life goes on, and thankfully both Walter and I were soon to be once again fully engaged in the sport we love - football.

I was soon home, to tell my wife, Cathy, what had happened. She said how happy she was, and thank heavens it was all over. She didn't like what was going on any more than I did.

The phone soon started ringing - Manchester United, Bolton, Liverpool, Steve Heighway, Les Kershaw. What did the future hold for FOD? Would my final stopping place be Blackpool?

Oh! One final note. The following Monday I got a cheque from North End for £15.00. Did I receive a letter of thanks from the Board? You've guessed it. No, I'm still waiting.

Walter Joyce sacked, FOD resigned

The Beck Style of Play Sent to Me by Mistake, a PNE Postal Error
Preston North Eend Football Club Limited

Our ref: GB/VA

Dear Scout

On behalf of John Beck and myself, may I thank you for the tremendous work you do for Preston North End. Without the support you give us, the coaching staff would spend many wasted hours pounding up and down motorways at the expense of their coaching and managers roles.

Because of our style of play, when looking at players please bear in mind we require the following:-

Fullbacks

Must be quick and 'brave' and competent in the air. They must be able to strike a long pass of good accuracy (Channel ball).

Centrebacks

Must be quick and 'brave', good in the air and able to strike a long pass of good accuracy.

Centre Midfield

Must be quick and 'brave' and able to play first time balls over opponents defence (Chipped Channel ball)

Wide Midfield

Must be quick and 'brave' and a good crosser of the ball. If possible two footed and likes to cross the ball early.

Striker

Must be 'brave', quick and preferably big. They must be mobile and don't mind running wide to cross for other team mates to score.

Glen Bonnell

Chief Scout

Mr John Beck
Manager
Preston North End F.C.
Deepdale
PRESTON

Dear Mr Beck

I wish to tender my resignation with Preston North End Football Club. I have been here for over 6 years working non-stop sometimes as much as 60 hours a week. I regret to say , Mr Beck, that you have not spoken to me about any ideas I may have concerning the youth Policy at Deepdale. I feel that any information you have received about me appears to have reached you second hand from various sources.

Having spent a lifetime in football I cannot understand the lack of teamwork and collaboration within the senior staff at Deepdale.

The clubs Youth Policy in which I have been greatly involved had operated successfully with quite a number of boys graduating to the First Team.

Another sore point concerns my wages, which have not increased with the cost of living for well over two years.

It would appear that both the club and yourself obviously require my services no longer.

Yours
Fred O'Donoghue

Copies: Chairman
            Vice-Chairman
            Chief Executive
            Lancashire Evening Post (Sports Desk)

Note:

I did not date the above resignation as I did not know the time or place when I would hand this in. No reply to this letter was sent to me, from any of the recipients listed.

Newcastle United

Chris Holland
(PNE) Lilleshall, Birmingham City.

I am writing a few words about Fred O'Donoghue because this is one way of thanking him for guiding me on the right road to hopefully a career in professional football. When a Chief Scout of Fred's experience says that you have potential to make the grade, you have got to believe him and set out to prove him right.

Fred signed me on schoolboy forms at Preston North End, one of the best youth policies in the country, where Fred's guidance and training helped me to be recommended for the School of Excellence at Lilleshall, where I spent two years improving my techniques in football.

When I returned, Fred was still in charge and things were still being run in the same vein so I slotted in as though I had never been away. Sadly Fred left and I and a lot of other people were sorry to see him leave. Preston's loss was Blackpool's gain, and I am in no doubt that Blackpool or any other club will benefit greatly by Fred's knowledge and expertise. Carry on the good work Fred.

Chris Holland

30 January 1994

Keegan snaps up PNE boy wonder

NEWCASTLE boss Kevin Keegan looked set to sign North End starlet Chris Holland for £200,000 today.

The England Under-18 international travelled to St James Park to talk terms after Keegan stepped in following rumours that new Everton manager Mike Walker was interested in the teenager.

PNE boss John Beck said: "We have tried everything in our power to get him to stay."

■ Kevin Keegan — £200,000 swoop

PNE Squad Plate Winners Northern Ireland 1992
Back Row L/R: S. Grand (Coach), D. Woods, R. Howarth, A. Howarth, K. Hayton,
F. O'Donoghue (Manager), J. Callighan, A. Lea, D. Lucas, T. Almond, D. Woods (Coach).
Front row L/R: G. Roberts, B. Andrews, P. McKenna, I. Stanley, D. Webb, P. Dean,
J. Price, S. Stewart.

Chapter Eight

(In Three Parts)

Part One
A Parents "must" (your child) and drugs with a code of sporting ethics

Part Two
A soccer scouts bible (Sam's Song) introduced by Sam Allardyce
Ex Blackpool FC Manager
with letters form Micky Burns PFA Nobby Stiles
and funny one to Ken Barnes at Man City FC

Part Three
Centre of Excellence Regulations by kind permission of the
Football Association with help from Alex Gibson FA

Big Sam with Cathy O'Donoghue the better half of the FOD

Part One

To all Parents
Drugs and Solvents - You and your child

If you don't talk to your child about drugs, someone else will.

Help Prevent Your Children Using Drugs

Most children don't get involved with drugs and solvents. But in today's world it's inevitable that your children will come into contact with them at some time.

Young people nowadays find out about drugs earlier than you think - from the media or from friends or older children. But it's much better if they learn the facts from you than from their classmates behind the bike sheds or from watching TV.

Simply by talking to your children, you can influence whether they decide to give drugs and solvents a try - and you can help them to stop if you do find out they are already experimenting.

Many of the reasons for trying drugs and solvents might seem ridiculous to us. However, they might seem very real to our children.

When you're young tomorrow doesn't exist - you live for today. You can help your children to see that drugs and solvents can be dangerous for their health and well-being in the future.

The following free publications are available from the Department of Health:

Drugs: A Parent's Guide and Solvents: A Parent's Guide

give the facts about drugs and solvents.

Drug and Solvent Misuse: a Basic Briefing

provides further important information for parents and professionals.

Drugs and Solvents: a Young Person's Guide

is suitable for children aged between eight and twelve.

Drugs and Solvents: Things you should know

is for young people aged between thirteen and eighteen.

It is my belief that the above publications should be nationally issued to all parents in Great Britain immediately. Let the lottery money pay for it.

To Administrators, Managers, Coaches and Parents of soccer mad schoolboys:

1. Treat children as children and not as mini adults.
2. Avoid placing expectations on a child unrelated to the child's ability or capacity to meet them.
3. Insist on players accepting referees, umpires or other match officials decisions without question.
4. Raise the awareness and place the emphasis on fair play.
5. Provide opportunities for the development of skills.
6. Ensure that all those taking part in competitive play know the rules.

Players:

1. Know the rules.
2. Accept the decisions of the referee, umpire or other match officials without question.
3. Respect your opponent.
4. Win with style, not "at all cost."

Spectators and Parents:

1. Support the referee, umpire or other match officials.
2. Remember; encouragement is a greater incentive than criticism.
3. Encourage the boys (Don't be a loud mouthed vault lawyer like some parents I know).

Everyone:

Above all ensure that enjoyment is an integral and important element in playing, training and watching sport.

Enjoy Sport
These points are fully endorsed by FOD Youth Soccer Liaison Officer at Blackpool Football Club

Scouts and Parents Section

"Fred, how can you tell a good player?" - This was the question put to me by the Referees Association at Blackburn in 1973/4 at the Cob Wall Working Men's Club. This is a question I have been asked many times, but to which there is no quick snap answer, although I find it a most intriguing question. Many scouts would answer that such skills as aggression, pace or first touch etc. are key factors, but rarely will they take the trouble to give a more complete definition.

In an attempt to give a more detailed analysis of the qualities of a top class football player, as we all know, the human being consists of both mind and body, so for the purposes of the following I will refer to the body as A and the mind as B.

First let us examine A, the body:

1.   Pace/Speed - much needed in today's game.
2.   Strength - of trunk, arms, legs and neck.
3.   Balance - required when turning and twisting.
4.   Touch - a must when receiving the ball.
5.   Technique - all of the ball skills, and there are many.
6.   Suppleness - this is something I have always allied to athleticism.

*Note: there are a total of six body factors.

Second, we will examine B, the mind:

1.	Enthusiasm	1a.	Commitment
2.	Temperament	2a.	Awareness
3.	Vision	3a.	Speed of thought
4.	Aggression	4a.	Confidence
5.	Composure	5a.	Mentally tough
6.	Game intelligence	6a.	Creative abilities.

*Note: there are a total of twelve mind factors.

As you can see, there are more factors concerning the mind than the body, I am not saying these deliberations are in a precise order but my answer to the original question would be that many factors of the body and mind determine the brilliance or qualities of an excellent player.

Good coaches are aware of these qualities and can often develop a shortfall of the required abilities that may be lacking in a good player, both in mind and in body. Has your child got the ingredients above? Not many have all of them.

Players with skills, Blackburn Rovers
Rovers on the menu. Modern players spend much of their time on promotional work. Simon Garner, Noel Brotherston, Derek Fazackerley and Ian Miller at the opening of a new restaurant

Paul McKenna signs Schoolboy forms for PNE, at home in Eccleston.

Part Two

Soccer Scouting Bible

Introduction to the book by Sam Allardyce

also

The P.F.A. letter of invite from M Burns, Chief Executive

Other Contributions by
Harold Super Scout Holburt

Various photographs by kind permission of The People/Morecambe Visitor/Lancashire Evening Post/and The Press Association, Fleet Street, London

Sam's Song

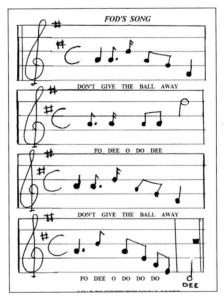

I had to write the vocal score for music lovers who may happen to read my book

The FOD

(1986 - 1993)

I first met Fred at PNE when he was appointed chief scout of the Youth Policy at the club. He came with a very good reputation from the previous clubs he had worked for. Fred started working very closely with Walter Joyce the Youth Development Officer, on building a Youth Policy. I was a player at the time, but very interested in coaching, and learning how the other side of the club was run behind the scenes. My first impression of Fred was of a man in a smart suit with a big handkerchief sticking out of the top pocket of his jacket. I thought "what a flash bugger he is", but as I got to know him I realised that was a bit of a front.

Fred and Walter created a Youth Policy that became too big for the club. In the words of the then Manager, John McGrath, "You have built a monster!" By the end of its first season the club had schoolboy teams ranging from the Under 14's to Under 16's and also ran a school of excellence for the Under 11's to under 14's. This was all done under very, very limited finance. By the end of the second season they had developed, along with Tom Hasty and his committee, the Preston Junior Football Federation, which had teams for Under 11's to Under 16's as well as the school of excellence. The committee raised the funds to help this monster run as smoothly as possible.

There were so many talented schoolboys coming through that the club couldn't take on as YT's as many boys as they would like to, due to the lack of coaching staff and financial restrictions. Fred and Walter were doing a great job.

Occasionally, Fred would get involved in something which didn't really have anything to do with his job and on one occasion Barney Campbell, a Director at the club involved him in one of his schemes, a senior citizen's club. Barney was one of those Directors whom John McGrath didn't get on with and as soon as he found out that Fred was involved, "the madman" (which was John McGrath's nickname), was on the warpath. We had just finished training when we heard him shouting for Fred up and down the corridor. Fred went into the referee's room and all the lads were saying "This will be funny", as the "mad man" was famous for his bollockings. We didn't have to get too near the referee's door because the noise could be heard nearly all over the club from 1.30 pm until 3.00 pm. Poor old Fred came out punch drunk, his face all red, huffing and puffing, saying "I've had a heart attack, I'm supposed to take it easy, I can't take these bollockings!"

I left PNE in 1989, having helped the club through the worst period in its history. In 1985-86 the club had to apply for re-election. I joined the club at the start of 1986-87. I could see that Fred had a good relationship with the schoolboys, also their parents and the coaches he had working for the club under John McGrath. We finished runners-up in Division Four and in the 1987-88 season we came tenth in Division Three.

By this time the young players were starting to come through, like Alan Kelly and Nigel Jemson. By the end of the 1988-89 season in which we missed out on promotion in the play-offs to Division Two, more youngsters were coming through. Alan Kelly, Nigel Jemson, Adrian Hughes, Lee Ashcroft, Martin James and Nathan Peel were all in the squad.

I left for West Brom, as coach and kept in touch as my son Craig was to sign YT at the club. They carried on producing youngsters right up to July 1992, when I came back as Youth Team Coach. Walter moved upstairs as assistant manager and I began to work closely with Fred, who's nickname was FOD.

I found out what it was going to be like to work at a club with restricted finances, as Walter and Fred and I ripped out the old drying room that had not been painted for some ten years or more. There was dust, spiders, cockroaches, dead rats and all sorts. We installed new cupboards and even managed to scrounge the paint free. We all thought we would get credit for this - we didn't, but we had some fun.

FOD that summer had taken the Under 14's to Northern Ireland, and his team had won the Shield in that competition against teams like Manchester United, Glasgow Rangers, etc. FOD did not even get a "well done" when he came back, and he was deeply upset.

However, Walter managed to talk him out of handing in his resignation, because we knew he would regret it later if he left.

Fred was liked by everyone. Before every game he would get them to sing his then famous song which went like this:-

> Don't give the ball away, fo de oh do dee
> Don't give the ball away, fo de oh do dee
> Fo de oh do, fo de oh do, fo dee oh dee oh do dee
> So remember, don't give the ball away....."

Fred was a good singer and the boys would have a laugh, but they knew what he meant.

FOD is a great character who has dedicated his life to schoolboy football and more importantly, he loves it. He gets a bit forgetful now and again, but there is no substitute for experience. I learned a lot from FOD on the schoolboy side, and I still ring him on a regular basis.

Nobby Stiles

I told Nobby about the book I was writing and he kindly sent me this following contribution.

Xmas 92

I would like to congratulate Fred O'Donoghue on the great job he has done in bringing through young players in every club with which he has been associated.

It takes a great deal of patience and understanding and Fred certainly has that. More personally we shared the same hotel, (well both teams did - Preston and Manchester United), in Port Stewart in Northern Ireland Milk Cup of July 1992. We both had taken a team of 14 year olds to compete in the competition. Harry Gregg our ex-keeper at Manchester United was the owner of the hotel so I can tell you that the three of us had many a funny chat. One thing I remember we had been beaten by Stella Maris, (a team from Dublin), in the qualifying rounds and Preston were due to play them in the Plate Final. Fred with all his experience asked me who the danger man was for Stella. (He was doing his best for his kids). I duly told him and Fred did the rest. Preston went on to win after extra-time and penalties. It's a pleasure knowing you Fred.

Keep enjoying it

Nobby Stiles

Nobby and the FOD,
Hotel Windsor, Port Stewart, N Ireland.
Photo taken by Harry Gregg, ex Man United goalkeeper.

The Footballers' Further Education and Vocational Training Society LTD

Ref: MEB/NJW/1

2 June 1992

Mr F O'Donoghue
7 Conway Avenue
Penwortham
PRESTON
PR1 9JR

Dear Fred

Further to our telephone conversation with regard to the above and your kind agreement to speak to the prospective Football League Managers on the course.

The talk title is "Scouting and Youth Policies" and I would be obliged if you would cover the whole system of schoolboy scouting, coaching and the associate schoolboy systems. As we agreed on the telephone I will pick you up at The Pleasant Retreat Hotel at 5.40 pm on Tuesday 9 June 1992.

I enclose a map of the venue for information together with an expense form which should be completed and handed to me on the 9th. I also enclose a cheque for £50 which is our standard fee for visiting lecturers. I look forward to seeing you on the 9th.

Regards

M E Burns
Chief Executive

Scouting

Instructions for "would be" Scouts and all soccer enthusiasts

An established part of football folklore suggests that a scout, to discover a star, should go to the top area for talent - the North East of England - shout down the nearest mine shaft and up would come a future England international. The abundance of top class footballers that have come from this area over the years has helped to encourage such sporting legends.

In a similar vein - albeit a different sport - Welsh folk singer and self-confessed Rugby Union fanatic, Max Boyce, wrote a ballad about a fictious factory in the mountains turning out outside halves for Wales!

All these stories add colour and character to our sporting traditions but, of course, the truth of the matter is far removed. Scouting for future soccer stars is a long, hard, painstaking business, only to be undertaken by the totally dedicated. It's a fallacy that young players who break through into the first team after progressing through a club's junior sides have "cost nothing".

A great deal of money is invested in scouting schemes, to say nothing of the time and effort put in by the scouts themselves. Often they do the job for expenses only, their only reward being the satisfaction of helping a young footballer make it to the top - the senior team of an English Premier, First or Second Division club.

There is more to scouting than meets the eye. Every soccer fan whether he watches Jimmy Hill and Co, with action replays to boot from the comfort of an armchair, or prefers his football live without frills from the stark reality of the terraces, thinks he can spot talent. Don't we all think we can pick a better team than the next man?

In reality, however, it is a specialised business that has its own particular qualifications, including patience, an eye for detail, determination and a fairly comprehensive knowledge of the game.

There is nothing haphazard about scouting for a Football League club. It's a cut-throat business; a competitive affair where, as the saying goes, "You get nowt for being second", especially if you are second to the door knocker and somebody else has beaten you to it. The aim of this part of the book is to fill in some of the gaps about this anonymous breed who rarely get the headlines yet contribute as much if not more than any other group to the well-being of our national game.

Hopefully, it will give anyone wishing to enter the world of scouting an introduction to the job. For those who are already scouts, it may help to make them better ones. For all others, and all soccer nuts, it will hopefully provide an entertaining insight to the subject.

Who to look at

From time to time, a non-league, unknown player will come along to confound all the theories but, generally speaking, the soccer scout's main attention will be focused on schoolboys in the 10-14 age groups. The story of Tony Book, Ex- Bath City player, who then became manager of the First Division giants Manchester City, really belonged in the pages of comic fiction rather than football fact. As a bricklayer and part-time footballer with Bath, he was virtually a veteran in sporting terms before he even entered League football, yet he went on to lead City to a string of honours as skipper before moving "upstairs" to boardroom battles with City Directors.

The Tony Book types are few and far between. Indeed, his story could well be unique. But the lesson should be well learned. Late developers in a soccer sense have been a source of heartache and regret among the legions of soccer scouts throughout the years. Similar problems are sometimes thrown up by the early developer. A big, well-built boy of 11 or 12, with a fair degree of football skills, shows up very quickly in schoolboy soccer. This can be misleading because the other boys are still developing. In many instances, they catch and often pass the early developer. Outstanding 12 year olds must be noted, but even if an early approach is made to the parents, the only form that can be signed involving a boy of that age is a Centres of Excellence form.

I think the first group of boys I would seriously watch would be 11 year olds. These are the youngsters under scrutiny for local teams and this is the group that often needs very special attention, especially with their local Sunday teams.

It is probably true to say that the general trend in recent years has been for clubs to look at boys at increasingly tender ages. Abroad, this is particularly true. The major club's often "sponsor" a string of junior teams, ranging upwards in ages from primary school boys. In this way, a youngster can be brought up in the traditions of a club and a careful eye kept on his progress. League clubs Centre of Excellence are an example of this.

Johann Cruyff, one of the greatest footballers the world has ever seen, came to the attention of Ajax Amsterdam when still really only a child but, then again, the Flying Dutchman was one in a million. My wife Cathy would have picked him out.

Whether a boy's potential or footballing future can be assessed at the age of seven, eight or even nine, before his character or personality has had time to develop, is a matter of opinion.

My own view is that the tendency to look for boys at earlier and earlier ages is not a good thing. There is an awful lot of wastage in football at the moment, boys being cast off when they reach 16 to 18, having failed to make the grade. However, club scouts' live in fear of missing a future star or, worse still, losing him to a rival club, has made the competition for the top schoolboys intense to say the least, and this is especially so in the case of the age groups I have mentioned (11-12), as these are usually the most productive ages for League club's Centre of Excellence Forms.

As these age groups come under the microscope so much more than the others, so much greater is the need for special attention, to detect the tell-tale signs that may reveal a potential star. Sifting through the hoards of youngsters who fancy themselves as the next Bryan Robson, Trevor Sinclair, Gazza, Ryan Giggs, Cantonas of this world, is the prime function of the soccer scout.

The semi-pro leagues have all produced a fair crop of recruits for the Football League. Paul Mariner, who went from non-league Chorley to a full England cap is a perfect example. Steve Galliers, Chorley and Alan Taylor, Morecambe and lots of others.

Club scouts are often sent to assess players who are, in fact, already established as League players. A manager will use his scouts to weigh up players he might be considering making a bid for, or players whom he hopes will become available - perhaps on a free transfer at the end of the season - at a later date.

At other times, he might be used to assess the performances of other teams (future opponents). Later we can look in more detail at the way a scout goes about these other particular tasks but, for the moment, we concentrate on his major role of finding future stars - the schoolboys with potential.

Where to look - The area of search

The golden rule for every soccer scout should be to know his home territory. It is of little use spreading his search far and wide until he is absolutely sure that he has exhausted all the possibilities in his own area and is sure that he knows it thoroughly. If course, some areas can prove barren and perhaps devoid of the right sort of boys or schools. It would be unusual for there to be no talent at all, but one of soccer's quirks is the fact that some areas, such as the North East, London, South Wales and Merseyside prove prolific providers of talent whilst in others, the South Coast for example, footballers are thin on the ground. By the same token, some clubs have earned a reputation for producing not only stars, but specialists. Burnley used to have a production line of young talent that was the envy of most Football League clubs, while little Chesterfield had a penchant for unearthing - and later selling at huge profit - great goalkeepers. Gordon Banks, perhaps the greatest of them all, is the top example. Then there has been Jim Brown of Sheffield United and Scotland, Alan Stevenson, formerly of Burnley, etc.

If by chance, the scout does find himself in a "desert" as far as talent is concerned then, by all means, he should move on. But check and check again in your own area. Setting up your scouting operation needs a methodical approach once you have settled on your area. But I repeat, your own area is best.

A good first step is to buy a town guide or area map, the kind which can be obtained from most large newsagents. Having acquired it, pencil in all the schools that teach soccer to boys over the age of 10 and are engaged in local schoolboy competitions. Also map out the playing fields, school grounds, etc.

Hold on a minute - which schools play football you might ask? In fact, how do you find out the schools in my area? Surprisingly, the answer is easy. Simply write to the local education department asking for a list of local schools and - most important - include a large, stamped, self-addressed envelope. The local authorities are usually most helpful and will normally forward a complete list of schools in their area.

As an example, I can quote Preston, which I have covered myself. The Preston authority (District 6 under Lancashire County Council) forwarded a concise yet complete register not only of schools, but also including names of head teachers, phone numbers etc.... a real goldmine of information to the scout.

A few enquiries, phone calls and a little bit of "local" knowledge left me with a list of what I reckoned were the most active soccer schools in the Preston district. Principally, they provided the bulk of the Preston representative sides that competed in the county and national competitions. In other words, the town teams and the district sides i.e South Ribble, Pendle, etc., have usually the cream of the local schoolboy talent.

When watching games, incidentally, it is always a good idea to introduce yourself to the teachers who run these school representative teams. Like a good newspaperman, a scout can't have too many "contacts".

After some painstaking detective work your list should be narrowed down to about a dozen schools, plenty to concentrate on for the moment. It will take perhaps a similar number of Saturday mornings to work through the 12 year olds, a few more for checking or covering someone's tips, also occasional schools outside the list. Then you can think of widening the net.

To ensure blanket coverage and a reasonably tightly-knit area of search, please don't go and start looking somewhere 25/40 miles away. Remember basics - know your own patch. Around Preston, for example, there is an abundance of competitive schoolboy soccer within a very small radius. Either side of Preston lie Blackpool and Blackburn. There is no end to the amount of Saturday morning watching between early September and the end of the schoolboy soccer season, not forgetting the massive explosion of Sunday games. So, the best way to set about spreading your search is, again I repeat - Begin at the local education department and take it from there. Then, secondly, contact the local Sunday League officials (under 11's to under 14's).

Apart from the local authority, however, there are many other valuable sources of information for the would-be scout in his chosen area. Almost always, the local newspaper can be relied upon to give reports of inter-town games and most major schoolboy fixtures. They also carry comprehensive reports on local youth and junior leagues. Read the results and league notes with relish. This is meat and drink to the scout, his all-important homework. Reading a newspaper, you get to know what is going on. Having contacts in the area gives you valuable knowledge.

Apart from these studies a scout must build up a library of reference books. Most counties promote their own competitions and most county associations publish their own handbooks which could otherwise be title, "A Scout's Saturday Morning Bible". The Lancashire SFA is probably as well organised as any and their handbook, published by enthusiastic volunteer teachers, contains dates, competitions, names, telephone numbers and just about everything a scout needs to help him cover schoolboy soccer in that area. This also applies to Sunday Leagues.

Not all professionals, of course, start off in the local schoolboy town team. They can be overlooked. It has happened with many, many boys in the past and will no doubt continue to happen in the future. Some youngsters prefer to turn out with their friends in their own teams rather than play for their school eleven and, in a good year at a particular school, a promising youngster might not even be in his own school's side for one reason or another. He might not be rated, either rightly or wrongly, very highly by a teacher in charge and, if not, he will not be playing in the school or town squad.

This is one of the principal reasons why it is vital to keep in touch with the various junior leagues as well as individual school teams and not only the representative teams.

Often a scout may be tipped off about a young player in one of the more senior leagues. There are simply thousands of amateur clubs and hundreds of semi-professional teams apart from the giants in the Football League.

It is necessary to make a breakdown of your own area. In my own part of the country, the Lancashire FA Handbook is a must for the names and addresses of teams, secretaries, leagues etc. Other major leagues which cover the area are the Northern Premier, the Cheshire League and the HFS- all semi-professionals. Then there is the West Lancashire League, the North Lancashire League and so on through the various town leagues like the Preston and District League, the Central Lancashire League, The Chorley Alliance etc. All produce handbooks or fixture sheets which can provide valuable information.

In other parts of the country similar operations can be carried out. Split up the area, working down through semi-pro leagues senior amateur leagues, junior leagues and youth leagues. It has been known for scouts to visit Centre of Excellence centres and pick up a good lad under the eyes of club officials concerned.

Basically, however, watching schoolboy soccer is just about the most important starting point for the novice scout. Most League clubs have realised this fact and competition for the talented boys to sign schoolboy forms is very, very intense. The work must be carried out thoroughly by the scout for there is fierce rivalry, and a cut-throat attitude certainly exists. Although there is a sort of camaraderie between scouts, don't be fooled by it and make sure you get to that door knock first.

What are we looking for?

Skills, talent, raw, natural ability - that's what we are looking for. Good, basic, early skills that can be nurtured and developed until they are second nature. You might only be given a brief glimpse of a player's talent during a game and thus the need to be constantly on the alert for the flash of real ability, perhaps even a touch of genius. Watch more than once - that's vital. A good player should always be recognisable but whether he is good enough to make the grade is another matter. The scout must assess his strengths AND weaknesses, so that he knows exactly what to look for and can spot the general skills which help to judge a player. Attitude and character is another ball game. Aggression, pace, most vital. Remember what I have written previously in an earlier chapter, 6 body factors and 12 mind factors are what you are looking for as a scout.

Apart from goalkeepers, we do not really need to go into detail about the different positions. Remember, we are looking particularly at very young players who probably still have to find their best position in many cases. Here, we put the basic skills under the microscope and they can be divided up into the following categories:- ball control, first touch, dribbling, passing, shooting, heading, tackling. Look at positional play and also pace, which speaks for itself. That is so needed in today's game. Today's pros are fitter and faster than ever before. Football Association made a start by recently asking all 92 League clubs to forward the names and positions of their best young under 18 players for a get together at Lilleshall close scrutiny, which can't be a bad thing for English Football. I hope the scouts and coaches can recognise their skills and abilities. There are so many donkeys knocking about.

The Approach

The first approach concerning any schoolboy player should almost always be made to the secretary or teacher in charge of the team. If the game is on your own patch, you might well know him. If not, introduce yourself and explain your purpose. It is possible that the teacher himself will be on the payroll of another club, perhaps a bigger one, and might not be too keen on divulging the boy's name and address. If this does happen, no need to worry, there are other ways. Parents watching the lads usually help you, also in many other ways as well.

Alternatively, write to the headmaster concerned, even ring up the school. Always explain precisely why you want the information. It would be very rare indeed if all of these avenues were blocked.

As a last resort, you could always try asking the boy himself if you could have his address to speak to his parents but, in that case, you might be backing a loser. If you explain to the boy why you want his address he's liable to run home full of notions about turning out for a famous football club in whatever division within weeks of being spotted by a scout. His parents - many of whom are not too keen on the prospects offered by League football as a profession - are not likely to thank you for that, so you've made a bad start. On the other hand if you ask a youngster for his address without proper reason, all you are likely to get in reply is a rude answer, and quite rightly too.

My advice is do not approach the lads. I don't think it is fair. I have never approached a schoolboy and I don't think it is the thing to do, especially with other boys looking on. I have come across scouts who, when all else failed, have hung around after the game and followed their "target" back to his house in true cloak and dagger fashion. Again, not advisable.

The initial approach then is to the teacher or secretary, followed by the parents. When the interview comes along, be prepared for anything. Explain as fully as you can the limited, yes LIMITED, opportunities of a youngster making the top in professional football, as well, of course, as putting over the benefits and advantages you believe he will enjoy by signing for your club. Above all, be honest with the boy's parents. This is why it is important to know what your club is doing for its young players and to believe that they will get every chance not only to further their football career, but also their education for life after football.

Usually, the practice is to invite the boy down to the ground for training and coaching, and importantly, joining the club's Centre of Excellence.

Reactions can vary enormously. The boy and his parents could be overwhelmed with delight simply at being offered a chance by any professional club. Then again, they might have had banking or insurance in mind for him. Or, the boy himself might be Manchester United mad and nothing else will do. TV glamourises the big clubs.

I cannot stress enough, however, the importance of pointing out the hazards of professional football and the very small number that actually make the grade. The average is reckoned to be three out of one hundred and it could be less than that.

Television has given professional football a very glamourous image that, at some time or another must attract the thoughts of most young boys, who wouldn't want to be Ryan Giggs, Gazza, Shearer, etc. But, whilst it can be a rewarding and profitable career, there are pitfalls. Most clubs take their responsibilities seriously and spell out the dangers. My own club, Blackpool, has a specifically prepared leaflet to hand out to parents and promising youngsters, taken from the PFA advice to schoolboys. Thanks are due to Gordon Taylor, Chief Executive, for some sensible and first class advice. I like to think of these as my useful commandments, directed not only at all schoolboys but also intending or even established scouts. Many of them, I am sure, have not read what the PFA has to say about young hopefuls in the game - the trickiest of businesses.

Top shelf advice from them all - The FA, The PFA
Schools FA, Football League and yours truly

The failure rate in football is very high. The majority of Associated schoolboys are not offered YT places and only a minority of YT's make a career in the game, so you can see why it is important to do as well as you can at school and to prepare for an alternative career whilst you are a young player.

In any event, professional football is a very short career, averaging less than ten years, and only a tiny minority stay in the game as managers, trainers, etc., so that it is vital for players to continue to prepare for a second career throughout their time as a player. I know so many ex players who try to sell insurance as a result of failing to take advice.

Scouts - Parents - Boys
Relationships

It is vitally important for the scout to strike up a good relationship with the boy's parents. He is possibly the first club representative that they meet and, as such, first appearances and impressions count for much. There must be mutual trust and therefore the need to be completely open and honest.

Once a boy has signed for you on schoolboy forms then you should also call round from time to time. Give the parents a report on his progress, liaise with the club's coaching staff, and also remind them occasionally of the large failure rate even after boys have signed as YT players; hence the need for a second string to his bow.

A boy's background can also tell you something about his character. Often, the boy from a big family who has had to battle to assert himself and fight for everything he has had, can have a distinct edge over, for example, an only child for whom life has probably been much easier; "though not always". All clubs like an aggressive, will-to-win type of lad. Even in these days of Social Security and the Welfare State, it is often said the "hungry" fighter nearly always proves the best. As I have said before, the will-to-win is a must. This will to win comes in all kinds of lads - white, black, rich and poor. It is something that is born and bred into them with no compass or boundaries.

Advice to Schoolboys, Parents and Scouts

1. It is a fact that scouts from clubs observe many school and youth matches and it is very rare for a boy with a lot of talent to be overlooked. In other words, if you are good enough there should be no need for you to approach a club, they will contact you, your teacher, your parents or your headmaster or club secretary.

2. However, you can write to a club asking for a trial or asking for someone to come and see you play. You should give details of forthcoming fixtures in which you are involved and it is as well to have a recommendation from your games master, or someone in a position of that nature.

3. If you are outstanding, you may be offered a chance to join a Centre of Excellence, the "Associated Schoolboy", signing for the club on your 14th birthday, in which case, you attend the ground for coaching and training sessions and the club has an option on your services when you leave school. However, you can only play for the club in that season if you have reached your 15th birthday by 1st September and then only by written permission of your Head Teacher.

4. When you reach school leaving age, you may be offered YTS terms. This is a much more permanent position involving full-time employment. YT positions normally last until your 18th birthday.

However, it is important to bear in mind that you can become a full-time professional at 17.

5.   If you sign as a YT player your contract will allow you to continue your further education or take up suitable vocational training. At present, this normally means that you will be able to attend a college on a part-time basis, for example, on a day release course. It is obviously in your interest to continue your education. If you sign as a professional, you can still arrange to be allowed to continue your education.

Good advice to Boys (and Parents or Guardians)
(This I Fully Endorse)

Before Signing
Have a meeting between yourself, your parents or guardians, your headteacher and the Club.

Look at the coaching and training facilities.

Experience the methods used by the club.

Look at the way other members of the club are reacting i.e. Is it a good atmosphere?

Think very carefully before signing for a club outside your area - accommodation problems.

If two or more clubs invite you to sign for them;

There may be greater or earlier opportunities available by signing for the "smaller" club.

There may be wider experience to be gained by joining a "bigger" club.

Facts you need to know
Who is responsible for the coaching of your group?

What are their qualifications?

Who is responsible for your welfare at the club?

What are his qualifications and experience?

How many schoolboys have signed for the club?

How many trainees are employed by the club?

How many boys from the club progress to the First Team or have done well with another club?

If the club is not near your home, what provision will be made for your football development?

If you leave home to join the club, what provision will be made for your welfare?

Is there a report system at the club to keep you and your parents informed of progress?

Remember that personnel at a club can change. You are signing for the club, not an individual.

If you do not make the grade what will the club do?

After Signing

Show a proper commitment to your club.

Do not forget your loyalty to your school and schools' Association.

Prepare for when you finish playing or in case you do not reach the required standard.

Do not forget your school studies.

Complete your external examinations.

Keep your club informed about your other activities.

Tell your club in February if you are likely to leave school later that year.

If you are offered a Trainee place or a contract

Give a reasonably prompt reply.

Ask what further training outside soccer you will receive.

Do not leave full-time education without a very good cause.

If you have an opportunity to take your studies further at school or college, investigate extending your link as an Associated Schoolboy.

Consider the loyalty you owe to the club, taking into consideration the training and commitment they have given you.

Consider the benefits you will gain from continued involvement with the club you know. Professional football can be very rewarding but it can also be heartbreaking.

The career is a short one, therefore look to the longer term future and try to obtain some security.

Look ahead to the close of your Traineeship or Contract.

You may be offered a further Contract.

You may be released. Are you prepared for that?

These pointers attempt to guide you when you have to make a big decision about signing for a professional Football League Club. Whatever the outcome of your footballing career, the English Schools' Association and the Football League hope that you are able to enjoy your involvement with the game.

**This is good advice to all boys and parents on joining a
Football League Club**

Ken Barnes

Ken Barnes, of Manchester City, the ex-chief scout of the well-known League club once said to me that if he could pay £5,000 a piece for three or four of the England schoolboys squad each year, it could save his club a vast fortune buying the established, ready-made, schoolboy stars. I believe him but, fortunately, both the Football League and the Football Association have drawn up strict rules to hopefully prevent anything like that happening and boys are freely able to choose which clubs suit them best - not just those that can pay the most money, but with due all respects, it happens. 'Cash in hand' is difficult to resist. Some parents are poor.

To contravene the rules, in any way at all, is to invite serious trouble. Financial fines are very severe. It goes on, we all in football know it - but try and prove it. That's a different ball game.

Preston North End FC LTD

Our ref: FOD/JLW

1 May 1992

Mr K Barnes
Chief Scout
Manchester City Football Club
Maine Road
Moss Side
Manchester
M14 7WN

Dear Ken

May I wish every good wish and success on your Testimonial game that also includes good weather, I hope it is a glorious sunny day. It doesn't seem that long ago, when I played in your City team at Rossendale at Outside Right in a charity game, when all I could hear in the first half was "CAR YA" "CAR YA" at half time I said to Roy Gratrix all I can hear is someone shouting "CAR YA" "CAR YA" and you was sat next to me in the dressing room, said "I it's me, I'm saying where the Fxxx are you and everybody laughed, including you.

Over the years you always seemed to get the best young players, but I'll miss you on the circuit. Best of luck Ken.

My very best regards.

Fred O'Donoghue
Ex Rovers - Now Blackpool FC

Scouts joining a club

If you are now thinking of taking up soccer scouting in a bid to get rich quick - forget it. The financial reward received for the time and effort put into the job is barely adequate. It might sound corny, but most scouts do the job because they love the game.

Certainly, some clubs are very generous in their rewards to the men who scour the local playing fields weekend after weekend in the never-ending hunt for that one boy who can go to the very top. As far back as 1969-70, in pre-inflation and pre-decimal days, one top First Division club was ready and eager to pay bonuses to scouts such as £50 for a schoolboy who went on to sign apprentice forms, plus another £50 when he signed as a full professional. After ten League games, another £100 would be forthcoming and there were further payments should your discovery reach international status. Since then, rewards have obviously increased, but not all clubs are so generous, far from it.

Still, the first step is to be accepted by a League club. Most Premier, First and Second Division clubs as well as some in the lower divisions of the Football League, are constantly on the look-out for good scouts; the bread and butter men who are regular spectators at the under 11's, 12's and all junior games. If you wish to join their ranks, it's quite a routine procedure, but you must prove your worth.

Get out and about and look for one or two good young players on Saturday mornings. Get the feel of things, speak to the teachers (remember their names, you'll meet again) and after you have found your way around and perhaps noted a couple of promising youngsters it's time to put pen to paper. I would suggest a letter something like this to the club manager.

Dear Sir

I have been watching schoolboy football for some time and am familiar with Anytown District and its schools.

I know quite a number of the teachers in charge of school teams and have also noted one or two boys from Anytown GS and Someplace Comprehensive. Would you kindly consider my application to become an assistant scout with your club.

(then give details of any playing career you may have.)

Although I am specialising in schoolboys for a start, I eventually hope to become a first class scout. I hope that you can give me a trial as I am keen and willing to work.

(then enclose the names of the lads you have watched and the details of their games.)

Yours faithfully

It might sound rather humble but the very fact you are prepared and are already watching schoolboys with one or two good boys under your surveillance should induce a favourable reply. It is possible that many clubs might not be interested and might prefer to dig out their own men but as the former chief scout of Blackburn Rovers and Rochdale, I would certainly write back to you and invite you for a chat about the boys you have seen. Finding men prepared to go out every Saturday and Sunday morning is no easy task, especially on the cold, wet and often windy mornings of mid-winter. A few men, unfortunately, are only in the game for the status of being a scout, along with tea and biscuits in the boardroom.

Assuming you are taken on by a club, the chief scout will very likely explain the main do's and don'ts. Make your own way to games, unless instructed otherwise, and give simple, straightforward reports on the boys you watch.

The point to remember above all is that any boy you recommend then becomes the yardstick of your standards and, believe me, it must be very, very high. It is quite a responsibility to say to a club "I have found you a good schoolboy player". Remember that they have heard it all before so only recommend a boy who has the ability to back your judgement.

Although there are incentives for scouts, such as those mentioned at the beginning of the chapter, most payments are much less handsome. Some clubs these days pay their scouts a small weekly wage of just a few pounds (which is taxable), plus travelling expense which can vary from as little as ten pence a mile to as much as thirty-two pence. Some scouts, of course, have full time posts and the salaries can vary enormously. It's a rat-race really. The majority, however, pay expenses only, with twenty five pence a mile being the average rate. Postage, phone calls, etc. are covered and, with a full Saturday and mid-week work, the busy scout could probably knock out £30, £40 or even £60 a month. this might sound a lot, but with the cost of running a car and other incidentals, not to mention the huge amount of time that is involved, no-one can tell me that scouts do the job for money. Unfortunately, scouts still have a very low standing in many clubs, despite the fact that if they are successful they can provide a much needed lifeline.

Especially with the smaller outfits, job satisfaction comes first. I had some great times at Rochdale and my most satisfying moment came as chief scout when Alan Taylor was signed from Morecambe and later went on to become an FA Cup Final hero (see Chapter and Verse).

At the other end of the scale, Arsenal, in my experience, have always given their scouts the best of treatment. For example, my wife and I were guests of the club at the FA Cup final against Leeds, including two nights' accommodation in a top class hotel.

Apart from any financial rewards, which must be regarded as a bonus, the chief benefits are the friendships that can be made. Working with such men as Jack Marshall, ex-Blackburn Rovers physiotherapist and former well-known manager, is a real pleasure. Honest, sincere, always smiling, "Jolly Jack" as he was known - and this is so true.

Naturally, it is not all plain sailing. Whereas most clubs are prepared to reward - lavishly in some cases - their scouts if they are successful, there is the other side of the coin. Soccer, after all, is big business and if the scouts are not doing their job then the employer, rightly, wants to know why not.

When I was working at Arsenal, I along with all the other representatives, received a typical chief scout's reprimand. It followed a Christmas holiday training and coaching period for 12 - 15 year olds that we had recommended to the club. Here are a couple of extracts from that chief dragon in charge of the scouting team, Gordon Clarke, Arsenal's Chief Scout

"To You!!"   From: Gordon Clarke, Arsenal Chief Scout

This year "The standard of the boys sent along was very poor indeed, the poorest boys we have had since I came to the club. If this is your judgement of boys for us I am afraid you are well below the standard of scouts I want here. Time and time again I have stressed only the best (underlined) is good enough for us here. I am sure some of you do not look hard enough, often enough or deep enough and if you got out of the street where you live you would get lost."

"I am afraid a few of you, unless there is a vast improvement in your 'scouting', your services will not be required here."

(signed) Gordon Clarke, Chief Scout 1971-72 Season.

Later that year, May 1972, I received the following invite to the Arsenal v Leeds Cup Final.

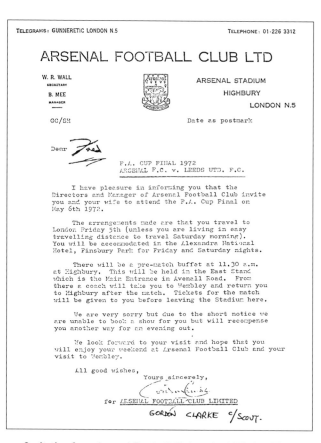

Invitation from Arsenal Football Club to the 1972 Cup Final

Assessments

Generally, there are three types of assignment that a scout is given by his club. He is usually sent to report on a schoolboy, a senior player (League or non-League) or to complete an assessment on a particular team.

The basic job is checking on potential schoolboy stars and the main principles to remember are to be brief and to the point. If you like the boy, check him again, make sure he is the best player in his team, then don't hesitate to contact his teacher, secretary and parents and get him to the club you represent as quickly as possible for trials. If you don't someone else will.

Most clubs provide standard printed forms for your reports, asking for basic details such as date and place of match, teams, name and position or player, height, general build and a space for special remarks. In your report give the score and a brief summary about the boy, taking guidance from the earlier chapter on what to look for.

Reporting a senior player is very similar but there are certain things to remember. Make sure he is playing in his normal position and, although it might sound rather obvious, that you are watching the right player. I have known scouts watch the wrong man because of a bad telephone line or a slip of the tongue by a chief scout who will always blame his scout for the mistake.

Get it right from the start and get there early. Keep your eyes and ears open and your mouth shut. It's surprising what you can learn about the staff and players of the club you are visiting. It is more than likely, however, that the man you are watching has already been under surveillance several times by your club, so remember when making your report to write about what you see and not what someone else tells you.

Be critical of his faults, moderate your praise and, above all, be honest. There are a lot of good racehorses but very few thoroughbreds and the same applies to football. Also note the player's "pedigree" if a pro, his previous clubs, which can be obtained from Rothman's Football Year Book, another invaluable guide for the scout. All top scouts have it.

Standard printed forms are usually provided for these reports but, in some cases, clubs might ask for a more detailed appraisal of a player.

As for match reports, assessing future opposition for your club is an increasingly important task in the modern day game. Few professional teams, if indeed any at all, take the field without a fair prior knowledge of how their opponents are likely to play (i.e. what formation they will adopt, and their strengths and weaknesses.) Thankfully, a game of football will never be decided in a dossier. It is still what happens on the day that counts, but today's pro generally believe in being prepared. (see Harold Holburt's report - a top scout in the game). (In this chapter)

Here are some typical reports

First a schoolboy player

From: F O'Donoghue

Saturday morning schoolboy report - High School v low School, Saturday February 1st.

Result 4 - 0

Player: A.N. Other; Position: Goalkeeper; Club: High School; Age: 14 Height 5'9"
Weight: 10 stone;

General build: good; Special remarks: a tall boy for his age, must watch him again in a tougher game as he has no crosses or high balls to handle.

Report: The boy, A.N. Other, did what he had to do with skill. He has a good kick to the halfway line, threw when it was on. I must watch him again for other aspects of his game. Nothing else of interest on view.

A brief report on a senior player would follow the same pattern but I was once asked to assess Blackpool striker Micky Walsh for a First Division outfit. Once you are established, these requests are not uncommon but always get clearance from your own club first. They wanted a detailed report on a player who had been linked with many top clubs.

This was my report:

Micky Walsh, Blackpool

On the whole, this player had a very good game and without any further ado, I like him. He combined well with his team mates and was responsible for many of the openings created by Blackpool.

Things I noted particularly were:-

a.   He had good, all round skills, especially heading ability. Work rate excellent. Good pace.

b.   Good positional play and good vision.

c.   Good "talker". Aggressive.

d.   Gave 100% for his side.

Walsh laid the ball off well with his head and also impressed me when heading for goal. I liked the lad's distribution and he is also capable of taking players on. Several times he took on and beat the cover man and hit the target area with his shot. I got the impression, and I am not on my own, that he is a dangerous, effective front-runner with a liking for scoring goals.

He also did well running off the ball to get into channel spaces. His running was simple and natural, he is an economical player but very effective. He also has the sign of a good player in that he is often in the right place at the right time to receive a ball. He gave the impression when he got the ball that something was about to happen and illustrated this with a first half run that brought the first goal.

Picking up a pass, he beat a man on the run and hit the ball first time. Although the shot was partially saved he managed to score at the second attempt - very dangerous player on this good showing.

Blackpool rely very heavily on him and no doubt he would be even better with better players around him. As the main Blackpool striker he looked good and is obviously worth a good deal of money. But I feel he is fit for higher company.

As for senior match assessments, it is important to note squad formations, obvious planned moves, throw-ins and all set-pieces such as free kicks and corners. Simple sketches showing particular moves, how the centre backs cover or in which areas the front men operate are useful, and if your memory is very good, the build up to the goals scored, both for and against. I sometimes use a voice recorder on occasions.

A typical match report would give the date, time, venue and weather conditions for the game, the line-up of the team in which you are interested (in formation) and whether there were any changes to this line-up during the game, such as when the substitute was used and also the opposition formation. Especially the way the defences play, this is most important to the manager.

That can be followed by a brief resumé of each player's personal contribution and how he fits into the overall pattern, noting strengths and weaknesses.

Set pieces come next. List corners and free kicks and any rehearsed moves from either of these positions. Every team has its own moves - note them very carefully, they are most important to your manager or coach.

Give a general summary, mentioning any special features such as, "Watch for midfield players coming in behind the front men and arriving late in the box,midfield men don't like to be rushed, need plenty of time and back four played fairly square."

All these details help in the final summary to a team before they go out to meet their opponents.

Crewe v Rochdale   Saturday 6 November 1993

Teams

Crewe		Rochdale
SMITH	1	HODGE
BOOTY	2	MATTHEWS
GARDINER	3	OLIVER
EVANS	4	BOWDON
ABEL	5	REEVES
SMITH	6	BUTLER
COLLINS	7	STUART
NAYLOR	8	DOYLE
JONES	9	LANCASTER
WHALLEY	10	WHITEHALL
ROWBOTHAM	11	WILLIAMS
WILSON	12	HOWARD
EDWARDS	14	MULRAIN

Team Report: - Rochdale

Rochdale were weakened by illness and injuries affecting both full backs Thackeray and Graham as well as Reid. They had Williams on loan from Stockport playing up front in a 4-4-2 formation, lining up like this:-

```
                    1
                  HODGE
    2         6            5          3
 MATTHEWS  BUTLER       REEVES     OLIVER
    7         4            8          10
 STUART    BOWDON        DOYLE    WHITEHALL
              9            11
          LANCASTER     WILLIAMS
```

They are definitely a side that plays football and although they looked a bit unbalanced in the first half, they persisted in building through midfield, getting men wide, and using the two big lads up front dangerously around the box. With Whitehall wide left midfield, the balance of the side seemed a bit wrong and this is the flank down which Crewe caused most problems. Both Doyle and Bowdon lack pace, and Crewe were able to threaten by running from deep, exposing the lack of pace in midfield, and getting into space between midfield and the back four. They scored a great goal exploiting this area, with a strong run from deep followed by a cracking long shot as the back four funnelled back towards the 18 yard box.

Rochdale settled down as the game went on, and got their act together. Across the back the two centre backs looked solid. Reeves is very mobile and covers ground quickly to get his challenges in and snuff out attacks, whilst Butler alongside him is improving all the time and looks strong and competitive.

Behind these, keeper Hodge talks and organises well and is alert to start attacks with throws to the full backs when it is on. Matthews at right back did o.k. He got forward well and varied his delivery - wide to Stuart in front of him or through midfield and bringing the big lad Williams on the blind side with some decent far post balls. Oliver at left back did better when Whitehall moved up front to replace the injured Lancaster in the second half and the side had a much better balanced look about it with Howard wide right in midfield. Stuart moving over to the left and Whitehall playing off the big Williams up front.

In midfield Doyle and Bowdon were very good on the ball and started most of the attacking build ups. They can both use the ball intelligently and bring other players into the game in all areas, either wide or through the middle. They have experience, they can get their foot on the ball and they are both very constructive.

They have Stuart in a wide position and in this game due to the re-shuffle mentioned earlier, he had a half on the right and one of the left. He likes the ball to his feet, comes deepish to pick it up and can go at defenders either inside on his left foot or to the line.

Up front the two big lads, playing together for the first time, were not getting close enough to each other in the first half, but both of them looked capable of playing as a target man. Williams also looked good when taking up far post positions on the blind side of defenders, and coming in with strong headers around the box.

They are a good all round side who knock it around well and they have the ability to play from the back. They also have big useful lads up front to hit from deep as a variation.

They defended against free kicks with everyone back, and against corners with just Whitehall upfield.

THEY ARE GOOD AT TAKING QUICK FREE KICKS AND CATCHING THE

OPPOSITION UNAWARES. THEY ATTACK IN NUMBERS DOWN BOTH FLANKS AND THEY HAVE BIG USEFUL LADS FOR HEADERS IN THE BOX. THEY ALSO HAVE WHITEHALL WHO IS GOOD AT TURNING PEOPLE AND HE HAS TO BE KEPT TIGHT NEAR GOAL.

I'm sure you know the individuals well enough without me going through them all, but I think you have to stifle them in midfield to stop them playing. If you sit off them and give them room they can play.

This report is typical of scouts doing match assessments and is followed by simple diagrams showing all set pieces taken during the game i.e. corners, free kicks, throw ins, penalties and the positions of players in each situation.

Well done, Harold

Payroll (Teachers on the make)

One type of scout of which I am afraid I do not really approve is the schoolteacher who is on the payroll of a League club. It's usually one of the bigger ones as they are the only ones who can afford this type of operation. The gain for teachers is money, the boy's interests become secondary.

The reason I am against teachers being employed by clubs is simple enough. A teacher is in a privileged and special position of influence as far as a youngster's future is concerned and if he is paid on a part-time basis by a particular club then, obviously, he is going to be biased (cash-wise) towards that club if a potential footballer comes along. I do not believe there is anything wrong in a teacher contacting his local club about a talented youngster or, in fact, helping a boy to find the right sort of club but, in my opinion, he should not use his privileged position for monetary gain. Some unfortunately do.

It goes almost without saying that some clubs treat their boys better than others, providing more homely accommodation and better further education opportunities. When a boy's future and welfare is at stake surely it would be better for the teacher who, after all, is probably second only in influence to the parents, to be strictly neutral. In that way he could be an invaluable counsellor when it comes to perhaps choosing between half a dozen League clubs.

All that glistens is certainly not gold in professional football and many boys have regretted signing on the dotted line with undue haste when they should have delved deeper into the facilities and opportunity offered. I know of many boys who have left the game after joining a faraway club and finding life was far removed from what they expected, sitting night after night watching TV.

The digs provided in some cases are poor to say the least and any chief scout worth his salt should check his own club's offerings. Ample time off for study is also a must these days.

(By Kind Permission) of the Football League a Copy of
THE FOOTBALL ASSOCIATION LTD REGULATIONS
FA CENTRES FOOTBALL

1.   Matches to be played between
- FA Premier League Clubs
- Football League Clubs
- Football Association Centres of Excellence
- Schools Associations

No more than twenty five matches in a season to be played on Sunday during term time and at any time during school holiday periods.

2.   Players must be registered in the respective age groups within the Registration Scheme under The Football Association Programme for Excellence or be trialists under the regulations set out in the FA Regulations.

3.   Clubs must not include boys who are registered with another club's Centre of Excellence. Clubs wishing to include "trialists" may only do so by giving 7 days' notice of approach to the registered youth team with which the trialist plays as per Football Association Rule. This will require clubs to "clear" the trialist seven days in advance. Breaches of this regulation to be dealt with through the normal procedures.

4.   Directors of Centres of Excellence are allowed and encouraged to develop games in the 9-12 age groups under these criteria. These games should meet the ruling of The Football Association regarding small-sided games.
       It is expected that in the 13-16 age groups games will be 11v11.

5.   Members of staff responsible for the work at Centres of Excellence should in the main be those who are conducting Centres Football with

the players. It is expected that those conducting F.A. Centres Football on behalf of both professional clubs and Centres of Excellence will be qualified either as Full Licence or Preliminary Award holders.

6. Matches.

    (a)   to be organised as coached games. It is recommended to play in three periods of twenty five minutes.

    (b)   the host club to be responsible for appointing qualified match officials.

    (c)   a qualified First Aider to be in attendance.

    (d)   to have unlimited substitutions.

    (e)   to allow players to return to the pitch after having been substituted.

    (f)   to have footballs and pitches of appropriate size.

    (g)   to have no results published.

    (h)   to be played on a "friendly basis" i.e. no competitions.

7. Information to be kept by each club through a scheme to be introduced by The Football Association

    - details of each match played

    - date

    - venue

    - names of all participating players - indicating those who are Associated Schoolboys.

    - such details shall be retained and be available to The Football Association for inspection at any time.

    Directors of Centres of Excellence will be required to report to The Football Association the details of matches in which individual players took part. A Scheme for reporting this information will be introduced.

8. It will be permissible for Centres of Excellence to play against each other:

    - under 9/10/11/12   (small-sided games)

    - under 13/14/15/16   (11v11 games)

All games to be conducted under the criteria as outlined above and

within the Rules and Regulations for the Programme for Excellence.
In the development of small-sided games the following details are
included as guidance as to the appropriate number of players, pitch
dimensions, substitutions and duration.

Age	No. of Players	Size of Ball	Size of Pitch	No. of Subs	Duration
9	6 v 6	4	40yd x 30yd	continuous	2 x 25
10	6 v 6	4	40yd x 30yd	continuous	2 x 25
11	8 v 8	4	60yd x 40yd	5	2 x 25
12	9 v 9	4	80yd x 60yd	5	2 x 30
13	11 v 11	4	full	4	2 x 30
14	11 v 11	5	full	4	2 x 35
15	11 v 11	5	full	5(2)+	2 x 35
16	11 v 11	5	full	5(2)+	2 x 40

9. Players registered through The Football Association Programme for
    Excellence will be registered with The Football Association and
    individual directors of Centres of Excellence will be expected to control
    he amount of matches played by an individual player throughout the
    Season, particularly with the release of a licensed player to Category
    "C" football. The Centre of Excellence director is responsible for this
    release and monitoring the number of games played by the released
    players.

10. Fixtures for F.A. Centres Football will be designed by Regional Co-
    ordinators and will include certain details which will be left free to
    allow members of staff to attend in-service training and meetings
    concerned with Centre of Excellence developments.

11.   Players must only play one match in one day. Clubs may include no more than two players from one junior team and no more than four in total on a trial basis in each match. The normal trial period shall be regarded as four matches after which players should either become signed to the club or released.

It will be in order for players to be combined in consecutive age groups to play against teams of a similar nature.

A fixture list will be compiled by the Regional Co-ordinator and forwarded to all Regional Committees, The Football Association Premier League, The Football League and The English Schools' Football Association.

Any matches subsequently re-arranged should be similarly notified.

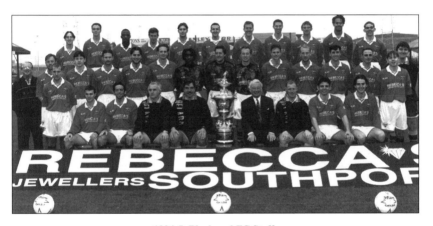

1994-5, Blackpool FC Staff.
Billy Bingham, Sam Allardyce, Neil Bailey, Bob Saxton and the FOD.
This side just missed promotion, Sam being sacked.

FOD and Terry Venables, Barcelona Manager, 1986.
Spanish Press Photograph Hotel Foyer. F.O.D. and Terry Venables, Barcelona Manager 198(
Hotel Catalina, Los Palmas. F.O.D. on Holiday. Terry in charge of his team playing the Los
Palmas Squad. They won 3—1. A good game. 2 free tickets for the F.O.D.

Chapter Nine

Liverpool Football Club

"Where do all our Football Youngsters come from?"

Well, they are spotted at a very early age by that quiet unsung band of scouts that scour schoolboy football, looking for that gem that will one day thrill millions of people with his particular brand of soccer magic.

Fred O'Donoghue is one of that unsung band of dedicated and committed scouts who can be seen most weekdays and always at weekends patrolling school playing fields and parks casting their eagle sporting eye over the crop of youngsters who are parading their soccer skills.

Without the likes of Fred, professional football would be the worse off and most certainly wouldn't be the most popular sport in the world. Without someone spotting those youngsters of the future, we wouldn't have here those superstars.

It's a pleasure knowing you Fred, keep up the good work and remember another George Best is just around the corner and playing on the next football field.

Best wishes,

Brian Hall
Community Officer, Liverpool Football Club
28th February 1994

Alan Taylor

The FA Cup Hero I helped to "Discover"

Remember Alan Taylor? How could anyone ever forget him after the way the blonde West Ham bomber virtually won the FA Cup single-handed for the East London side, sinking gallant but outclassed Fulham with two opportunist goals in the 1975 Wembley final.

Well, many tales have been told as to how Alan took the first steps on the road to the top, but I have always classed him as one of MY discoveries...despite stories to the contrary. The first I heard and saw of Alan Taylor was when he was playing for a Preston North End junior team as an apprentice. He reminded me of a newly-born colt - pacey, wiry, leggy and lean. At the time he impressed me as being very quick and I made a note of him for the future.

Alan Taylor, celebrating West Ham's 1975 FA Cup win

I was working at Rochdale, as Chief Scout, the following season and when one of the teams came up against the North End juniors Taylor was missing. A quick enquiry established he had been released and was playing somewhere in Morecambe.

After phoning round contacts in the area, it was Sean Gallagher (ex-manager of Northern Premier League side Lancaster City) who told me that Taylor was playing in the Morecambe reserve side and pushing for a senior place. I watched him for a few games, liked what I saw and was glad when he made the Morecambe first team.

I distinctly remember taking in a couple of Sunday matches standing with Sean and analysing Taylor's game. He was just what Rochdale needed, a flying winger. He could catch pigeons in his flights down the wing.

In due course I sent my reports in to the then Rochdale boss, Dick Connor. He dispatched Dennis Butler, ex-pro at Port Vale, Bolton etc., and Angus McLean, Secretary, to have a look and it was eventually agreed with Mr. "Benevolence" himself - Rochdale Chairman, Fred Ratcliffe - to enter negotiations.

Taylor's ability was further confirmed by men of standing in the local non-league game. Stan Howard (assistant coach of Chorley) stood with me at Victory Park watching Alan and asked, "What the hell are you waiting for?" - not knowing that I had already set the wheels in motion.

Jimmy Birkett, the ex-manager of Cheshire League side Darwen and a friend for many years, backed my judgement with a glowing report from a game against Bradford PA when Alan scored three goals.

Alan eventually joined Rochdale, was subsequently transferred to West Ham and the rest of his story belongs to football folklore.

The one note of discord as far as I was concerned was sounded in the post-final press coverage, when Alan Taylor's meteoric rise to fame, not surprisingly, stole all the headlines. It's unfortunate, but a fact of life, that the man behind the scenes, such as the scout, rarely gets the credit he might deserve.

It seemed that, according to the press, various people from all levels of soccer life had been responsible for finding Alan Taylor in the first place - depending on which newspaper you took. Many, I have no doubt, would have liked to claim the credit for spotting him but, for my own part, the Lancashire Evening Post writer, John Morrell's version got to the heart of the matter. Nice one, John

Here are some appreciative letters from very personal friends

Father of Jim Willis - Ex-Leicester City FC Various Clubs

Dear Freddie,

Just a few lines as promised. We first met back in 1982 when you were representing Blackburn Rovers Football Club. With you was Big Jim. We were in the living room of my home at the time when you offered my son James, schoolboy forms, but we could not find a pen for him to sign.

You pulled a parker pen out of your top pocket, and my son used your pen to sign his name.

I happened to say, "What a lovely pen it is. We'll do well to keep hold of this. It's worth a few bob". By this time the pen had ended up in Jim Furnell's hand and afterwards in my wife Christine's hand who was admiring it.

By this time the conversation was more about Freddie O'Donoghue's pen than the signing of James. I then took the pen off my wife and said, "Enough of this pen business. It's doing my head in." Freddie stood up and laughed and said, "Keep the bloody pen". At that moment in time my other son Paul, who later turned a Professional Footballer came running down the stairs with a boxful of pens.

I suppose at the end of the day the pen had the last laugh, because fifteen minutes later after Freddie and Jim left my home, famous Everton Scout, Les McGray, appeared on my doorstep. It was quite obvious what he was after, the signature of my son James. I told him, "Les you could have signed him, only that a certain pen was at fault, you know our family are Everton daft."

However unknown to yourself Freddie, this magic pen did the business once again, you see Les McGray did not leave empty handed. He signed my other son Paul. Yet again this pen has proved to be a lucky pen even twelve years later when Tranmere Rovers signed my third son Scott. Yes, you've guessed it, we used your pen.

Seve Grand (Coach) - PNE & Blackpool

When friends asked me to write about Fred I thought, should I write about how honest and fair he is to the boys and parents he brings to the club? Should I write about how he has helped me in my match and player analysis reporting? Should I write about how wherever we go he always seems to know everybody? No, I'll write about the night in Northern Ireland when he got completely rat-legged (Drunk).

We were there with Preston North End Under 16's and Under 14's teams for the Northern Ireland Milk Cup. The night of finals day, all the clubs staff were invited to the Tournament H.Q. at the Eglington Hotel in Port Rush. The night evolved into a drinking dual between Scottish and Irish Clubs and Fred seemed to be drinking for both sides. Fred having acquired a taste for Bushmills was well lubricated and holding centre stage of a conversation between myself, Walter Joyce, and anyone else who was nearby. The room was long and narrow and we were positioned at the far end when suddenly as Fred threw his head back in a guffaw, he started to stagger backwards. I don't know whether it was his low centre of gravity or his natural balance but he went the full length of the room, sending unsuspecting drinker's sprawling as he picked up speed, sprinting backwards towards a window in the gable wall. We will never know if it was luck, or whether his legs just gave out but he disappeared backwards into a large armchair and was asleep before his back touched the leather. The next hour was spent trying to carry him back to his hotel, leaving his draped body over and leaning against various objects during rest periods.

During the next morning when everybody was getting ready for the trip home, Fred was sat in the front of the bus with his head in his hands. It was then the local armed constabulary came up the road in their usual, Northern Ireland staggered formation, and I stopped the lead man and asked if it was possible for them to arrest the ill-looking man asleep in the front seat. He did say he had more important things to do, but couldn't resist when he saw what a state his victim was in. The sobering effect of three sub machine guns placed against your temple is astounding. They told Fred that he answered the description of someone seen acting very suspiciously the previous night. Knowing what he had done since about 8.30 that evening he coughed and spluttered all sorts of excuses to prove that whatever it was, it wasn't him that did it.

I've since been to the same competition another few times with Fred, the last one in 1992, when the PNE Under 14's Team won the Northern Ireland Plate. My assistant, Darryl Woods had to return home with one of the boys, Ian Stanley who had broken his leg. With Fred now accompanying me in the dug-outs there was never a dull moment, as whenever we scored, Fred leapt up and promptly hit his head against the concrete roofing.

It was 1987 I first met Fred and have enjoyed his company and friendship during my time at Preston, and look forward to many more enlightening experiences now we are together at Blackpool Football Club.

Ted Taylor (Senior Youth Scout) - Blackburn Rovers

It gives me great pleasure to say a few words in praise of Fred O'Donoghue whom I have known as a scouting colleague since 1978.

My memories of Fred are memories for cheerfulness and joviality, always a friendly smile, a cheerful hello and no semblance at any time of the thought that he had any cares in the world.

Fred always got on with the job in a professional manner and with his ever present smile.

His car journeys when I joined him were invariably undertaken in an operatic atmosphere, usually Gilbert and Sullivan.

Long May He Scout!

Signed
Ted Taylor

David Lee - Bolton, Southampton, Bury and Wigan FC

Thank you to the late Bernard Snape and Fred for giving me the start I needed on the long hard road to becoming a professional.

After meeting Fred for the first time I was sure his professionalism and advice would stand me in good stead, and that it has.

All the best Fred.

Signed
David Lee

A Few Footballing Cameos

The Great Bill Shankly

When Bill Shankly died in September 1981 at the age of 68, the football world mourned the loss of a unique personality. In a career lasting over forty years he reached the top of his profession as both player and manager. His commitment and dedication to the game were legendary, while his lacerating wit made him one of the greatest characters football has ever produced. If the country as a whole remembers him best as Manager of Liverpool, it was in Carlisle that his career began as both player and manager.

He was the youngest of five brothers who all played professional football.. So did two uncles on his mother's side and one of these, Bill Blyth, was a Carlisle director when the 18-year-old Shankly arrived on a month's trial at Brunton Park from his Ayrshire home in August 1932. He made his debut in a 6-0 defeat for Carlisle Reserves that same month, but kept his place. On 31st December 1932, he made his full league debut against Rochdale. He played sixteen league games in 1932/33 at right half for Carlisle and though the team struggled, his performances soon had other clubs taking notice. In July 1933, Carlisle accepted a £500 fee from Preston North End for his services. For a 19 year old player in a team at the wrong end of Division Three it was a sizeable sum for those days.

Bill Shankly was to spend the rest of his playing career at Deepdale. Preston gained promotion to Division One in his first year there and thereafter he remained a First Division player.   All in all he made over three hundred first team appearances at wing half for Preston and gained an FA Cup Winners' Medal in 1938, having been in the losing team twelve months earlier. He also won five caps for Scotland in 1938/39 and captained his country. But for the war he would surely have won many more honours.

Early in 1949 Carlisle player-manager Ivor Broadis joined Sunderland for an £18.000 fee. Bill Shankly, one of forty applicants, succeeded to the post and after some protracted negotiations took over as manager at the end of March. The Broadis fee had put Carlisle in a reasonable financial position but it did not take 'Shanks' long to make his own mark at the club.

His hallmarks were commitment and dedication to his players and to the job in hand, while he was an obsessive student of football in general as others can testify.

Carlisle full back Norman Coupe for example recalls him buying all the Sunday papers each week just to study the football pages. Jackie Lindsay remembers that you could be eating a meal with him when your plate would suddenly disappear - only to re-appear elsewhere on the table as he moved all the crockery around to illustrate a series of tactical points about the game.

Bill Shankly was one of Carlisle's most successful managers. He built on the foundation laid down by Ivor Broadis to produce a team that came close to winning the Third Division title in 1950/51 when the club finished third in the League as well as holding Arsenal to a draw at Highbury in the FA Cup. The great Bill Hogan and Paddy Waters were among his most notable signings along with full back Alex McIntosh and winger Alec McCue. He also built up a rapport with the crowd with his regular pre-match talks over the loudspeaker that began, "This is your team manager speaking...." delivered in his rasping Ayrshire voice.

In June 1951 he beat 170 other applicants for the manager's post at Grimsby Town who were newly relegated from Division Two. In two and a half years there he twice narrowly failed to win promotion before he returned to Cumberland to manage Workington. His eighteen months at Borough Park saw a sharp upturn in the Club's fortunes before he moved to Huddersfield as coach, then manager for four years. Whilst at Leeds Road he signed both Dennis Law and Chris Balderstone. Finally, in 1959, his last managerial move took him to Anfield and a Liverpool team still in the Second Division. His achievements there have been well chronicled but his haul of trophies included, three League Titles, two FA Cups and a EUFA Cup before his retirement in 1974.

Bill Ayre - Ex Blackpool FC, Southport FC, etc.

Anyone who has had the Managership of Halifax Football Club knows a lot about managing on a shoestring. Greatly respected by all the top men in the game. A 'Geordie' with a sense of dignity, humour and pride. A pleasure to work with, and a man who knows the game on and off the field.

Jimmy Quinn - Ex Blackburn Rovers FC, Reading FC and Peterborough FC

Goal-scoring centre forward at Blackburn, also Northern Ireland. I helped Jimmy to look for a house in the Blackburn area, and found one he liked off Revidge Road in Blackburn. Played in my Testimonial Match - good lad for me.

Derek Fazakerley - Blackburn Rovers FC

On a wet cold miserable November night in 1985 a 'FOD' Quiz Night was arranged for me by the landlord of the pub, (Hyde Park) in St Pauls Road, Preston. About twelve people attended the event. Rovers players, Terry Gennoe and Derek Fazakerley turned up for me as they were the stars at that time of Blackburn Rovers. They stayed at the pub all the time when it would have been easier for them to have a pint and then buzz off, but they didn't. Words cannot express my admiration and feelings for the real men of the soccer world who gave me time with no pecuniary gain. Would some of today's players do likewise? I wonder. The event raised £20 but I was richer in friendship. That was the bonus plus.

Vince O'Keefe - Ex Blackburn Rovers FC. PFA Top Man

Goalkeeper - He played for Rovers and guested also for Northern Ireland, in the match for me at Ewood. Thanks Vince you're a good friend and one of the lads. PFA? Top Man in Agent's Advice. I remember Majorca and Frank Lord - great days Vince with you and the lads.

Tim Parkin - Ex Blackburn Rovers FC

Ex-Rovers apprentice from the Kendal area - a young lad I very much helped at the Rovers. Found him his digs in Manor House Lane in Blackburn. He became a pro-footballer and bought his own house near to his original digs. Tim did well in the game, made a bob or two. It's nice when the lads do well like Tim Parkin.

Bob Saxton - Ex Blackburn Rovers

Nicknamed - "Sacko" - a shrewd manager at various clubs. I must say I can't thank him enough for suggesting a Testimonial for me to the Rovers' Board of Directors, but I will never be able to understand his decision not to include me on the Rovers payroll on my retirement from local government in 1985. He's done well in the game, made a bob or three.

John McGrath - Ex PNE FC, now sadly deceased

I was always on edge when John stalked the corridors at Preston North End, Deepdale. He was, as the popular saying goes, "a larger than life character." Terrific, great coach when in the mood, also fearless and outspoken. He did a great job for Preston North End in winning promotion in 1986/87. A strange man. Those in the game often refer to him as the "madman", (so does John). A magnificent after-dinner speaker, one of the best.

Neil Bailey - Ex Blackpool FC, now Man United FC

Ex-Burnley apprentice - Ex-Blackpool Youth Officer, ex-pro at various clubs. I got to know Neil at the Milk Cup in Northern Ireland in July 1992. We quickly became friends and I joined him at Blackpool in February 1993. Good worker, patient with the lads, knows the game at all levels, a pleasure to work with. I predict Neil to go far in the game. Calm, dignified, a sense of purpose and optimistic. Strong and firm with the YTS lads under his care.

Noel Brotherston (sadly deceased) - Ex Blackburn Rovers FC

Flank man, a Rovers and International Northern Ireland star. Quiet, modest, affable and unassuming. Noel helped me in the many quizzes I had in the Testimonial Year. Had a great career in the game.

Lee Cartwright - PNE FC

A Walter Joyce soccer academy product. Midfield player from Rossendale; efficient, unassuming lad. Found him digs at the Preston North End Club, and took him to France. Over 100 appearances for the Preston North End Club. A quiet lad, he is fitness itself, a good 'diesel' engine in that body of his.

Billy Bingham - Ex-Blackpool FC Director of Football

Ex Everton player etc., -ex Northern Ireland Manager. I am greatly indebted to Bill and his team who played on my behalf in 1985. Bill is one of the game's great characters.

Alex Ferguson - Man United FC

The phone rang at Deepdale. A pleasant female cheery voice rang out, "Could I speak to Walter Joyce please?"

"Who's speaking?" said I in my best Preston tenor voice.

"I'm Mr Alex Ferguson's secretary," she replied daintily. My heart pounded, not the female quality of the voice but really Alex, "Fergie", wow!! I was all ears and excited. Walter came rushing from the ref's room at Preston North End. "Hello, Walter speaking," he said. After a few minutes of dialogue, Walter spoke, "Yes I'll get my scout, Fred O'Donoghue, to meet you at the Tickled Trout at Samlesbury." Jason Ferguson he revealed was going to attend Preston Poly for further studies and his Dad, Alex, was looking for accommodation in Preston. My job being the accommodation officer at PNE, it fell to my lot to meet and escort Alex and Jason to a big house in the Ashton area of Preston. I had seen Jason play football and I suddenly had dreams of him playing for our 'A' team at Deepdale. I thought he was a good young player when I had watched him.

Alex arrived bang on time, 7.00 pm. Both father and son looked smart with a very positive handshake and nice broad smiles as well. I immediately felt at ease in their company. They followed me to the house, the best I could find on PNE's books. I spent a pleasant half an hour with Alex and Jason talking about this and that, mainly football in general terms. Now the odd time, not often, when I've seen Alex at Old Trafford, at Youth and Reserve Team Games, he smiles and gives a nod. I often wonder does he remember me? Alas, my hopes for Jason, of whom I was dreaming and hoping to play for the PNE squad were to be dashed. Jason left the Poly and went into television work. My opinion of Alex Ferguson was a canny Scot who knows the game. A pleasant, cheery, distinguished, optimistic sort of man who made you feel comfortable in his presence. Bill Shankly was a completely different ball game, yet both were successful in their chosen profession.

When I resigned at Preston in January 1992 I was offered a position with Manchester United as a Scout in this area by Les Kershaw, the Chief Scout, another equally respected, capable man.

I can understand why staff at Man United FC think the world of Alex. As Nobby Stiles put it, "Alex, different class Fred, different class."

Jimmy Smith Derby FC, Ex-Blackburn Rovers FC Manager

The chapter on Rovers will reveal all about my good friend, "Jimmy Bald Eagle Smith". One of the best Yorkshire lads I've known, and I have kept in contact with him over the years. Thought my singing was better than my scouting, (a shrewd man), probably right.

Glen Keely - Ex-Blackburn Rovers FC

Centre back and tough. A 'Rover' and radio star, who served on my Testimonial 85 Committee with great credit. Spoke with clarity and knowledgeable authority of the game at the different functions. Another old cliche, "He was a friend in need, a friend indeed."

Howard Kendall

Player and Manager. His career stands out as a great player; as a manager I couldn't say we met eye to eye, but I respect his success, both on and off the field at every level.

Ron Atkinson - Ex-Aston Villa FC, Coventry FC

I met him once in the Small Directors Room at Ewood. A lot to say, knowledgeable, a lot of grin, a lot of gold about the man. He was manager at Man United at the time. Chief Scout, Tony Collins was with him at this particular Reserve Team game. I wrote to him about my Testimonial Game asking if he would play. I didn't get a reply. He's done well for himself. On radio and TV.

Paddy Sowden - Ex-Blackpool FC

In the Book see Chapter No. 3, (Stanley Matthews' young understudy), my mentor and the man who started me scouting at Darwen Football Club.

Terry Gennoe - Ex-Blackburn Rovers FC

Top of the Pops for me - my remarks about "Faz" equally apply to this old friend of mine.

Bill Fox - Blackburn Rovers FC

Ex-Rovers Chairman, (sadly deceased). My wife Cathy said, "Fred, a chap, a Mr. Bill Fox, called at the shop." We then lived at Whalley Range in Blackburn at the Lion off-licence Shop., He was a potato/fruit merchant on Blackburn Fruit Market. We bought all our fresh vegetables from the firm, i.e. Fox and Sons. He told her he was a Rovers dedicated fan and was glad I had been appointed scout for the club. I later met him when he became a member of the Board. A tall man, 6'1", ginger hair, straight talker and a down to earth man's sort of approach. We got on well, always, "Hi Fred, how's it going?" When Rovers signed on some of the young lads as pros which I had taken to the club he would take me to one side, "Well done Fred." When I look back at players like, J. Butcher, J. Bailey, J. Waddington, Paul Round, Tim Parkin, M. Salmon, M. Patterson; (S. Garner I helped to rubber stamp); S Galliers, F. Carr, L. Johnrose, P. Comstive, Jason Wilcox, David Lee, J. Willis, I felt that the years spent at the Ewood Club had not been in vain. I was most surprised when Bill allowed me to go in 1985 without calling me in for at least a talk about why I was leaving the club. But that's football. I liked the man just the same. It wasn't until December 1986, a year and a half later that I got an appreciation letter from the Board of Directors. Bill died at a very crucial moment in the Club's history but his deep spade work, i.e., wooing Jack (the Millionaire) Walker. He also became Chairman of the Football League, his prompting and orchestration on behalf of the Rovers was showing a fruitful future. About sixteen months before he died he came to PNE, for a Manx Cup game. He spotted me at the door. He beckoned and I took him into the scout's room. He said, "Fred we've missed you, but watch Rovers now we've got the financial punch." How right he was. Well done Bill Fox-RIP, a Rovers giant.

Dusty Miller Ex-Blackburn Rovers FC and other various clubs

Outside right for Rovers. A Scot; a flying machine. Dusty and I hit it off from the first day we met. An honest player, gutsy, he helped out at all the testimonial quizzes, a clever lad and right good company.

Glen Johnstone - Ex-PNE FC

A very unlucky young man. A PNE player/goalkeeper. A young keeper Rovers turned down. He was 6'3" and 14 stone. I signed him on schoolboy forms the same time as Franz Carr and David Lee. Glen was unlucky, having knee injuries whilst pro at Preston. He just didn't get those vital lucky breaks you need as a player in this game of ours.

Franz Carr - Aston Villa FC, Ex-Blackburn Rovers FC

A Preston Lad - an England Youth International. A Rovers boy under 14. Showed great promise as a young pro player at Notts Forest under B. Clough. Nickname, "Franny." Still has possibilities; a good lad with skills and frightening pace. Sends me a Xmas Card every year. If he missed his bus to Blackburn as an apprentice he would run through the centre of Preston, 2 miles, to my house. He knew that I would drop him off at Ewood, on my way to work at the Town Hall in Blackburn.

David Lee - Bolton Wanderers FC, Bury FC, Southampton FC now Wigan FC

Bolton F.C., spotted by Dennis Snape, my old pal at Bamber Bridge. He joined Rovers as an under-14 schoolboy. I signed him on a New Year's Day at his home in Hoghton. Great skills on his day, unflappable, a terrific young lad. Plays snooker as well, not bad at that either. I was most upset when Rovers let him go.

Simon Garner - Ex-Blackburn Rovers FC

Mr Arthur Fryars, Rover Director wasn't too keen about our Simon, being so small. Jimmy Smith's scout sent him from far away, Boston in Lincolnshire, (I rubber-stamped him). What a good player; he scored goals for fun. I loved Simon and have spent many happy years at Ewood at home and tours abroad, with this prolific net finder. Well done Garns. What a player! Likes a pint and a woodbine, as I did, in those busy days at Rovers.

Walter Joyce - Ex-PNE FC, Bury FC now at Man Utd FC

Walter contacted me about the Preston North End position, as his part-time assistant on the 'Youth Scheme' he proposed to introduce at the club. I began with him in December 1986 and continued for six years and two months. The School of Excellence at PNE with Peter Warburton in charge was already in existence. Peter did sterling work along with Mick Finn, Steve Grand, not forgetting Stuart Pilling, Glen Bohanan, Darryl Woods and a host of helpers - Walter's pals, teachers, contacts, also friends of PNE., i.e. Tom Hasty, the Federation president, Frank Hewitt, and firms of every kind sponsoring the PNE Football Federation. Also the PNE Junior Federation (91) under the direction of Steve Borwick, Dave Borland (Chairman), Jim Dean (Secretary) and Keith Neilson (Treasurer). All these people and some local firms paid for all PNE youths immediate cash problems. Travel expenses, kit washing, fees for referees, trips to Croix in Northern France, trips to Northern Ireland. The small job now became 60-70 hours a week. Walter and I, at times were at loggerheads, and clashed several times. He accused me of being too involved with the organisations raising funds for the Junior Federations. I organised three Sportsman Dinners helped along by Dave Borland, Jim Dean, Steven Borwick and Keith Neilson and also other fund raising events, quizzes, lucky cards etc. Walter at times to my mind was not in the world of reality with the club's contacts in the game and the Show Biz characters on the club circuits. The Federation 91 needed my help and I gave it, to Walter's annoyance. Manager, Les Chapman used to intervene with words like, "I thought you two were friends." Roy Tunks, who was coaching at the time, also chipped in with Tunks-type tattle as did big Sam Allardyce after Tunksie had got the sack.

Walter was sometimes strange. He never had any money on him. He liked a secret bet on the horses and only told you what he wanted you to know. He had another side to his character which he carefully disguised but I loved the guy and I think he knows that. Scouting, we went everywhere. Three days with Les Chapman scouting at London, Luton, Charlton, Wimbledon and Oxford, staying at the Henry VIII Hotel, swimming in the hotel pool at 6.00 am, leaving Les Chapman snoring his head off, returning at 9.00 am, to the bedroom with Les Still snoring. We did match assessments all over the old Third Division football league grounds, spent hours and hours at PNE Deepdale, with every credit to Walter for devising the Youth Policy at Deepdale. We are still the firmest of friends. Over twenty-five years we have kept in contact with each other. Walter is a tip-top Youth Coach and many players in the game today must surely be grateful for his coaching techniques and expertise. Also his time spending hours with all who came into his care. Well done Walter. The proof of his outstanding PNE Youth Policy success came when Micky Burns, the Professional Football Association Education Director, requested that Walter and I give a lecture at the two-week Residential Course in Professional Football Management. A tremendous honour for us both. Personally for me it was the highest accolade from the profession that I could only dream about.

Franz Carr, England Under 18's International

The Footballers' Further Education and Vocational Training Society LTD

MEB/CR/1

27th May 1994

Mr F. O'Donoghue
7 Conway Avenue
Penwortham
Nr Lostock Hall
Preston
PR1 9TZ

Dear Fred

Football Management Course

Further to our telephone conversation with regard to the "Youth Development" lecture on the above course.

The lecture is arranged for 7.00 pm on Tuesday, 7th June 1994 and I hope Walter Joyce will be able to join you to give a joint presentation.

Please find enclosed course brochure together with a map to assist with travel.

Should any problem arise, please do not hesitate to contact me.

Yours sincerely
FFE & VTS Ltd

M E Burns
Chief Executive

Gordon Taylor

Chief Executive of the PFA

Hoghton's Football Club Chairman spoke to me about coaching his senior players for the club. I was working many hours for the Rovers, so I had to decline the offer, but suggested one of the Rovers players may be interested. He asked me to enquire. £10.00 1 hour sessions on Thursday nights in the season, in the Hoghton Village Hall.

Gordon Taylor was my choice. He was buying his house at Mellor with a young wife and family, he jumped at the chance of earning £10.00 for training the lads. Gordon with his skills as a professional, and his gift with words, I felt he was the man for the Hoghton Football Club coaching job.

The large Village Hall at Hoghton, opposite the castle, has many windows round the large rectangular building. It was Gordon's first night of coaching.

The following morning after his coaching efforts my phone rang angrily. It was the Secretary of the Hoghton Football Club, "Fred, who the bloody hell is the coach you sent?" he said.

"Gordon Taylor" I said, "Why, what's to do?"

"Five bloody broken windows that what's to do," he repeated. "Five bloody broken windows. It will cost a fortune to do the repairs. Fancy kicking balls round the place, with all those windows. Has he no sense." I tried to placate a very, very upset Secretary, which eventually I managed to do, after a couple of days, with help from the Club Chairman.

Gordon told me after, it was only a passing exercise but didn't reckon on his squad's skills and footballing abilities. They forgave Gordon his clanger, and he did manage to hold the job down with the club.

When I have occasionally met Gordon, cheekily I always say, "Fancy a job coaching." He smiles and says, "you daft bugger".

I like Gordon. He was always cheery and helpful to his players and boys in the PFA.

Sons of Phil Neal and Frank Casper

Burnley/Bolton/Coventry/Cardiff Football Club Managers

I first spoke to Phil when his son, Ashley, was playing for the Sefton Boys Under

14's at Southport. He knew who I was, as we had met several times on the scouting circuit, "Phil," I said. "What about your lad signing for me at Preston North End?" Neal replied, "It's up to the lad really Fred, but this plastic pitch doesn't help your cause." However, I managed to quickly arrange a game for his son on the plastic pitch, at Deepdale with some of the other Sefton Under 14 Schoolboys I was interested in. Ashley looked the pick of the crop at that time, with Phil, Walter Joyce and myself watching the game from a Deepdale box overlooking the pitch.

Walter and I tried to convince Phil of the advantage of being with a small club like PNE. Phil just smiled at me, slowly changing the subject. We both knew it was a no go area. Phil had other top line contacts.

I've kept in touch with Phil over the years, we get on well. With snippets of information, exactly, and I mean exactly the same was repeated word for word with the then Burnley Football Club Manager, Frank Casper. Both of them were concerned about their son's well being on that plastic pitch. Both of them signing for the bigger clubs. Liverpool for Ashley Neal and Man United for Chris Casper.

Frank Lord

Ex-Player Manager etc.   Profile of an Ex-Chief Scout
"The Lord's Failure"

Frank Lord is a real character in the football world. He had a flashy, toothy smile, a large solid gold bracelet, purposely on view and a gold watch given to him by an Indonesian or Malaysian King - I can't remember which! If you're in his company, he glances often at the valuable watch fingers from time to time, smiling as he does so.

6'0", impeccably dressed, a real dandy of a man, Frank was earning at Rovers about £180 a week. I was probably on about £10 for petrol expenses, but I did not mind that. I was in the game I loved best. Bob Saxton, I and the rest of the Rovers staff used to enjoy Frank's many funny stories and observations of life itself. He really was a card. The value of his watch and bracelet we reckoned to be at least £10,000.

Now Frank prided himself on getting players, staff, referees and people in all walks of life to open their hearts to him, rather like the penitent sinner in the confessional box with the priest. To be honest, I sincerely thought he had this conversational, skilful knack, a valued gift for all club managers, or as in his case the chief scout of Blackburn Rovers. At that time he could get people to talk - that was sure - he told us so!

"Surely, Frank" I said, "There must have been one specific time or place when all your conversational entreaties and talking skills have fallen on deaf ears or stony ground?"

"Yes", he said, "I am human. Just once and only once."

"He must be modest sometime", I thought.

"I'll tell you," said Frank.

So he began.

"It was on a train from Manchester to London many years ago. A well dressed city chap got in the same compartment as myself and sat opposite me.

"Morning", I said. He just nodded and grunted "Morning".

I opened, later to realise, a one way conversation.

I spoke about the usual weatherisms, the newspapers, local news, international news, farming, hill sheep farming, literature. He never spoke or replied back to me. He just stared and grunted "Mmm.....Ugh." I was getting nowhere. Crewe station flashed by and the train came slowly to a grinding halt. Fog! I had visions of the next three or four hours sitting opposite to a person who would not come out of whatever unbelievably protective shell of non-communication, with me, the 'master' at creating conversations. As there was no-one else nearby in the almost empty train seats, I continued my ploy, hoping for a conversation to pass away the time during the infernal fog.

I was amazed at Frank's Oldham type, eloquent oratory. I tried to interrupt him.

"Hold it, Fred, I haven't finished yet", he said. He continued.

"I spoke about sex, murder, Tory politicians, power, the labour government, trade union power, philosophy, gays, lesbians, TV, the royal family, Picasso, Turner's English scenes, Michaelangelo, music, jazz, Mozart, big bands old and new, Beatlemania, religions in general - Fred, I was determined to get the lad to say something to me. The more I tried, the worse it got. He just sat there. I went on again - football, my own pet subject, cricket, golf, grouse shooting, holidays in Spain, America, the Lake District, Blackpool, dog and cat management, atomic power, railways, swimming, boxing, films, horse racing, dope, drugs!

Finally, Fred, I was completely and utterly baffled by his bland and complete silence and non-participation in all my conversational efforts. I felt demoralised, defeated. The train by this time was arriving at Euston Station, 3 hours late. I was worn out and mentally and vocally bruised."

"What happened next, Frank?." I said.

"The chap quietly stood up and said "Thank you for your company. It's a pity you were not able to talk about a bankrupt going to the Old Bailey for fraud and other matters. Goodbye." And he walked slowly off down the platform."

Frank was OK in my book. He had a sense of humour and didn't miss a trick. We got on well together. Has a bob or three I should think.

Postscript 93/94/95 Seasons

Blackpool Football Club

(January 1992) As I have said, I resigned from PNE and I had been at home for about a week. The phone rang. It was Les Kershaw at Manchester United. "Fred what are you going to do now?" he said.

"Les," I replied, "I really don't know".

"Well don't be stuck for a job," he quickly said.

I thanked him for the offer, and said I would think about it.

Nobby Stiles rang, "Fred get on board with us. It's a different class". I was tempted very much.

This was followed by other inquiries from Bury-Bound Walter Joyce, Les Chapman/Manchester City, Dean Crombie/Bolton, Harry Wilson/Burnley, Jim Furnell/Rovers even John Pickering at Middlesborough rang me up. It was nice of old friends. It was on the grapevine the F.O.D. was out of work, resigning from the PNE Club.

Pat Lynch the Blackpool scout I had befriended when he worked for me at Blackburn Rover's had told Billy Ayre and Neil Bailey about me, and he asked me if I would be interested in going to Blackpool. I was interested. Blackpool is a lot nearer than Manchester United (Preston is where I live). Neil Bailey's work load was unbelievable: A/Team/B Team/Youth Team Reserve Scouting/At Junior Level/Centre of Excellence Director. I had met Neil in Ireland at the Milk Cup Competition and took an instant decision and joined the Seasiders.

Bill Ayre, what a nice chap, with great knowledge, and strength, certainly the boss with a great sense of humour. We gelled almost at once, I started clearing mail for Neil, and of course Bill. The number of trialists that write to Blackpool for a trail is in the hundreds, as I found out over that season.

With the contacts in France I had made over the PNE years, I arranged a trip for the Blackpool Under 18's in Northern France. May 1994, the Croix International. It was a great trip for the lads with under 18's Teams like Anderlecht, Barcelona, U.S.A., Benfica, Crux Athul from Mexico, Chile de Santiago etc. Terry Churchill, Steve Potter, Terry Eccles and myself raising funds with a dinner at the Sheraton Hotel with Steve Kindon, ex-Wolves/Burnley, giving us a great night along with the Preston Comedian Syd Tait. Everything at Blackpool was looking good. But

Blackpool has its problems - MONEY. With poor gates not helping without Mr. O Oyston's helping hand I shudder to think what would happen. I remember Accrington Stanley FC who? you may ask precisely.

The Agents (In Football)

Two agents which come to mind are Mike Morris and Nick Young, whose job it is to get the best possible deal for young players. Another one is Paul Stretford, owner of the Pro-Active Sports Managements, with an estimated 50 players on his books, also with top players at many premier clubs. Legions of agents are now operating in this country.

Players acquire the names of agents from other players. These quick-witted men are silver tongued and have acquired a vocal skill that most of the younger players do not possess and are unable, unfortunately, to express themselves or "barter" as to what their particular club.

I have often been asked by younger players to take up for them an agent's role, but I have always told them to get the PFA i.e. my old pals at Blackburn Rovers Vince O'Keefe, Brendon Batson, Mike McGuire, Mickey Burns, etc, etc. They are your union, with the guile and experience. Top TV personality players like Ince, Giggs, Ferdinand, Batty etc., in my opinion, should employ the PFA as their professional business and contract managers. I am sure Chris Sutton will echo these sentiments of mine 100% as well as many other top players in the game today.

After the recent Bung Fiasco etc, the investigation into the existing set up of agents activities is a must for the FA and should be closely monitored and controlled for the benefit of football, it's clubs and players and the paying punters. Top stars I realise do need much advice and help in business acumen and commercial dealings, again I say to all the top star players let the PFA put you on the right road. Other agents spring to mind Jerome Anderson, Mel Stein, Eric 'Boom Boom' Hall, Peter De Sisco, Athol Still, Kevin Mason, Maydn Evans, and I am sure there must be lots of others that I have missed. All players, and YTS lads, who are usually PFA members, be sensible, use your own unions officers. In a recent newspaper article it was estimated that the Blackburn striker "Sutton" had saved himself a 1/2 million by allowing Vince O'Keefe of the PFA to negotiate his personal contract terms with Blackburn Rovers, "£150,000" is a lot of money. I have been told that £1,000 was the fee charged by the PFA. Well done Vince and the PFA At international agents level all foreign countries have the FIFA approved agents list I'm told to check with, I wonder.

Cameos of other Scouts

Simply because they have played the game at the highest level does not automatically mean that ex-professionals make the best scouts; in many cases they do not. However, their background does give them an obvious advantage over the lay man and, it's a fact that they can usually spot a good 'un! They know the basics.

A typical example in the North is Verdi Godwin, one, as I have mentioned before, of soccer's behind the scenes characters. Not only does he scout, he can sing, tell funny stories and even play the spoons! Instantly recognisable in an old Russian type fur hat, Verdi has worked for numerous clubs and I was with him for a time at Liverpool. Think of Paul Mariner and that's Verdi Godwin, Peter Beardsley, etc. What a scout!

Colin McDonald - Ex-Goalkeeper Burnley, Ex-Chief Scout Oldham etc.

Blackburn Rovers "B" team were playing Oldham's youth team, who were due to visit Crystal Palace the following week in the quarter finals of the FA Youth Cup. I was looking at the Rovers squad when two blokes approached me and introduced themselves as representatives of Palace. We chatted for a while and they asked if I knew the Oldham team. I was able to give them three or four names but, unfortunately, was overheard by one of the Oldham boys' parents who immediately reported to Colin that I had been giving away secrets to the Palace scout. At full time Colin came up to me in the tea room and blasted me in choice language, not even giving me a chance to explain that I only knew a couple of names anyway. One of his milder comments was "If anyone wants to know MY bloody team he can see ME". He was right, and it is a lesson I have always remembered. Shut your mouth! Palace's team incidentally, went on to beat Oldham in the subsequent match and I have always wondered if I was just a little bit responsible for helping them to get through.

Colin and I have since made it up, however, and are the very best of friends. We often used to arrange matches between our younger players on a coaching basis and he has helped me from time to time with good advice. I believe he is now retired. I've not seen him in a long time.

Tom Saunders - Liverpool FC

Even the best scouts still miss players from time to time and not all the boys they recommend are taken on; far from it. One scout, who must remain anonymous, passed on to me a tip about a promising 15-year old because his own club had turned him down. We gave him a chance and the youngster went on to make the first team. There's no harm done when this sort of thing happens. One club's loss is another's gain and the all-round winners are the boy and the game itself and the paying public.

It's a similar situation when a club give the thumbs down to a boy after his trial. I well remember the once a month regular trials that Liverpool held on Sundays, some years ago., 1970-71.

After the games, the names of the chosen few were called out, possibly three or four out of 60 or 70 boys, by that well-known figure in Merseyside schoolboy soccer, ex-headmaster Tom Saunders. To cushion the blow, he would call all the boys together, thank them in a gentlemanly fashion for coming along, remind them that football was a game of opinions and state that if they had not been selected for further trials not to be too despondent as the staff could be wrong in their assessments.

The talk would always be rounded off with his story of Ted MacDougall whom Liverpool let go (along with others) only for him to reach the top with another club, Bournemouth FC. Tom is now a Director at the Anfield Club.

In recent years Liverpool have been concentrating on their local area more than ever before, covering Merseyside as comprehensively as possible which, to my way of thinking, is the best way, S. Heighway, the ex-Liverpool winger, doing a fair job for a great club, i.e. Fowler - McManaman etc.

A few of the Scouts far & wide
(Past and Present with some sadly deceased)

Two of the biggest names in the North-West were Jimmy Milne of Preston North End, and the famous Gordon Clayton, of Burnley. Less well known was Jim Davenport, who was with Bury for many years working on all fronts, both non-league and the schoolboy game. He worked very, very hard for Bury, but sadly is no longer with us.

Gwylin Morris, who came from Pwllheli, worked from Blackburn Rovers and was responsible for bringing Mike England and Roy Vernon. He asked me down to see him when I was appointed Chief Scout for the Rovers. He made me very welcome, offering Cathy and me a caravan for a weeks holiday.

Then, of course, there was the effervescent Gordon Clarke who took me on as a scout for Arsenal the single year I was there. Gordon was a Manchester chap who had played for one of the Manchester clubs.

If I may, I'll just go through a few of the North-West scouts I've met (just a few there must be hundreds), Colin MacDonald, Harry Woodhouse, Stuart Diamond, Eddie Quigley, Harry Hodges, Jim Mooney, Joe Armstrong, Charlie Walker, Jack Chapman, Harry Potts, Verdi Godwin, Les Rigby, Joe Brown, Leonard Wiseman/Northern Ireland, Ron Armitage, Roy Hartle, Ted Taylor, Ian Hanson, Alan Spavin, Gordon Clegg, Dusty Miller, Colin Grainger, Brian Symington, Phil

Hedreth, Bobby Todd, Harry Boyle, Harry McShane, Tony Collins, Bert Edwards, Arthur Bellamy, Frank Taylor, Bob Parkinson, Geoff McDougal, Graham Hollinshead, Gordon Robins, Jim Madden, Jim Dean, Jim Hayhurst, Pete Mumby, Tony Griffin, Tommy white, Glynn Davis, Wally Mawdsley, Steve Walsh, Harold Jarman, Mick Finn, Pat Lynch, Colin Fairhurst, the Rovers scout is one of the best in my area. Some I am sure I have missed out. If so, please forgive me. Others are now deceased or retired.

When Bob Saxton came to Blackburn Rovers, he sacked Eddie Quigley, Rover's Chief Scout. Bob Saxton thought that possibly Blackburn Rovers was going to go into the First Division at that time so he then appointed football's jester Frank Lord, ex-PNE/Oldham, an experienced man at all levels.

When I arrived at Blackburn Rovers, there was a chap called Harold Readett who was Chief Scout. He was on £3 or £4 a week. He worked along with Jimmy Baldwin, his assistant. When I was appointed Chief Scout Harold Readett resigned. Baldwin also resigned shortly after. They'd been friends at Rovers for many years and I don't doubt the hundreds of hours those guys put in for Blackburn Rovers, when Rovers had no money. There was Jimmy Murphy of course, of Manchester United. Jimmy and Sir Matt Busby were actually responsible for the original scouting in a fairly big way. They were responsible for the first Busby babes. When I met Jimmy he was an old man, but very friendly, very knowledgeable. There's a lot of other scouts that I'm going to mention like Frank Pickford who did a hell of a lot of good work at Bolton Wanderers for peanuts. Harry Parkinson, LFA member also at Bolton. George Knight at Burnley and now at Manchester United, a smashing guy who is seen on the circuit regularly. Then top man Ken Barnes of Manchester City. Leeds man Brian Edwards was a former school headmaster, then there was Ian McMinn, a Skelmersdale lad who I got to join Blackburn Rovers, he was a smashing lad, we got on well together. We nearly signed Liverpool's McManaman, Ian making an early approach for him after both of us watched him play on Chorley's ground in an Under 14's game for Liverpool Boys against Chorley Boys. Ian was upset when I left Rovers, ringing me up, and trying to change my mind.

Other names spring to mind, like the friendly Jim Cassels, Chief Scout at Oldham. Dave Crompton was one of the top men at Wigan, and George Smith used to work for Manchester City.

Richard Dinnis, ex-Blackburn Rovers, was also Manager at Newcastle for a short time after being assistant to Gordon Lee. He has a very good eye for young players.

At Bolton the names of Steve Carroll, also a coach, and Jack Gruffog deserve recognition. Likewise, Steve Smith at Bristol City, and the well-known Norman Bodell, who always knew what he was looking at, and still does.

John McGrath's right-hand man at Preston was Nigel Brown. He did a great job for John McGrath, and left the club when John went.

Few scouts, or coaches, can match the know-how and experience of the popular Dave Bushell of Manchester United.

Walter Joyce's main man as far as scouting goes was Harold Holbert, who really knows the game and understands how to put together a match report.

Finally, the great Peter Doherty, Northern Ireland, would arrive at a schoolboy game saying, "Top of the morning Fred". Can I have the teams?" He knew I had already made a note of them.

I think that summarises a few different scouts that I've known personally, each one bringing back individual memories.

The number of scouts in these islands of ours are countless, and their numbers ever changing week by week, day by day. They are the life-blood of our national game. Scouting for Glory is this book's title. For the glory is a welcome complimentary letter, from their appreciative club, managers, parents, players and fellow scouts, who ply the trade.

Quiz Night Feniscowles Cricket Club
L/R: The FOD, Chairman Cricket Club, Keith Malkin, Miss Blackburn Rovers, David Jones and Peter Doherty

Chapter Ten

Other Interests and Final Conclusions

Boxing

As a schoolboy, as I have earlier mentioned, I joined the boxing "Boy's Club" at Starch House Square in Preston and achieved a fairly reasonable standard of skill in the noble art. The Club entered me in the Lancashire and Cheshire Boys Club Championships and I took part in that prestigious boys tournament, narrowly being beaten in the semi-final at schoolboy catch weight, at Fulwood Barracks, on points. My large nose twitches when I think of that night's hard bruising battle. Frank Holland of St. Ignatius Boy's Club went on, if I remember correctly, to win the schoolboy Northern Title, his brother Bert Holland being St. Walburg's youth and boxing coach.

Often I trained at the Croft Street (Vic Maudsley) gym, but my wise old father persuaded me that boxing was not for me. However, I still continued to train with the boxing fraternity for a few years during the war. I enjoyed the camaraderie of those Preston pro battlers. The fitness that boxing gave me most certainly helped me in football matches. (I was a super fit nut at that time.)

Several years later when I left the Merchant Navy in 1950, I rejoined St. Augustine's Boys Club. Leaders, Louis Caton and Frank Pyke invited me to become the boxing instructor for the club. This would be a paid position as and when I qualified as an instructor with the Amateur Boxing Association as a Grade 1 Instructor.

Training and studies of the noble art took a lot of my time, boxing at the Croft Street gymnasium off Marsh Lane (Vic and Cyril Maudsley's pro stable) with my old school pals, Ronnie Sinclair, Stan Macarthy and the other pro boxers at the gym. Dick Knowles was the trainer and also sponge man for the local team, Higher Walton Mills FC. Two shillings a week was the charge to train.

Finally, after hours of studying ABA rules and all the regulations, examination day arrived. It was held at the YMCA in Manchester. I had been told to take my boxing gear with me, for after the theory and written part of the exam a practical demonstration of my own skills would take place before three of the North West ABA officials.

Frank Casey and George Barton of the St. Joseph's Boys Club were also taking the exam at the same time as me. I changed quickly, ducking under the ropes. Grinning at the side of the ring were my Preston buddies Frank and George, then looking across to the opposite corner of the ring I felt a cold, steely gaze from a tough looking face coming my way. God, the boxer opposite was none other than (well known in his day) Max Shacklady, A British Olympic champion. All nine and a half stone of me turned to jelly. My goose pimples had other goose pimples. Max was kind to me however. Three two minute rounds were scheduled, but after two rounds the three officials of the ABA called time. Max just said, "Well done son". I'd passed the course and became an ABA qualified Grade I instructor on fifteen shillings an hour, with Preston Borough Council. I was so pleased. My wife, Cathy was pleased too. We needed that money for our up and coming family.

I duly thanked Mr Caton and Mr Pyke for helping me on my way. St. Augustine's produced some very good young boxers and the club went on to win the ABA Championships and the Lancashire and Cheshire titles. Two boys, Jackie Butler and Jimmy Powell turned professional at sixteen years of age, Jackie going on to fight for a British Championship.

Boxing at Pontins, Morecambe

Dick Knowles, the Vic Maudsley boxing stable coach had arranged with the Pontin's Holiday Camp organiser, a series of Monday night boxing for the campers. He came round to see me.

"Fred, do you and your lads want to make a bit of easy money?"

"How?" I puzzled. "What do you want us to do?"

"Boxing, exhibition sparring - eight bouts, sixteen boxers I am looking for. I know you and the club can raise four boxers for me. Just think, Fred, your lads in front of lots of Pontin,s camp spectators. £2.00 a round (2 minutes) three rounds (6 minutes) £6.00, for yourself and whatever lads you can get to come to the camp. Think of the experience you'll be giving them. I asked who else got up there. "Jackie Fairclough, Johnny Black, Ken Duckworth, Ronnie Sinclair, Stan Mac, Paddy Walmsly - loads of others - it's easy money (£6.00)."

I thought it was not bad for a sparring session. "How's my team going to get up there?" I asked. "That's the least of your worries, Fred. The camp boss puts on a bus for all the Preston boxers. It leaves Croft Street, off Marsh Lane at 6.15 pm on Monday nights and gets back for around 10 pm."

So I asked the lads. It was held twice a month during June, July, August and September. The boys at the club agreed and Jackie Butler, Gerry Peacock, Tony Walker, Jimmy Powell and one or two others that I can't remember, took up the challenge. Believe me that £6.00 was well and truly earned! It didn't work out as sparring, it was more like street fighting. With other boxers they brought in, weights were nearly all silly catch weights and some of us were black and blue! It lasted a few weeks and then I ruled the club and my lads out.

Bert Holland, the St. Walburg's coach pointed out to me that we were being used, and also, the ABA were becoming suspicious of my semi-pro activities. Most of my lads at St. Augustine's turned professional. Jackie Butler with Harry Woodward, and also Jimmy Powell. They all left the stable. The boy's club was now losing its members and so reluctantly, I closed the door at St. Augustines. The local authority gave me a football post coaching St. Maria Gorrettis youth club and also at Penwortham Holme, along with Jimmy Kay and Bert Holland, two good coaches. They paid me the going rate I had been receiving at my own St. Augustine's boys club, fifteen shillings a night, the same nights as well, Tuesday and Thursday each week. But it was so sad to see my beloved St. Augustine's parish declining very very rapidly. I've never thought of boxing coaching again, football was my real love and began to take over my life.

My philosophy of the noble art is that it is the loneliest place on earth in the boxing ring when that bell rings and you face your adversary. Is it primeval urge? It's you or him. The moment is fearsome in its stark, brutal truth. The same applies I would think in another sport in another place, the bull ring. The matador, the bull - a ton of beef, with horns. I've often thought that both boxer and matador are similar - universal manly brothers (homo sapiens) in a common union of fear.

Sir Tom Finney OBE, MBE

The Preston Guild is held every twenty years when the town celebrates its Guild Merchant. In the 1972 Guild year I was living in Higher Walton, near Preston and working at the Town Hall in Blackburn. My local newspaper shop was owned by a certain well-known footballer, Roy Gratix of Manchester City and an ex-

Tom passing to the FOD, Benefit Match, Preston Guild, 1972.
Preston Greyhound Track

Page 181

Blackpool Football Club player. Roy delivered our daily newsheet, and he knew I was the Chief Scout at Blackburn Rovers. Of course we quickly became firm friends through both our love for football. Roy, along with Joe Dunn ex-PNE star of the fifties and sixties, and Brian Pilkington ex-Burnley player, asked me to become a member of the Willie Cunningham ex-PNE and Scotland, his Charity Football XI. I felt most honoured to join this select band of ex-footballers who had raised thousands of pounds for the various local charities and I was lucky to take part and play in many local charity games along with Willie Cunningham, Eddie Brown, Sammy Taylor, Lindsay Wallace, Alec Ashworth, Stan Howard, Les Rigby, Terry McDonald, Les Dagger, Leo Gornall etc., etc. Willie was the organiser and the team captain. Football was his game. A hard man was our Willie.

Preston Guild Year (August 1972)

If I may return to Tom Finney and Preston Guild in the opening remarks, the local authority at Preston had arranged a big charity game. Roger Hunt, Liverpool FC XI -v- Tom Finney XI on the Acregate Lane Greyhound Track. A phone call from Roy Gratrix the same day of the match sent me rushing around to his house. "I" was picked for the Tom Finney XI as first reserve. ELATION, cloud nine, to sit in a dressing room and get changed for a star-studded match and actually sitting next or near to my idol, Tom Finney. No explicit descriptive words or eloquent oratory will ever be able to describe the feeling I had that day. Roy and I arrived at the ground. The game started. After five minutes Leo Gornall, ex-PNE player, playing

Willie Cunningham XII

Standing L/R: Willie Cunnigham, Linsay Wallace, Les Rigby, Lady Unknown, Joe Dunn, Barry Dilworth, Stan Howard, Terry McDonald, Eddie Brown. Kneeling L/R: Les Dagger, Sammy Taylor, The FOD, Brian Pilkington. Photograph by Roy Gratrix

at outside left fell with torn ligaments (we found out later). I was on the pitch taking Leo's position, outside left.

Imagine me playing on the same side as our Tommy, the pride of Preston, the flying England Plumber. As for the game these old pros made it so easy for me. How they talked to me. Fred, square, foot on it, man on, your ball, I'll have it back, go wide, take him on. The value of talking is so paramount to the old pros that made the mouth and ball work together in harmony. Tom Finney firmly calling, "Fred," the ball arriving at my feet with the right weight on it, what a ball artist. The best. How they helped me, a forty-five year old amateur. They made me make the ball do the work.

After the game which resulted in a 7 or 6 - 3 for the Tom Finney XI all the players and officials were invited into the Greyhound Club for drinks and presentation momentoes. Players received pewter tankards, but somewhere down the line my name was not called out by the organisers. Roy who was stood next to me said. "Go up to the stage and tell them Fred, where's my cup".

"I can't do that Roy. I'm only the reserve player", I replied. Roy in a loud voice shouted to Tom. Tom Finney who was assisting the organiser to hand out the cup replied back, "Yes Roy". Roy in an even louder voice said, "Where's my mates cup?" He has played eighty-five minutes for us, no cup?"

Tom looked at the organiser who in turn, red faced, beckoned me to the stage. There was one left, both men shook my hand and thanked me for my efforts. I could have killed Roy Gratrix at that time. Roy is one of my best pals, outspoken, funny. He gets mad and he calls a spade a spade. I got the tankard engraved, Preston Guild 1972, Tom Finney XI.

A would be Tenor

Music, singing, opera, Gilbert and Sullivan, the stage. "Where words fail, music speaks." (Hans Christian Anderson).

In the boyhood part of the book the love of music was instilled in my very being as a choirboy and watching the famous Gilbert and Sullivan operas. In the early fifties I joined the Preston based St. Augustine's, my own church G & S Society. John Mercer was the society's musical director, a competent man with the necessary letters behind his name, that complemented his brilliance on the piano and musical directional expertise.

The Mikado (Audition Time 1953)

John Mercer sat at the school piano. Fred in his warm friendly voice, "Would you like to sing these scales for me? Ooo, Ho, Ha, Ay, Ee," rippling his large expressive

Trial by Jury, St. Augustine's Operatic Society

Defendant, Fred O'Donoghue, with Marion Russell plaintiff

St. Augustine's Society on stage.
FOD, the defendant, with the plaintiff, with St. Augustine's Chorus.

fingers deftly over the keyboard. "What a nice pleasant light tenor voice you have." He then proceeded to take it to its upper top range and its lowest audible register. He looked up and smiled, "Ex-choirboy?"

"Yes" I gladly replied.

"Thought so. You've a good musical ear as well. You are in tune and you pitch your voice well. Would you like to sing me a song? Have you brought anything?"

"Yes" I said, "I have brought Cesar Franks Panis Angelicus."

"Good" he replied. I had secretly been rehearsing the piece with the church organist, Mrs Collins, ready for the operatic audition. (I was accepted). "Come to rehearsals next Monday, 8 pm till 10 pm he said "put in for a part." I like what I've heard, there is a lot of Irish in your voice, the Ee's and R's and I bet you have got John McCormack's records", he said. I laughed, "Yes, a lot. I have also got Benjimino Gigli, Peter Dawson, Taubers, Kathleen Ferriers and my favourite tenor, Jussi Bjorling". Smiling, I left the audition room feeling very happy at my acceptance with the society.

The society held its Easter offerings of operas in the girls school in Carr Street. How I found time to play football, do youth club coaching, boxing, sing in the church choir, take parts in the G and S operatic world and bring up my very young family, working fifty hours a week at the drawing office, I get a sweat on just thinking about it.

The years rolled by and many operas followed, Mikado 1953, the Gondoliers, Yeoman of the Guard, Ruddigore, Trial by Jury, HMS Pinafore, Pirates of Penzance and again Mikado in 1964. By 1965 I had moved to Blackburn, when I was sadly made redundant with the cancellation of the T.S.R. 2 aircraft, by the Wilson Labour Government and my wonderful operatic days came to a close.

However, four of my close G and S school singing pals, John Judge, my life-long school friend Jack Garner, Gerard Connor and Jimmy Charnley, formed a close harmony singing group known as the Exiles and performed at many local charity functions. Possibly the highlight of the group was at the Mayor's Gala Variety Show in 1975. We however broke up due to the many pressures on all of us. Our work commitments and personal family matters. Here are a few bric-a-brac items of those busy years. Shakespeare once wrote - "The man that hath no music in himself nor is not moved with concord of sweet sounds is fit for Stratagems and spoils. The motions of his spirit are dull as night and his affections dark as Erebus. Let no such man be trusted.

**County Borough of Blackburn
Mayors's Gala Variety Show**

**Tuesday, 31st October 1972, at 7.30 pm
Windsor Hall, Northgate, Blackburn**

Artistes

1.   LEYLAND MOTORS BAND - VOCALISTS MAUREEN MURRAY AND KATHLEEN WATKINS

2.   THE MELROSE SINGERS

3.   THE PAT EAKETS SCHOOL OF DANCING

4.   BRIAN WHITTAKER AND IRIS DOWNHAM

5.   TERRY BARBER - COMPERE

6.   CHRISTINE LEES AND PETER ROSE -VIOLIN & PIANO

7.   DAVID BROWN TRIO

8.   TERRY BRAMLEY & FRED SPENCER - COMEDY DUO

9.   THE EXILES - VOCAL GROUP

Production Staff

Producer	F O'Donoghue
Assistant Producer	T A Best
Stage Manager	Norman Stevens
Choreography	Pat Eakets
Lighting	M Eccles

Steering Committee

His Worship the Mayor, Councillor T Ellis J.P.
Mr J Charnley
Mr W W Yeates
Mr G A Poole
Mr F O'Donoghue
Mr T A Best

Mayors's Foreword

October 1972

I am very happy to welcome you to the Gala Variety Concert this evening, and I want to express my sincere appreciation to you for supporting this charitable event.

The Producer of the Show, Mr Fred O'Donoghue, has arranged a first class programme, with artistes of the highest quality who will, I know, ensure for you a delightful evening.

May I take this opportunity to express my thanks to the artistes who are giving their services this evening, and to everyone who has, in any way, contributed to the production of the Show. I am deeply indebted to you and I know that everyone will join with me in showing their appreciation at the end of the evening.

Thomas Ellis
Mayor

THE EXILES - This will be their third welcome visit to the Windsor Hall. The Exiles consist of John Judge, Bass, John Garner, Baritone, James Charnley, Tenor, Gerard Connor, Tenor and Frederick O'Donoghue, Tenor. These Exiles are singing in various shows and also with their work for different charities. This group have been offered various professional contracts but have never taken the stage as a profession seriously.

All of them are members of the St. Augustine's Amateur Operatic Society, Preston and at some time have either played leading parts or produced for the Society. An audition with Harry Secombe in London was offered to them after the N.A.L.G.O.

Silver Jubilee Celebrations in this hall but due to the Group's domestic, professional and business reasons they declined the offer. All of the Exiles are Prestonians and have been firm friends for over 40 years.

John Judge and Gerard Connor now sadly deceased.

July 1994
Enter Sam Allardyce

The sacking and resignation furore and the demise of Billy Ayre followed. Blackpool were looking for a New Manager. Many big names appeared in the press. I knew that Sam wasn't happy at Deepdale with John Beck, and I also knew that Sam wanted to be a Manager most of all. I lobbied again, Billy Bingham first of all, Ken Chadwick, Jimmy Wilde, Gill Bridge. Derek Allen the Secretary, did likewise as also did Tony Ellis (Ex-PNE star). We all felt Sam was the man to do the job.

When the job became vacant I alerted Sam, who was about to go out to Florida coaching at the organised venues over there. By the time he came back all the interviews had been carried out. I rang him up at PNE Deepdale and said, "Sam, ring Gill Bridge up and ask could you be a late entry for the job right now", and of course he did.

Sam I believe, had a great interview from the remarks that were made. Sam, my old pal, became Blackpool's Manager. What a wonderful outcome for this old scout with a dream I had, come true only to be shattered when Sam was later sacked.

July 1994 - Big Sam, Blackpool's New Manager

The man who has a dream

The Chairman of Blackpool Football Club is a person of unique personality, the founder of the largest family owned Estate Agents in the UK. An ex London and Blackpool hotel waiter (his parents were the owners), he became a radio mogul when he founded Red Rose Radio, covering Lancashire. He added to this the Leeds based Radio Ayre and two South Wales based stations which he amalgamated into Red Dragon Radio. He then turned the loss making Radio Ayre and Red Dragon Radio into profit making radio stations, followed by the addition of Piccadilly Radio, Manchester to the Group, winning the first contested take-over of a radio company, thus making the Group one of the largest radio groups outside of London. This then became Transworld Communications, which at one time included Miss World plc.

He has many other business interests, not forgetting the Yorkshire, Cheshire and Lancashire Life magazines. He is a man of exceedingly high profile in a jungle of commerce and financial wizardry.

A well known millionaire in the North West, Mr Oyston has many friends in the local Labour Party hierarchy, i.e., Jim Mason of Lancashire Enterprises (who worked with me for many years at the Town Hall in Blackburn); Louise Ellman, Chairperson of Lancashire County Council, and many other top MP's. He is indeed a man of wealth.

Many years ago, I took part in the Gilbert and Sullivan Opera "Ruddigore" with the St Augustine Operatic Society in Preston. A character in this comic opera is the awesome Roderick Murgatroyd. When I first met Mr Oyston my mind immediately cast him for the part, with his tall stature of 6'1", a distinctive moustache and goatee type beard, a large dark fedora style hat, and his 'long' hair flopping loosely around his neck. The place was Blackpool Football Club Boardroom, April 1993. His voice was clear and theatrical, his eyes steely and piercing as he welcomed me aboard in my new position as part-time Youth Liaison Officer with the Club. My mind was made up, he was a natural for the part. My vivid imagination ran riot as I could hear his voice singing 'When the night wind howls in the chimney cowls, and the bat in the moonlight flys'. Alas, I eventually came to my senses. I stammered and stuttered "Please to meet you", embarrassed by my delayed reply. Having said that, on the odd times that we do meet, Mr Oyston always smiles as he shakes my hand and enquires in a quiet voice, mostly about my health. He is a man under great stress, with vast demands on his time and a workload which I am sure would break a man half his age. With all this he seems to cope admirably.

His contributions to the Club have been gigantic financially, mentally and physically, of this I am sure. He has been outstanding in the Club's service to the youth teams, supporting boys from the Under 9's through to the Under 16's, giving financial support and personal commitment, qualities which have not gone unnoticed by his employees.

Original Cover design for the 1st Edition

Chapter Eleven

Trials and Tribulations of your Author

In one of the Blackpool FC home programmes (January 1999) Mr. Oyston wrote, that the Oystons have one major fault, that is a long love affair with the club, and whatever faults, they have poured their own private money into the club. As an employee regarding scouting, expenses, i.e. kit, medical, bus travel and a variety of other very costly expenses, I was never turned down by Mr. Oyston or his family. Indeed my first meeting with him, in the Blackpool F.C. Board Room, in February 1993, I reported we needed three kits for our scruffy looking U/14-U/15-U/16 Blackpool Schoolboy Squads immediately, we looked rag bags. A cost of £600 plus was mentioned to him. He then grilled me as regards shopping around for costs, etc I was ready for him with three positive quotations, his eyes flashed across the boardroom straight at me, speaking clearly and very positively he said "go ahead get them". Manager Billy Ayre the following day said "Fred the Chairman says you screwed him for a new kit £600 quids worth for the kids" I said "yes I did" he laughed and said "well done, remind me to take you to my next board meeting, you must have something I haven't" The Oystons have supported the Youth I cannot complain.

1994/95 :- Sam Allardyce (Manager), Phil Brown (Assistant Manager),

Bobby Saxton (Coach), Mark Taylor (Physio.), Jack Chapman (Chief Senior Scout), Neil Bailey (Youth Coach), Fred O'Donoghue (Chief Youth Scout), Billy Bingham (Director of Football) were the back room staff at this time. Players were bought and a number sold, but I always felt that there was discord between the Manager and some of the Directors of the Club. You could sense it and feel it. Sam failed in the bid for promotion that season because of a very bad run of results at the season's end. I always felt one or two of the players let him down at the crucial time. The back room staff at the club were the best squad of professionals I have ever worked for and with. I could not believe it when my old friend and colleague, Sam Allardyce, was dismissed. I was devastated and very, very sad.

Soon other staff were leaving the club. Neil Bailey went to Manchester United, Phil Brown to Bolton Wanderers, Bobby Saxton and Jack Chapman to Sunderland to join Peter Reid, Mark Taylor to Blackburn Rovers. A complete break up of a fabulous back room team. This was not a good time for Blackpool Football Club and its loyal, ever optimistic band of supporters.

Neither was it a good time for me. I had a brush with Kenny Dalglish.

```
CB

28th February 1995.


Mr. K. Dalglish,
Manager,
Blackburn Rovers Football Club,
FAX. 0254 245189.


Dear Mr. Dalglish,

I have recently written a book of my football
experiences over the last 50 years; 15 years
working for Blackburn Rovers which culminated
in a Testimonial game for me on 12th May 1985.

The Publishers have asked me to enquire if you
would be able to say a few words of Introduction
to the Book.  You will probably not remember me
but your son will when I was employed at Deepdale
by Preston North End with Walter Joyce and Les
Chapman coaching.

Thank you in anticipation of your kind assistance.

Yours sincerely,

Fred O'Donoghue.
Youth Liaison Officer
```

TEMPUS FUGIT ET FRAGILIS GLACIES INTERIT IRA MORA
AD08 (PUBLIS OVID NASO-POET)
MR K DAGLISH-BLACKBURN ROVERS

"TIME FLIES AND LIKE FRAGILE ICE, ANGER PASSES AWAY IN TIME"

Monday, 19th March 1995, a day of hypertension, and not a good day for your author.

The Pride of Place Publisher, a certain Mr John Booth, suggested I saw Kenny

Daglish about my forthcoming book,and would he be kind enough to say a few words on my behalf, i.e.with being at Rovers for fifteen years I thought that this was a reasonable request from my Publisher.

As I had spent a little time with his son, Paul, at under-14's youngster at Deepdale (Preston North End),along with Keith Neilson's son, Chris, and a few other lads from the Formby area,near Southport, I wrote Dalglish a letter to this effect.

A reply came back from Rovers that he wanted to see the contents of my efforts in the book. I arranged to see him and give him the book at the Rovers training ground at Blockhall village, near Blackburn.

I arrived at the ground.Jim Furnell,offering me a welcome cup of coffee. Jim told me that the manager was in a press conference and advised me to wait(the time was then 10.15 am).11.00am, he was still in the press room with a posse of reporters. To kill the time, Jim said, "Fred,come on.Lets have a walk round until he has finished. Just come and see these marvellous pitches we have here." As I slowly observed,they are indeed.Jim Furnell had also told the manager of my arrival,as I was informed later by Jim.

On arriving back at the complex area, Dalglish was playing pool with Graeme Le Saux. His sharp piercing type eyes caught my profile as I entered the dining room (pool table area). He knew I was there.

Three frames later I was still sitting waiting for the man to at least say hello. No such luck, a man of my age could ill afford to waste time.

Dalglish will find out it is a precious commodity, which should not be wasted with such bad manners. I was fuming, my blood pressure, every second rising to new heights.

Finally, as he left the area, I quickly followed him to his office, knocked on the door, trying to keep as calm as I could. I said to him, "this is my book". I could not tell exactly what he said about the matter. I then enquired about his son, Paul I was informed that he was eighteen years of age working at Glasgow Celtic. I put the carrier bag, containing my manuscript, down near his desk. I didn't like his harsh, brackish tone of voice at my intrusion, and I walked out of his office, completely drained by the mannerisisms of this man.

Kipling (I feel I must quote) "Walk with Kings and Queens yet not lose the common touch".

12.30pm back home to good manners, good lunch , good people.

A fortnight later on 2nd of April, I rang up his secretary or receptionist Susan, to tell her that I would be coming to pick up my valuable manuscript that day. I arrived at Brock Hall to be told that he didn't have time to look at the work I had done.

End of story.

P.S. He was, however a successful manager, and was a player of football merit. That I admire

The company that had promised to publish my book, 'Pride of Place' at Chorley collapsed. Nearly 400 people, consisting of family, friends, football colleagues had each paid their £11.99 subscription for the book and they all lost their money. The next article I wrote was from a hospital bed, illustrating that this was not a good time for your author. I had had another heart attack.

"Pride of Place"
Profile notes of publishers bankruptcy

As I was nearing the end of my book writings, my mind began to think of publishing my humble 15 year effort of writing my very own book. This is what happened.

In the Lancashire Evening Post, a Preston based paper, a book launch appeared. Gail Newsham a local author, had written a book about Dick Kerr's Ladies Football Team, which if I may add is very well written. The title was a "League Of Their Own", a hardback, and the publishers were, of course, "Pride of Place" plc, based at a works unit in Chorley. I knew Gail from local football ladies competitions, I thought being local at Chorley and seemingly successful, would be an ideal vehicle for a local author like me to make contact.

In early April 1995 I rang the firm of publishers "Pride of Place plc" and spoke to a certain John Booth, the Managing Director, about the book I had written. He asked me if I would take the manuscript round and leave it with them for a couple of weeks. This, of course, I promptly did. Retrospectively, looking back, I should have recognised his incompetence, the office mismanagement, a fearful lack of tidiness, dusty office equipment.

I sensed this man was under great stress, at my age Id seen it before and felt the undertones of deep personal problems. My basic instincts told me to pick up the manuscript and get out quickly. Speaking in a low soft, flat colourless voice, no timbre quality in it whatever. John Booth the publishers MD at 6ft plus tall, told me he liked what I had written, and would publish the book October/November for Xmas 1995 that year. To help the circulation and costs of the publication, John Booth told me it would help to form a subscribers list of all in football that knew me and would I partake in this really worthy exercise. Being the egotist I was, and dreaming of fame at last, ("Wow my very own writings") to be published, I agreed (foolishly) why didn't I shop around?? I still wonder at my lack of savour faire.

The application form for the subscribers list was written by an acquired partner to the firm a Mr. George Harris and was forwarded by me to all my family, friends, 92 League Clubs, schools, FA Headquarters, etc. etc. Over a 1,000 forms were sent all over the UK. Nearly 400 subscribers sent and paid (£10.00 and £11.99). This was now the end of September with no book draft in sight. I began worrying about the firm's validity.

A contract was sent to me (not signed) and at a meeting that was arranged with the plc, we agreed the book would be £9.99 shelf price (paperback). John Booth said that the deal would be based by normal standards as dictated by him, a £10.00 book -£3.00 for the printer, £3.00 for the publisher, £3.00 for the distributor and £1.00 for the author. Yes £1.00 for yours truly. I the asked Derek Quigley, a local Solicitor, to give me some legal backup. He updated the contract and forwarded the papers to Pride of Place plc. It was now early October 1995. Solicitor, Derek, the son of the famous PNE/Rovers Eddie Quigley footballing star, never received any form of answer to his communications. My worries increased. I was told I had nothing to worry about. I was however still worried, it was now early November.

By early December, I had spoken to authors Eddie Cotton at Liverpool, Gail Newsham, Charlie Lambert and other authors. Alas, they all informed me that my money, like theirs, was being used to payoff massive debts, as scouser Eddie Coton put it robbing Peter to pay Paul. Obviously I vigorously remonstrated with George Harris and tried to make contact with the by now notorious John "difficult to get hold of" Booth. I also joined the Book Author Society in London in the hope of some kind of protection from publishing predators or failures. No such joy. Two letters I sent to the society were never answered, I have cancelled my yearly subscriptions. I had spoken to a Susan Blishen about the subject matter, but she never followed up my doubts or worries. "Ah well", it doesn't matter they must have their own problems.

The telephone rang one night in March. It was George Harris of Pride of Place plc. I suppose I expected what he had to say "Fred" I want you to be the first to know that Pride of Place is going into liquidation. I was devastated. After asking all my friends to buy my book,a fifteen year effort,it made me very,ill. My own integrity I felt had been taken from me and I felt so stupid at allowing these people to exploit me and my friends in this way. I visited the local GP for stress,high blood pressure and heart palpitations.Friends reassured me"Fred it is not your fault". I stayed away from work to recuperate for a couple of days.

Therefore, for all the subscribers who lost their money I have made an arrangement for their names to be printed in the cover of this book, the cost to be borne by me. Inclosing to all my initial subscribers may God bless you all and thank you for your support.

Fred O'Donoghue

May 7th 1996

Royal Preston Hospital,Cardiac Ward.

The capital needed to fund the book and publish it myself was about £4300. This I was determined to do so I wrote to Blackpool Football Club, asking for a loan of nearly £2000. Gill Bridge kindly presented my case to the board and the Directors agreed to my request. I was happy for their support and the book was published to my delight and relief.

MIKE LANGLEY
SPORT

Fred O'Donoghue,
Blackpool FC

August 26, 1996

Dear Fred,

Ever since taking my leave of you at Bloomfield Road last month, I've been hoping to find a quiet hour to reflect on your misfortune and offer well-deserved sympathy.

Vanity publishers (a name that's a warning in itself) prey on amateur writers, few of whom make any profit from their labours--although not many can have been as unfortunate as yourself in suffering a 100% loss.

My golf club in Hertfordshire intends to publish its centenary history in a couple of years; when the committee's eyes turned towards me, I backed out on discovering that all similar vanity projects in our area had lost heavily.

A friend from boyhood, a professional wrestler who competed until 62, had a great story to tell. It embraced D-day as a paratrooper, sprint cycling, a top-of-the-bill year in Singapore, car dealing and its many strokes, as well as the night when, after breaking his neck falling backwards over the ropes in Bristol, he slipped out of hospital and drove himself home to Crewe.

Unfortunately for its literary merit, he let his new wife do the writing and they finished up with a glossy production by a vanity publisher but no reviews and few sales. He, of course, was rich enough to meet the bill without batting an eyelid.

I don't suppose you'll try again or, if you do, fall into the same traps; nevertheless, I quote this warning from the Writers' & Artists' Yearbook:

"Those who pay for the publication of their books should realise that what they are paying for is simply the manufacture of copies...The true publisher invests his own money in the publishing process; the vanity publisher invests the author's money ...Often the contracts will provide for printing 2,000 copies at an exorbititant cost to the author, but will leave the 'publisher' under no obligation to bind more than a limited number."

Next time, if there is one, write a synopsis first and then find an agent prepared to interest a publisher; meanwhile, hang fire until signing a contract that's been approved by a solicitor. Then write like crazy.

With best wishes,

"Mirror Group"

ONE CANADA SQUARE CANARY WHARF LONDON E14 5AP
switchboard: 0171-293 3000 / 0171-510 3000 Fax: 0171-293 3939 / 0171-510 3405 Telex: 27286 Cables: Mirror London E14
MGN Limited Registered Office: One Canada Square Canary Wharf London E14 5AP Company Registered in England No. 2571173
Daily Mirror · Sunday Mirror · The People · The Sporting Life · Weekender · Daily Record · Sunday Mail

Youth Scouting

By this time my work with scouting was beginning to blossom. The team of scouts and helpers were raising funds for our Youth programme by organising Quiz Nights and Sportsmans' Dinners. With the tremendous help received from stalwarts like Terry Churchill, Terry Wood, and Steve Potter, we were able to organise trips to

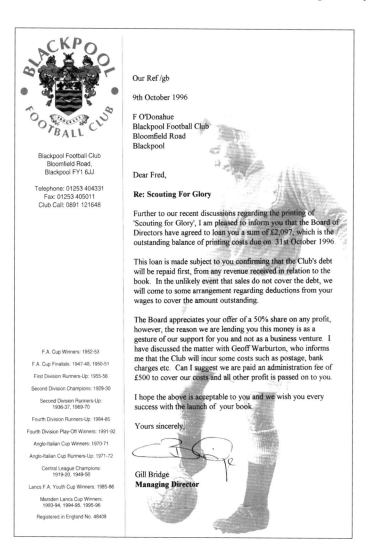

Blackpool Football Club
Bloomfield Road,
Blackpool FY1 6JJ

Telephone: 01253 404331
Fax: 01253 405011
Club Call: 0891 121648

Our Ref /gb

9th October 1996

F O'Donahue
Blackpool Football Club
Bloomfield Road
Blackpool

Dear Fred,

Re: Scouting For Glory

Further to our recent discussions regarding the printing of 'Scouting for Glory', I am pleased to inform you that the Board of Directors have agreed to loan you a sum of £2,097, which is the outstanding balance of printing costs due on 31st October 1996.

This loan is made subject to you confirming that the Club's debt will be repaid first, from any revenue received in relation to the book. In the unlikely event that sales do not cover the debt, we will come to some arrangement regarding deductions from your wages to cover the amount outstanding.

The Board appreciates your offer of a 50% share on any profit, however, the reason we are lending you this money is as a gesture of our support for you and not as a business venture. I have discussed the matter with Geoff Warburton, who informs me that the Club will incur some costs such as postage, bank charges etc. Can I suggest we are paid an administration fee of £500 to cover our costs and all other profit is passed on to you.

I hope the above is acceptable to you and we wish you every success with the launch of your book.

Yours sincerely,

Gill Bridge
Managing Director

F.A. Cup Winners: 1952-53

F.A. Cup Finalists: 1947-48, 1950-51

First Division Runners-Up: 1955-56

Second Division Champions: 1929-30

Second Division Runners-Up:
1936-37, 1969-70

Fourth Division Runners-Up: 1984-85

Fourth Division Play-Off Winners: 1991-92

Anglo-Italian Cup Winners: 1970-71

Anglo-Italian Cup Runners-Up: 1971-72

Central League Champions:
1919-20, 1949-50

Lancs F.A. Youth Cup Winners: 1985-86

Marsden Lancs Cup Winners:
1993-94, 1994-95, 1995-96

Registered in England No. 48409

France (Under 18 International Tournament at Croix) and to Keele University (Under 14 Tournament). This augured well for the Blackpool F.C. Youth Policy. Names like Steve Longworth, John Hills, Clark Carlisle, Phil Thompson, Adam Nowland, Phil Robinson began to appear in the various squads. The age groups became progressively lower, reaching Under 9 by 1997. The club then had squads of boys from Under 16 to Under 9 playing against other League Club Centres of Excellence.

In September of 1997 I felt that I well underpaid for the work I was doing, and more so for the work that had been done and what had been accomplished over the last four and half years. I decided to write to the Chairperson (Vicky Oyston), to the Chief Executive (Gill Bridge), and a copy of my wage claim to my Manager (Nigel Worthington) who had heartily approved of my application to the Board of Directors for a pay increase.

To accompany this letter I produced the following profile :-

Name :- Fred O'Donoghue

Salary :- £3600 p.a. (weekly wage £75 after tax)

 50% of telephone bill

 Up to £125 petrol

26th September 1997.

Mrs. V. Oyston,
Chairman,
Blackpool Football Club,
Bloomfield Road,
Blackpool.
FY1 6JJ.

Dear Mrs. Oyston,

I enclose herewith my four and a half year report on Youth Scouting, together with my claim for a 20% increase in my basic salary.

I have not had a rise for three and a half years and feel justified in this request.

I would like you to discuss this request at the next Board Meeting.

Yours sincerely,

Fred O'Donoghue

Request :- An upgrade in my salary consistent with my success with the number of young Professional and Youth Training players with the club. Also the work that has been carried out over the last four and half years

Paul Carden	Now at Rochdale
Steve Longworth	Now at Accrington Stanley
Clark Carlisle	Second Year as a professional
Jamie Skeock	Second Year Y.T.
Tamas Byrne	Second Year Y.T.
Ian Dickinson	Second Year Y.T.
Adam Nowland	Second Year Y.T. (Professional contract)
Simon Bridges	Student signed schoolboy
Michael Bamber	Second Year Y.T.
Mark Fahey	First Year Y.T.
John Hills	Professional
Stuart Parkinson	Now at Lancaster
Paul Ashcroft	Now at Chorley
Pater Croasdale	Coach at Centre of Excellence
Matt Greer	Now at Bamber Bridge

Survey of Efforts

1. Centre of Excellence / Schoolboy Level Scouting (Main Task)

Scouting at all levels U11,12,13,14,15,16. This includes visits to school games, local junior league games, league representative games, games in the Central Lancashire area (Morecambe to Manchester and Merseyside).

2. Scouting at Senior Level

On the instructions of the Manager and/or the Chief Scout, I regularly visit Non-League and League matches, making reports on players and teams in the Central Lancashire. I also assist Alan Crawford in his work with the Youth Trainees. Whenever possible I try to my finger on the button on the movement of players at this level without it interfering with my main task of signing the best schoolboys in the area.

3. Administration

On arriving at the club four and half years ago, I found a lot of the administration late and not being done. I produced several standard reply letters for various types of trialists. This allowed Neil Bailey more time for coaching. When the Centre of Excellence was created I, along with Neil Bailey and Steve Potter, created a very good filing system whereby boys can easily be traced with full details i.e. date of birth, home and school addresses, telephone numbers etc. I enrolled Terry Churchill as Centre of Excellence Administrator and he is proving invaluable.

4. Trialist Accommodation and Travel

Terry Churchill and I deal with the accommodation and travel for the schoolboy and senior trialists, liaising with the approved Guest Houses etc. I am also responsible for the preparation of order forms. I also collect the various trialists from the bus station, train station, and airport when required to do so.

5. Scouts

I brought several of my scouting colleagues with me when I came from Preston North End :-

Steve Grand (U14 coach and scout), Daryl Wood (U14 physio and scout), Dave Woods, Brian Fairclough, Dave Hind, Brian Hewitt, Steve Elliott.

6 Fund Raising

With my own £10 note I formed The Tangerine Junior Football Academy Account on 8th August 1993. Terry Wood became Chairman of the Academy Committee, Terry Churchill (Treasurer), and Steve Potter (Secretary). I was unable to serve directly on the committee but I was able to organise and direct their efforts on behalf of the club.£11000 was raised for the club's Youth Policy and I cannot praise Terry Churchill, who is par excellence, Steve Potter and Terry Wood, enough for their help and support. I came as a part-time scout and administrator but now I am doing much more.

A Short Book Review 1996/97

I would like to thank the Club for backing my recent book publication of "Scouting for Glory". The Club has received the sum of £500 from me for its administration purposes and a further £2.50 for each book sold. From February 1st 1997 all the creditors (typists, printers, distribution agents) have been paid close to the sum of £6000 and the book is now in the black. A National Publishing firm has now offered to take over the publishing rights. This I intend to allow.

The outcome of this was that the Club granted me the 20% rise I had asked for. We were now embarking on a bold scheme of producing our own players under the edicts of Howard Wilkinson and the Football Association. Squires Gate Training Ground became the venue for the Centre of Excellence during the lighter months of the year, and Ansdell Arena and Kirkham Grammar School All Weather Floodlit Pitches were hired for the winter months. Qualified coaches were appointed to work with Under 9, 10, 11, 12, 13, 14, 15, 16 age groups. Alan Crawford is now in charge of these, and he along with Terry Churchill is doing a sterling job. My Scouts List was growing in size. I now had 30 scouts and contacts on the list from various parts of the British Isles, including Scotland, Northern Ireland, and the Republic of Ireland. The work involved in organising this has become colossal but we have done well with a number of our youngsters already playing First Team football. These include John Hills, Clark Carlisle, Adam Nowland, Phil Thompson, Phil Robinson, Steve Longworth.

The 1st Edition of my book sold out to my happy and obvious delight. Preston North End, however, had refused to stock it in their souvenir shop and in January 1997 these two articles appeared in The Lancashire Evening Post

Following the appearance of the articles, sales of the book "shot through the roof." Advice to all budding authors therefore is to get you book banned! Various other articles appeared in national and local newspapers, reaching places as varied as Liverpool, Manchester, Newcastle, Dublin, and Belfast. Reviews also appeared in several football magazines. I appeared on television, both B.B.C. and I.T.V., as well

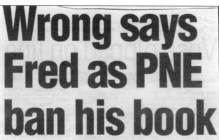

Wrong says Fred as PNE ban his book

FLY-catcher Fred O'Donough has done a Spy-catcher with his autobiography Scouting For Glory.

The soccer talent-spotter has had his life story banned by Preston North End.

And now, like Peter Wright's controversial book, sales are expected to rocket.

Economic

Fred, who quit his scouting job at Deepdale three years ago in protest at the sacking of youth development officer Walter Joyce, claims North End's decision not to sell his tome in their two club shops is down to vindictiveness.

"I don't know what I've done to them, but there's something behind this," he said.

BANNED: Fred O'Donough

But a profit of three quid a copy isn't to be sniffed at."

North End, who two weeks ago assured Fred his book would be given shelf space "subject to our usual cut," have now announced they don't want it.

Managing director Derek Shaw said: "We've discussed it and decided we don't want to stock it.

Selling

"It is not a Preston North End venture and we prefer to use the space in the shops for PNE lines.

"I don't think it's anything to do with what's in it or who's written it."

Fred disagrees. "All the other clubs in the area are selling it, so why not Preston?

"Still, can't do any harm. Spycatcher did all right after they banned it!"

"It's upset me really. This is my home town club and one very dear to my heart.

"They've told me it isn't economic for them to sell my book.

Fred tells the secrets of life as a talent spotter

ACE talent spotter Fred O'Donoghue has unlocked the door on the private world of soccer scouting.

In a no-holds-barred autobiography, the best-known face on the North West circuit gives fans a unique insight into one of the worstpaid, least glamorous, yet ultimately most invaluable jobs in professional football.

Famous

Fred, 69, has been a scout for Liverpool, Arsenal, Blackburn Rovers, Preston, Rochdale and now Blackpool.

And in three decades squelching on touchlines and shivering in stands, his story is, according to Manchester United manager Alex Ferguson, just "amazing."

Scouting For Glory (The Inside Story) is a frank account of Fred's time in the

BY BRIAN ELLIS
Sports Editor

game and includes some enlightening tales and forthright opinions of the famous and the not-so-famous.

The author isn't afraid to have a dig at himself either - hence the story of how Kevin Keegan might never have gone to Liverpool had Bill Shankly listened to Fred. And how he also failed to spot Paul Mariner's talents.

International

But there were many more instances where the opposite happened, with Fred responsible for launching scores of professional careers, some which would one day make the international stage.

Scouting For Glory, published by Fred O'Donoghue.

as being heard on the radio. For these I received fees but more importantly the appearances contributed towards a complete sell out.

Meggy / Pheely / Harry Mac

With Sam Allardyce's departure from the club a new manager was appointed. Not only had Sam departed but so had Phil Brown, Bobby Saxton, and Jack Chapman. Garry Megson became the new manager, with Mike Phelan as his assistant, and Harry Macnally as the senior chief scout.

Billy Bingham rang to tell me of the appointments and asked me to go and meet Gary and Mike Phelan in the manager's office the next morning. When I walked into the office Billy Bingham introduced me to the pair. Garry, or 'Meggy' as I call him, said " Bloody Hell, it's the F.O.D.!" This puzzled me. I knew his face and had seen him several times as a player (Ginger hair and a cocky, confident playing style). I looked into his face, his eyes twinkled, and he broke into a huge grin. "Think back to the P.F.A. Football League Managers' Course, to which you came as one of the lecturers." He turned to Billy Bingham who by this time was 'all ears' and also to other people in the office and said, " This guy (pointing at me quite boldly), he and IAN GREAVES were the best lecturers on that managers' course at Chorley. Both of them were brilliant. No bullshit, just honest to goodness facts and unbelievable clarity of thought about our beautiful game. I tried to make a joke of it by offering to buy him a whisky and dry. Suddenly it was then that I remembered him also. 'Browny', now at Bolton, and one or two others who were on that managers' course went for a few drinks with me after the lectures. 'Meggy' was one of them. Good for 'Meggy', you'll do for me! We got on very well together. Alas I always felt there were differences between 'Meggy' and Billy Bingham (Director of Football) and that the manager was not happy with the set up at Bloomfield Road. Again, I could feel it and sense it, as I had with my old pal Sam Allardyce during his reign at Blackpool F.C.

All change once more! Meggy, Pheely, and Harry Mac left to join Stockport County. Even Craig Madden, the Community Officer, joined them!

Scouting for Glory---The Book

They say that lightening doesn't strike twice in the same place. IT DOES, BELIEVE ME!

Readers of my book, as well as friends suggested that because the 1st edition sold out I should contact a Sports Book publisher to produce a 2nd edition. The company I chose were called Two Heads Publishers. It was an unfortunate choice! They agreed to publish the book and I signed a contract for the publishing rights to be handed over to them. The contract was signed and sealed, or so I thought, and sent back to the company. Unfortunately I did not take a photostat of my signature nor of Charles Frewin's (The Company's Director) signature.

The idiot I am I trust human beings! This last part of the book saddens me. I must keep my chin up and be cheerful and optimistic. Hopefully this 2nd updated edition will be published by someone, somewhere!

---

15 Dec

To: Fred O'Donoghue

From: Charles Frewin

Scouting For Glory

Just to let you know that there is little chance of the printers being able to get copies of the book to you for tomorrow due to the huge workload at this time of year.

It's likely that the book will go to the distributors early next week but they will probably wisely decide to send it out to bookshops in January to avoid the mass returns bookshops make on stock unsold after Christmas.

I'm relaxed about this as it is not a Christmas book.

Hope your event goes well tomorrow and compliments of the season to you.

Jenny

Mr F O'Donoghue
7 Conway Avenue
Penwortham
Nr Preston
PR1 9TR

Dear Fred

Ref: Scouting for Glory

Unfortunately I have had to take action to halt the production of your book.

I have become aware that the Distributor may not be able to deliver the required service, leaving me without a sales and distribution channel into the book trade. Despite exploring all possible options I would also add that it is not possible to make any alternative arrangements because no worthwhile distributor will take on just the one book.

Given the effort and resources we have put into *Scouting* it is with great regret that we will not now be able to publish it as as we are prevented by cirumstances beyond our control (as per paragraph 5 of the publishing contract). In these circumstances all rights revert back to you forthwith.

My recommendation would be for you to reprint the book as it stands as you would then be in a position to benefit from any local and regional demand, as this is where the majority of any sales would come from anyway.

I am reminded that Scouting has endured a number of unexpected setbacks since you first put pen to paper and hope that you will be able to find a way forward with it from here.

I return the original clippings/letters and a copy of a cassette tape we had on file.

Yours sincerely

Charles Frewin
Two Heads Publishing

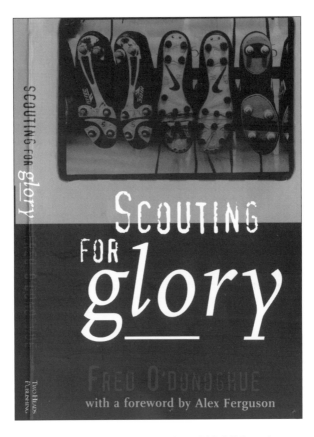

Cover design for the 2nd Edition, which fell through.

Chapter Twelve

The Future

With the recent advent of the football academies in our national sport I did a study
of the teams that are now academies or about to take part. This is the list to date.
In alphabetical order Premier League Clubs and others as of April/May 1999 with
football academies.

1. Arsenal FC	2. Aston Villa FC	3. Blackburn Rovers FC
4. Charlton FC	5. Chelsea FC	6. Coventry FC
7. Derby FC	8. Everton FC	9. Leeds FC
10. Leicester FC	11. Liverpool FC	12. Man United FC
13 Middlesborough FC	14. Newcastle FC	15. Nottingham Forest FC
16. Sheffield Wed FC	17. Southampton FC	18. Tottenham FC
19. West Ham FC	20. Wimbledon FC	

Other league clubs who followed suit are as follows i.e. 14 in all

21. Barnsley FC	22. Bolton FC	23. Bristol FC
24. Crewe FC	25. Crystal Palace FC	26. Fulham FC
27. Ipswich FC	28. Man City FC	29. Millwall FC
30. Norwich FC FC	31. Peterborough FC	32. Queens Park Rangers
33 Sunderland FC	34. Watford FC	

Total number of academies now is 34 with 4 more clubs with plans approved.
They are

1. Birmingham FC	2. Huddersfield FC	3. Reading FC
4. Stoke City FC		

The final total 38 which is far far to big.

I began to ask myself is this fair to smaller clubs i.e. Blackpool, Scunthorpe, Wigan, Bury, Tranmere etc, etc. The big clubs have enrolled a scouting system where by talented young lads of 9-10 years old have been spotted and targeted by the big boys. If you don't believe me, talk to my ex boss Sam Allardyce about the lad at Notts County, Jermaine Pennant and many others that clubs can reveal if you dig deep enough. To play football for your town team was in my days the ultimate pinnacle of footballing success with loyalty being part of a young lads make up. I am hopeful however that young good players have a better and bigger chance of footballing success with the small league clubs than internationally minded big boys of the premier league.

I am not happy at Howard Wilkinson's Academy ideas at all and decided to speak to Dave Crompton of Wigan FC about these monumental changes. We had long discussions, Dave is one of soccer's knowledge giants and I have respected all the work he has done for the sport over the many years I have known him. Dave illuminated me with his wonderful thoughts of academies so much that I asked him to write his thoughts on the subject. After reading his wonderful, thoughtful, illuminating reflections on the football academies, I tore my own aggressive, sad, insignificant report up. I wasn't able to match his superior thoughts on this subject. I then rang Dave up asking if I could include his work in this 2nd edition of my book, Dave readily agreed his report adds a bit of class to my humble scratchings. Thanks Dave, you're a real pal.

The Birth of the Academies
by Dave Crompton of Wigan FC

A decade or so ago the football authorities set up Centres of Excellence which were mainly based at League Clubs. They enabled boys of above-average ability from ten years and upwards to receive coaching for one hour per week at clubs within one hour's travelling distance of their homes. The emphasis was entirely on the coaching of basic skills and techniques with no 11-a-side football between one club and another allowed. Gradually, however, more coaching time was made available for these boys and club v club games were introduced for the older players in the first instance and eventually for all age groups over 11 years of age. It would be true to say that the majority of clubs welcomed the scheme and were pleased with the progress that was being made in youth development via the Centres' coaching and matches.

Much more recently in the late 1990s further major changes in the provision for talented young players from Under 9 upwards were instigated by Howard Wilkinson in his role as Technical Director at the F.A. His "Charter for Quality" programme attracted a great deal of publicity and interest not least, as he admitted himself, for its proposals for the setting-up of over thirty Football Academies during the 1998-99 season.

The new Academies represent a massive investment in facilities and staffing, including doctors, physiotherapists, and education specialists as well as coaches. They also involve changes in regulations and practice concerning young players that are intended to result in clubs rather than schools or youth clubs having control over their development. Boys, for instance, will not be allowed to play 11-a-side football until 12 years of age and then they will play a maximum of 30 games per season. At 16, clubs can offer boys three-year scholarships including far more educational programmes than was the case with two-year traineeships.

The setting up costs of these Academies will differ from club to club with those in London, for example, experiencing difficulties over the cost of land. Although grants from the F.A. and the National Lottery Commission assist in the funding, costs will run into hundreds of thousands, if not millions of pounds, as shown by the recent unveiling of Liverpool F.C.'s multi-million pound complex. Costs are obviously less of a problem for the wealthier clubs but nonetheless it is mandatory for rich and poor clubs alike in the Premier League to establish an Academy.

All this seems a far cry from the system which prevailed throughout the country prior to the mid-eighties. From a North-West perspective in particular it seems amazing that clubs from the region's lower divisions produced so many quality players. The inescapable conclusion must be that the whole ethos with regard to young players has changed and will go on changing; only time will tell if it will be for the better.

Youth Development Officers of that period or their equivalent (usually Chief Cook and Bottle Washers) will confirm that they were happy if they got their share of youngsters who developed into good professionals, which usually amounted to one or two players per season but not every season. As the appended list shows, Walter Joyce at Preston, Warwick Rimmer at Tranmere, Colin McDonald and later Jim Cassels at Oldham, were among those who produced players who went on to make solid careers in higher. We too were fortunate at Wigan. Steve Walsh(Leicester), Peter Atherton(Sheffield Wednesday), Joe Parkinson(Everton), head a list of youngsters who not only wanted to play for their local club but also realised that early First Team opportunities were more likely to come their way if they started in the lower divisions. Both the player and the club were in line to make good money later in their careers if progress was maintained, since transfer to a bigger club was usually a natural development.

Is it Fair to the Lower Division Clubs?

If we now turn to the effects of the development of the Centres of Excellence, Football Academies and the inter-club matches involved we see that it has created a scouting network which the big clubs can easily exploit. They become aware of the best individual youngsters elsewhere and can entice the most talented boys from 9 and ten upwards away from their local Centre. What in effect was once an illegal approach has now been legitimised (with only Constraints of timing) under the "window of opportunity" as the giants of the game can now "poach" players on a regular, and even systematic, basis. The payment of compensation is supposed to render this acceptable but clubs agree that the sums involved are derisory given the millions of pounds that young players could command if they came through to First Team football.

More importantly, as the Jermaine Pennant case at Notts.County illustrates, lower division clubs ideally want to see boys whom they have discovered and nurtured playing in their First Team even if it proves only a stepping-stone to progressing up the divisions later. Otherwise what is the point of smaller clubs running Youth Development programmes?

There are implications also in such cases with regard to the ethical standards surrounding the development of young players. The system seems ill-equipped to cultivate loyalty to the people and clubs which have to the boys' development in their formative years. On the contrary it will surely help to foster a "get what you can" philosophy among individual young players, not to mention inflating transfer fees. If a 15 year old is worth £2million, what price is a brilliant 21 year old?

Will Academies be Value for Money?

Cost effectiveness is an issue with all new developments. Nevertheless it is astonishing to hear

That Leeds United's manager, David O'Leary, whose team contains some highly rated youngsters, has recently that clubs are spending too much money on their football academies. O'Leary, forced to breed his own players because of lack of transfer money, says that in principle the academies are a good idea. He thinks that clubs have gone overboard on them and at the big outfits, the kids are spending less time on the football pitch and more on education. " That may be what the clubs want," says O'Leary, " but chairmen will soon be asking why they are spending all those millions and only producing the same good players who would have come through in any case."

On the other hand, as the P.F.A. et al have argued, football is an extremely precarious profession so that boys need to pursue further educational qualifications to provide them with alternative options if they are unable to make a career in the game for whatever reason. As David O'Leary admits , the failure rate is still enormous. Six years ago his club, Leeds United, won the F.A. Youth Cup against a Manchester United side which included Beckham, Butt, Scholes, and the Neville brothers. None of the Leeds kids made it to the First Team and only Noel Whelan at Coventry is still in the game. "They simply weren't good enough," said O'Leary.

This experience does lead some credence to the view of the P.F.A. that more should be done for youngsters who don't make it, but this view itself seems to ignore alternatives and current trends. It has been acknowledged at Prime Ministerial level that young people entering the world of work should not expect to have a job for life but to retrain at least four times during their working life. Thus it seems a little ironic that professional football believes it has a duty to provide ready-made alternative careers for all their aspiring youngsters. Given the plethora of college courses, apprenticeships and training opportunities, it is still open for 18 and 19 year olds to decide for themselves, with the support of their Youth Development or Education Officer, to do their A-levels or a vocational course after having devoted themselves full-time to attempting to fulfil their ambitions in the professional game.

Doubtless we all differ in what we would consider an "acceptable wastage rate" in football, but it is inevitable that there will be wastage since that is the nature of the beast. It does make you wonder, though, what some Chairman will be thinking when a boy in his third year of a scholarship is spending more time training to be a plumber than a footballer at the club's expense.

Will the England Team Lose Out?

There are other slightly disturbing implications stemming from the establishment of Academies and again it concerns the really big clubs. Not are they signing boys from overseas but are even taking steps to do so on a more systematic basis over the long term. Manchester United are reported to have signed a feeder club deal with Belgian side, Royal Antwerp,"to grow their own stars." It is alleged that United will set off on a transfer spree for young players from all over the world, who will then play for Antwerp with United footing all the expenses. Meanwhile at Arsenal, having signed Jermaine Pennant from Notts County, Arsene Wenger has also raided France's National Academy for one French youngster. Wenger considers this perfectly legitimate since we are "all Europeans now," whilst French clubs have been signing youngsters from Africa for nothing.

If these great clubs institute a trend for trawling for young players in Europe and elsewhere what chance will English youngsters have to play for them? If their opportunities to play at the highest level are restricted wont the quality of the England side suffer in the years to come? The strongly cosmopolitan teams of the Premier League, like Chelsea, now find it difficult to field more than the odd one or two English players. Given this situation the logical development might see the big Premier League clubs farming out native youngsters to Nationwide clubs - where they may well have been better going in the first place to have a real opportunity of first team football.

Conclusions

The raison d'etre of academies will continue to be a contentious issue. There is bound to be suspicion that both short and long term costs will limit them to the bigger, wealthier clubs. Of course if every club had one then Academies could no longer claim to be superior to Centres of Excellence as many of them do now. Surely it would be simpler and more equitable for the Government to use Lottery funds to provide standard basic facilities such as all-weather pitches for the use of every club and its local community. Then we really would have the proverbial level playing field, giving every club the chance to show what it could do in terms of youth development without recourse to arguments about lack of resources and restricted opportunities. At the same time such provision would enable every young player to fulfil his maximum potential at the club of his choice, which would frequently be his local one.

Neither clubs, parents nor players should feel that they are being offered something second class in terms of football development. If the ultimate aim is to improve the quality of native players at the highest level then the stronger and widespread the base needs to be. Attempting to create an elite at an age when it is almost impossible to make definitive judgements on potential would seem to be a self-defeating exercise destined to result in an even higher wastage rate than the present one.

It was not surprising that comparisons with our European counterparts in terms of technical skills in the 1980s led to the demand for more widespread high-quality coaching of talented young players, as it was not an area of financial priority at most clubs at that time. Centres of Excellence, and subsequently, were seen as the answer and there have undeniably been many benefits. The basic skill levels of large numbers of young players have been improved and some of them have been given the chance to progress along the route leading to a professional career. It is too early to judge whether it has increased the numbers who have "made it" but there are certainly people in the game who doubt whether it will make much difference. Change obviously rarely suits everybody and seldom provides equal benefits but it is usually accepted if it is seen to be in the best interests of football as a whole. There is a feeling among League Clubs, however, at the present time, that academies in particular are part of a "hidden agenda" to change the face of English Soccer for the benefit of a few very wealthy (and often greedier) clubs at the expense of the smaller ones.

I then decided to look at some of our North Western footballing gates, over many years, as to who were the giants of footballing areas in which our young people watched and tried to emulate the players in these teams. It is a very interesting study imagine Blackpool in 1955 38,000 gate. If clubs have success on the park with good team's cup and promotion runs they come out of the woodwork to follow.

A survey of yesteryears gates (N/West Clubs)
(Sleeping Giants) by Fred O'Donoghue 11.04.99
In order of crowd numbers.

Most of them league members and other ex League members.

No	Football Clubs & Grounds	Gates Recorded	Dates
1	Manchester City, Maine Road	84,569	03.03.34
2	Everton, Goodison	78,299	18.09.48
3	Manchester United, Old Trafford	76,962	25.03.39
4	Bolton Wanderers, Burnden Park	69,912	10.02.33
5	Liverpool, Anfield	61,905	02.02.52
6	Blackburn Rovers, Ewood Park	61,783	02.03.29
7	Burnley, Turf Moor	55,775	23.02.24
8	Oldham, Boundry Park	47,671	25.01.30
9	Preston North End, Deepdale	42,684	24.03.38
10	Blackpool, Bloomfield Road	38,080	17.09.55
11	Bury, Gigg Lane	35,000	19.01.60
12	Stockport, Edgeley Park	27,833	11.02.50
13	Wigan, Springfield Park	27,500	12.12.51
14	Tranmere, Prenton Park	24,424	05.02.72
15	Accrington Stanley, Peel Park	17,634	15.11.54
16	Nelson FC, Seedhill	14,000	10.04.26*
17	Darwen FC, Anchor Ground	14,000	03.1882*
18	Southport FC, Haig Avenue	20,000	26.01.32
19	Barrow FC, Holker Street	16,840	09.01.54
20	Workington FC, Borough Park	21,000	05.01.59
21	Stalybridge FC, Lower Fold	9,753	13.01.23*
22	New Brighton FC, Tower Ground	10,060	14.01.1899*
23	Northwich Victoria, Drill Field	8,080	10.1892

24	Carlisle United, Brunton Park	27,500	05.01.57
25	Rochdale, Spotland Ground	24,231	10.12.49
26	Bootle FC, Hawthorn Road	20,600	26.12.1889

In the first edition of this book I wrote it's time I was going, it's time I moved on, after a recent Triple By Pass Heart Operation on February 29th 1999 at the Cardiac Thoracic Department, Blackpool Victoria Hospital I must make things more easily, advice I have been given by my doctors who have very kindly attended to me, not being one for compiling statistics apart from the bits and bats within this book, I have always had the greatest respect and deep admiration for those who carry out (time consuming) meticulous attention to precise details of whatever subject.

I remember Father Geoghan my old friend and catholic priest at St. Augustines pre war Preston telling me of one such person, was one, who spent many years in prison, in Spain, reading and recording the holy bible and its contents both Old and New Testaments. There are a few facts and figures of his colossal task. No computers in those days.

The Old testament has 39 books, 979 Chapters, 23,214 verses, 592,253 words and 2,178,100 letters.

The New Testament has 27 books, 270 Chapters, 7,967 verses, 132,253 words and 933,380 letters.

The statistician responsible was the (prince of Granada), who by the way was heir to the Spanish throne, spent 33 years in The Prison of Skulls in Madrid his only companion the bible. He faithfully read, digested, dissected and perused it every day of his exile producing the facts and figures for posterity to peruse the study. His work and findings must be one of mans greatest statistical monumental works. Yes I admire all those who turn out very accurate statistics especially with precise football details year in year out, the Rothman Yearly Football Handbook, is approaching close to monumental levels. Great stuff by all concerned in its production. Well my time is coming to a close, I will continue to serve Blackpool FC and Football as long as my health prevails. I hope that Chairman Karl Oyston of Blackpool FC whom I met recently maintains his obvious interest in this famous old club, it would be a shame to finish yes, as a non league outfit, like Darwen, Accrington Stanley "etc" if you know what I mean, Nigel Worthington, manager and Mike Hennigan, Assistant Manager, I am sure will benefit the Club in a long term situation, as they say Rome wasn't built in a day neither is a successful Football Club. Thank you for your time and trouble in reading my efforts I am yours in Sport.

Fred O'Donoghue, Born 17-6-27

**Fax From the
F.O.D.**

Fax

To: SIR ALEX FERGUSON	From: FRED O' DONOGHUE
Fax: As BELOW	Pages: ONE
Phone: `'' ''`	Date: 12 - 6 - 99
Re: KNIGHTHOOD	CC: PERSONAL FAX TO ALEX.

☑ Urgent ☐ For Review ☐ Please Comment ☐ Please Reply ☐ Please Recycle

DEAR ALEX.

MANY CONGRATULATIONS ON
YOUR KNIGHTHOOD WELL DONE AND
WELL DESERVED.

YOURS SINCERLY
Fred O' Donoghue.

FROM: FRED O'DONOGHUE

PENWORTHAM
PRESTON

TEL: 01772-498738
FAX: 01772-498739
MOBILE: 07971-445779

BLACKPOOL FOOTBALL CLUB
BLOOMFIELD ROAD
BLACKPOOL
FY1 6JJ
TEL: 01253-405331
FAX: 01253-405011